4.–

Sisters Three of Montana

Helen Shenefelt DeLong

6-15-98

Helen Shenefelt DeLong

Dedicated to my two sisters who without there would be no Sisters Three

Sisters Three of Montana

Acknowledgments
References and read

Early Flathead & Tobacco Plains 1977
By Marie Cuff Shea

Tobacco Plains country 1947-1950
Editor Olga Weydemeyer

Sisters 3 family cookbook 1981
Sharon LaBonty compiler

Published by Scott Publishing Company
Kalispell, Montana

Publisher's Note

Helen Shenefelt DeLong writes her life story with the charm and clarity of a woman bonded to her family by her heart and her mind, with details uncommon to most. Her remembrances are sometimes mischievous, and sometimes a solemn memoir of younger days in a frontier era. In order to establish the character and integrity of her journal entries, and upon her request, our editorial staff has not attempted to change her original manuscript. This story should be read and enjoyed with that in mind.

Scott Graber
publisher

How we came to be

As I see it through my eyes and remember to the best of
my knowledge.

My parents moved to Eureka Montana in the early 1900's. Dad's family on the train to Kalispell, then on to Jennings and north to Hayden. Arriving in Eureka March 3rd. 1903. They had sold there home in Redfield Kansas. Dad had an Uncle Monroe (Roe) Shenefelt who had a homestead just north of where the Eureka Cemetery is now. When he first arrived his family lived in a tent under the pine tree that still stands east of the house, while he built a small house and later the large white house that stands there today.

The Indians came past here going south and to the river. One day there was a young Indian woman left behind under the tree. She was in labor and they left her to take care of herself while having her baby. She didn't want any help and after she gave birth she rested awhile and then got on her horse and followed the rest of them south.

Monroe picked up Dad's family in a horse and buggy and took them to his home. Grandmother did not like the looks of the area in and around Eureka. Grandfather told her not to unpack the trunks, they would visit a while and then go home. But they never left.

After they had been on the homestead for awhile a very homesick young lady wrote the following song.

This was sung to the tune of "*Beaulah Land*" and was written by Sara Shenefelt. As is evident, she was very homesick for Kansas.

MONTANA LAND
I've reached the land of wind and heat,
Of cactus pie's and gopher meat.
I got my land of Uncle Sam.
And I am beat, you bet I am

Chorus
OH, Montana Land, Dry Montana Land,
As on the highest Butte I stand,
I look away across the plains, and wonder
Why it never rains,
Then turn around, and view my wheat,
And almost wish I was back East.

The wheat won't grow, the spud's won't sprout,
My Sunday pants are all worn out,
I sadly think of my Eastern home
As I gnaw the meat of a coyote bone.

chorus

III
And when I lay me down to sleep,
The mosquitoes and bedbugs o'er me creep,
Sink prospects holes all o'er my hide,
And chew my ribs like they were fried,

My Grandfather and Grandmother chose a home stead on the west end of Black Lake. It had been owned and approved on by the Jim Breeding family. This family were not in the area very long. Grandfather took over the homestead, by pre-emtion. The other homesteaders at the Black Lake region south of Tobacco River, and Iowa Flats had a number of lakes, stretching through miles of timber land and onto Pinkham Creek Mountain. In the Black Lake area were the Seth Maddens, John Shenefelt, Clifford Eayrs, O.H. Fluharty, Fred Lampton, Jake Greens, Uncle Billy Baker, Emile Pijeau (not Pigeon), Earl Rhodes and brother Roy Rhodes, and Charles Palmer.

Grandfathers farm had a lot of open land, they summer fallowed every year. This was done with horses, it was a very hot dusty and tedious job. When they came in from doing this job, they washed up at the wash bench by the back door before entering the house for meals. Dad said with all the borax in the water in Black Lake, Grandmother would soak the overalls in the lake all night before wash day and it would take all the grease out of them. They planted winter wheat and hoped to get enough moisture to get a good crop. They often got thirty to forty bushels to the acre. After all this was done in the fall of the year, then Dad could go to school till it was time to start in on the farm in the spring, then school was done for the farm boys for that year.

They raised hogs and horses on the homestead also. For their own use they butchered three hogs each fall, weighing from 225-250 lbs. each and were approximately six months old. If they did not weigh that much in six months, there was not any money to be made in raising them. Also a "lard hog" of about 450—500 lbs. would be butchered. This was made into lard for the year. All lean meat would be saved for sausage, hams, and shoulders, which were smoked by Grandfather in his out—of—doors homemade smoke house. (They usually looked like a outhouse with a pipe sticking out of the roof). Grandfather would get all the apple wood he could find for the year, as this is what he liked best for smoking his hams and shoulders. Sometimes he went as far into the foothills as the old Rich place (Scott and Rumble Place) for apple wood. (Above Quirks and Shea's) He would prune the trees and occasionally got a dead apple tree, and would bring all of this many miles home where he would cut and split it, carefully getting it ready for fall. If he could not get enough apple wood, he would then use birch wood. After hanging all of the hams and shoulders from the butchered hogs in the smokehouse, the three days of night and day smoking fire must be kept going. This meant several trips out each night tending the fire. When the required time in the smoke house was over, the meat was taken down and placed in clean muslin sacks that grandmother had made for this purpose. Next came the job (with our father, Francis Shenefelt helping). They would carry all of the meat to the Grainery, where it was buried deep in the grain where it remained until it was needed. This must have been the for runner of refrigeration.

The hams were used along with many other pork products and a lot of venison to keep the family well fed during the coming year.

Grandmother Shenefelt was a wonderful cook and a most gracious hostess. Her home was attractive and cozy. People liked to drop in and she loved company.

They had not been on the homestead very long when they had a fire. They had a frame cabin made of pine lumber with an upstairs. They had a few acres of wheat north of the house. The wheat binding was done early so it would be cool for the horses, They worked until 9 o'clock then came in for breakfast. John had came in and sat down at the table to eat, when the chickens started making a funny noise. He walked out to see why and came running in and said "every one out, the house is burning". He took two pictures off the wall, and Sara grabbed the four corners of the tablecloth, breakfast and all and took it outside. The house burned very fast as it was of such dry lumber. Francis (Dad), was left with only a pair of overalls as he did not even have on his shoes. The only things saved were the two pictures and the jelly dish, (which my niece Sharon LaBonte has now). All the other dishes were broken. There was a neighbor came by and broke a window into the bedroom he reached in and got a hold of what he could, it was a feather tick on the bed. This was made by grandmother before she was married, she and her mother picked the goose down to make it. It was then made into pillows as all their pillows had burned. These pillows are still being used today. My sister Esther has two of them.

Now the family moved into the blacksmith shop, it was a low log building with the roof made of poles with dirt and long root grass on it. Dad said in the summer it was cooler, and the rain did not come through the roof. But in the winter thaw the melting snow did drip through. Jake Green, Ory Fluharty and grandfather cut, peeled, and hauled in the logs for a new house. One day many neighbors with tools, and food appeared and the house went up in a hurry. That night the Shenefelts slept in their new log house. This house is still in the middle of the house that stands there today. It is entirely built over now. The neighbors brought a collection of $175.00 and a cook stove. Later on grandfather wanted his wife to have a new cook stove, so he ordered one for her for Christmas. When it arrived in town he wanted to surprise her, he made arrangements for someone to take her to see Mrs. Madden for a visit. While she was gone they brought a beautiful Monarch range with a water reservoir on it, when she came home she was a very surprised and pleased woman. This stove was used by her the rest of her life. My cousin Darrel Roose later ended up with it, they used it for some time and then put it out in the shed to store it. In the early 1970's my middle son, Dennis DeLong was building a house in rural Eureka and needed a wood cook stove, he heard Darrel had one so went to see about it. Well, it turned out to be his great grandmothers monarch range. Darrel sold it to him for very little, but told him if he ever wanted to get rid of it he had to sell it back to him. Dennis and Susan used it for many years and it now sits in its place of honor in their kitchen beside an electric stove, and is still used once in a while to make the kitchen cozy or to cook a Thanksgiving turkey.

In 1977 while visiting with my sister Esther Dad told her about a cattle drive he went on. (He was now in a nursing home) It was late October of 1914. He was 17 years old at the time.

Hahn and Kelley, the owners of the Skookum Ranch in Pleasant Valley, which is about 8 miles from Marion, hired Charles Workman, Jim Wilt and myself. They bought 81 head of cattle from various people and places, and rounded them up at Demar's Corral. Arrangements had been made for us to stay at the Billy Lloyd place, the Gaylord camp, the Bett's place, and Sinclair's Ranch along the way, and they would each have supper for us, and a place to corral the horses and cattle. We were to head over the Wolf Creek Trails, being no road to follow, and go on down through Pleasant Valley, and end up around Marion, and the Schookum Ranch. We started out on a Tuesday morning from Demars's Corral and got to Fortine that night, to a place owned by Dr. Burnett (the old Winkley place). We had to milk 26 head of the cattle. Hahn and Kelley did not want milk cows, but bought them anyway. These cows were pretty wild some would let us milk them, but others had to be roped and tied up. The reason for milking was so they could travel easier, their bags being so full. The first night we gave the milk to Billy Lloyd (he lived there at the time), the other times we just milked them onto the ground. We had supper that night with Billy Lloyd. The next day, Wednesday, we started on the trail as soon as it was light. We were supposed to hit the Gaylord camp for the night, but we drove the cattle till dark and no camp in sight. So, we took the cattle across the small bridge. One of us night herded during the night and kept the fire going. The other two slept while they could. While Charley Workman was taking his turn at sleeping, he rolled over close, too close, to the fire and burned all the angora off of one side of his chaps. We all had a good laugh about that, and his chaps were not so pretty from then on. We had no grain for the horses, but we picketed them for grazing grass. For our own supper, we split a can of beans between the three of us, plus gave a couple of bites to my dog, Turk, who had come along with us, and was a pretty good cattle dog. Next morning, Thursday, as soon as it got light, we started going down the trail to pick up the cattle, they were strung out a mile or more. Old Jim said that we'd surely hit the Gaylord camp for breakfast. We drove till noon and no camp. Jim admitted at noon that he guessed we missed it. We drove all day and about mid afternoon we came to a little cabin with a small garden that had carrots and Turnips. We helped ourselves to a couple of each and ate them along the trail. At about 8:30 that night we got to Sinclair's ranch and got the cattle corralled and had supper. We had nothing to eat, except the carrots and turnips, since dinner on Tuesday; and the horses had no grain. Does a can of beans count? We slept in a bed that night. Friday morning we drove all day till about 6:00 that night, when we got to the Bett's place (as it was later known). Rather a good day of riding for the cattle and us.

On Saturday, we rose with the sun and drove the cattle along the trail till about 3:00 or 3:30, when we got to the Scookum Ranch, we took care of the cattle and horses, had dinner and slept.

The next morning, Sunday, Kelley said that we had a pretty hard trip, and since the haystack needed fenced in, and the horses needed to rest, why didn't we just plan on staying on another day. So, that took about two hours to do, and then we laid around the bunkhouse for the rest of the day, and planned on heading home on Monday morning.

Well Monday came, and Jim said " I think there is a buck waiting for me to find him up on that mountain. Kelly said " Go get him." So, Jim went, and hunted all day with no luck. Charley and I were just lazy and laid around all day. On Tuesday morning, Kelley wanted us to ride a sorrel mare that had never been ridden. Jim said that he would if he could use my saddle; I had a good one, so I told him to go ahead. Jim wanted Charley to snub the sorrel; Charley did, Jim got on, and it started to buck. This all took place in a big meadow, and Charley had to let go. Boy, was Jim ever pulling leather, but he rode it! Jim rode the mare around for a couple of hours after they caught it. Then all that we did was lay around for the rest of the day.

The next morning we headed for home. Hahn and Kelley had hired us for $3.00 a day, which was good wages, but ended up paying us at $3.50 a day, plus also paying us for the two days to get home. Really, two days we rested and played, with riding the horse and Jim hunting. We got to camp 6 the first day (above Trego), the Pierson's Camp (where George Shay has now got his chutes and corrals); we put in the horses and fed them and got our supper. We got a couple of blankets from the commissary, and had to sleep in the hay bunks in the bunkhouse. We got graybacks (lice!), and were all lousy. We got home the next day and my mother made me take a bath and change clothes every day for a week. She also washed my bedding every day. It took us a week to get rid of those darned things. That ended the cattle drive!

Grandfather and grandmother Shenefelt had four children. Francis who was our father, Marie who was married to Earl Roose and later Alfred Dionne. She had five sons and two daughters. The boys are Darrel, Everett Lloyd, Clarence and A.J., the girls were Gladys and Jackie. Aunt Marie lived in the Eureka area for many years then moved to Libby where she owned a Cafe. Then they moved to Aberdeen Washington and later Fortuna California. She retired there after many years of owning a very popular cafe. Alfred retired as a log truck owner and driver. They stayed in Fortuna till they both passed away. Darrel stayed in Eureka, Everett lives in Oregon, Lloyd and A.J. live in Washington, Clarence and Jackie live in Fortuna California. Gladys passed away while living in Oregon.

Uncle Harold passed away from bleeding ulcers at age 13. He is buried beside his parents in the Eureka Cemetery. Aunt Blythe was years younger than the other children, Grandfather built a house in town after suffering a heart attach and was advised to get off the farm. He worked as town policeman for a while and was ditch rider for some time. This is where they were living when he passed away. This left Aunt Blythe and grandmother alone. They had a struggle but made it. Aunt Blythe worked at the theater and grandmother baked cakes and sold then at a store in town for 35¢ each. The stale ones they picked up were the ones they ate at home.

Aunt Blythe graduated Valedictorian of her High School class. The next fall she started teaching at Black Lake School. I believe she told me she received $1,000.00 for her first year, but things were getting worse with the depression and her wages went down after that some what. She still worked at the theatre in the summer time and did manage to go to Dillon to Normal College and get her Teaching Degree. She became a very good and much loved teacher.

After grandmother passed away she married Vern Amondson and moved to Washington. They lived many years in the Vancouver area. They raised two children Wayne, and Loris. Aunt Blythe retired after years of teaching. Vein retired from the telephone company. They have traveled all over the world. Much of it with the fellowship of their church.

Grandfather Shenefelt was the middle child of a family of 13. The Shenefelts were of the Dunkard Faith. Dad said as a young man he had the fastest horse and buggy in the area. Guess they did some racing then also!

Mothers family arrived on the New railroad from Kalispell to Eureka. They moved from Montreal, Canada to Iron River, Michigan in 1899. Then to Montana. Arriving in Eureka on Easter Sunday 1908. The Baillargons were of the Catholic faith.

Jessie Morrison said every one in town was watching for this French family to arrive. She said the first time she saw mother she had long black curls below her waist, and the bluest eyes she had ever seen. Really a beautiful child.

Sinai and Stephonie Baillargon had eight children. Three died in infancy. They raised three sons and two daughters. Marraine Yvonne Oliva (Eva) Baillargon was our mother.

Celose married Ora Green, they raised four daughters. Velma, Edna, Cecelia and Elyn. In Bend Oregon.

Raymond never married and passed away in Michigan as a young man, he died of pneumonia.

Corade married Signa in Bend Oregon, they married late in life. Both of our Uncles were working at the Brooks-Scanlon lumber company in Eureka when it closed in 1925. They were some of the few that transferred with the company to Bend Oregon. They both retired from the mill there. This is where they lived the rest of their lives.

Blanch married Dow O'Brien they had one daughter, Leona, and five sons. Frank, Fred, Leo, Louis, and Richard. They raised their family in the Black Lake and Rexford area. Both of them passed away while they lived at their home in Rexford. Fred spent most of his adult life, until he passed away in Seattle area. The rest of the family live in Libby and Rexford.

Eva our mother grew up to be a beautiful young women. She married our father when she was 17 and he was 18. What brought the Baillargon family to the area was that grandmother had a cousin that lived here, Joe Peltier, who owned the Pine Grove ranch. They came so grandfather and the boys could work for him, which they did for many years.

Mothers family lived on the Tobacco River on what was known as the Pidgeon place. Mother and Dad talked about what fun the young people had walking down the tracks to LOST HALL to dances. Dad said they would dance till dawn, and mother was an excellent dancer. Then they would start home and get there in time for him to do his chores. Mother was allowed to go to the dances if she went with her two brothers. Aunt Marie would tell about going to dances with mother and dad when they were young. To get to the dance, they would walk along the railroad tracks for several miles. After dancing until the wee hours, they would have a long walk home again, Grandmother Baillargon could hear them coming, the singing and Eva's laughter would carry in the quiet morning air. Being Devout Roman Catholics, she had to go to mass. Eva would come in and lay down on her bed on her back, still in her dress and rest until it was time to leave for church. Then the family would walk about four miles to town to attend mass.

When mother's family started school in Iron River Michigan she could understand very little English. The teacher would say something to her and she would smile and not have any idea what was said to her.

When the teacher asked her what her name was she said Marraine Yvonne Oliva Baillargon (with a very French accent). The teacher picked up on the "Iva" in

Oliva and called her Eva and that was her name from then on.

Grandfather Baillargon later went to work at the Brook-Scanlon lumber company. They had a home in East Eureka. Shortly before the mill shut down in Eureka in 1925 our grandfather was killed in the mill. Grandmother said when she heard the whistle in the middle of the day she knew it was an accident and she knew it was Sinai. She later moved to Bend Oregon and lived with Uncle Corade for many years. We called our grandmother Baillargon "Maimi" that is French for grandmother.

After many dances, picnics, boat rides, box socials, pie socials and etc. Mother and Father married June 30 1915, at her parents home. They set up house keeping in a small house across the road from the homestead. The house sat in the field at the fork of the road that goes down sand hill and on to Rexford. They were there for over a year, that is where they lived when our brother Harold was born. He was born at Maimi house in town, on April 11 1916. They moved to the little house behind Uncle Roe's when Harold was still a baby. Dad must have been working there as a farm worker. Mother became very ill after Harold was born and the Dr's sent her to Spokane where she had surgery and she finally recovered. Our Dad also was a rural mail carrier at one time he hauled the mail in a horse and buggy but I don't know exactly when. Then he went to work in the woods in Idaho at Bottle bay on Lake Pend Oreille they had not been there to long when the camp cook quit and mother took on her first job cooking for lumberjacks in a camp. They were there approximately a year. Since Harold was a tiny baby, with men to cook for and diapers and other wash to do on a scrub board, she was a mighty busy young lady. They did manage to go to Saturday night dances across the lake, they put Harold in a pack sack and dad took him on his back. Mother was a little apprehensive of this transportation of her baby boy but he survived nice and warm and safe.

When Mother and Dad were in Idaho Mother was 18 or 19 years old and she had her first experience off being a midwife, This is where she delivered the first of many babies.

Mother and Dad returned to Montana from their time in Idaho, I am not sure where Dad Worked they were living in the log house on the homestead in 1921. Here they were blessed with a baby girl my sister Esther. She was born in town at Maimi's house. Mrs. Boorman lived close by and she thought Esther was the most perfect little girl. Years later she had a girl of her own she named her Esther. At this time when babies were born and the mother was in bed for ten days, every one came to see the new baby, so Esther has been told by people that they held her when she was only a few hours old.

Now Harold had a little sister 5 years younger than him. He probably was not too thrilled as he had been the only child for a long time. One day mother wanted Harold to watch the baby, he didn't want to, so mother told him she would just give her to the Indians then and didn't think any more about it, till Harold came running into the house and jumped in the crib and lay on top of the baby. Mother didn't know what had gotten into him till she looked out and saw that some Indians were coming up the road. He was going to hide his baby sister. When she started to get dolls, the ones that had a Ma Ma in them when you bent them forward, well Harold decided they needed surgery. So he took out their appendix... but the incision was on the back and sewed up with big black stitches and they didn't say MA MA any more but he had a new toy to play with. Now this is hear say as I was not born yet. But I do remember Esther having dolls with black stitches on their back when I was very young.

The family now moved to the Ovid Peltier place where Dad was working. They had a very small house to live in. Mother gave Esther her locket to play with which she dropped down a crack in the floor and they never did get it out. My class ring went the same way I will tell of that later.

While living here Harold and a friend went up on top of the bald hill behind the house and they rolled a rock down from the top and knocked a wheel off from the county commissioner's car.

From the Ovid Peltier Place Mom and Dad moved to Eureka on the hill in East Eureka into one of the square mill houses. Mom liked this house as it had two bedrooms. She made a cover for the day bed in the front room that Esther remembers as having red cherries and green leaves on a light colored background. She also made a round pillow out of the same fabric that tied on her rocking chair. They had ruffles on them and Esther thought them to be so pretty, that every time some one came she had to take them in so she could show them the new prettys. This is the rocker that Mom rocked her in. Mother rocked all her children and sang to all of us Then before long they were packing again and this move took them to Fortine. Dad must have had some cattle now as they moved to the ranch that is now owned by the Burgess family. The house was a duplex and the other family living there was Dewey and Thelma Schuck Green they also had two children. Harold was in school in Fortine it must have been some walk for a 8 or 9 year old. While they lived here Mother would shoot venison from the back porch, they were feeding on the haystack. She would dress them out by herself. One day Dad invited the game warden for dinner and he ate fresh venison with them. (out of season). He thanked them for dinner and never said a word.

This is where Myrtle Marie joined the family. Mother had two very dear friends Aunt Marie and Myrtle Rhodes, this is who Myrtle was named after, Myrtle Marie. The night she was born Harold who was 10 years old was sent up the Marrow Lake road in the dark to get Mrs. Nutt to come and assist in the birth. This was September 14 1926. Dad took Esther out to clean the barn, she woke up, she always wanted to be in the middle of every thing, they wouldn't let her go into Mothers room. When they came back into the house she was told she had a new baby sister. She informed them that she knew that because she had seen her hair in the Dr.'s bag but she had thought it was a brush. So now Harold was 10 and Esther was 5 and they had a new baby which made Esther take a back seat.

Before Long Dad wanted to go back to the woods to work so the livestock were again sold and they moved to Kinchilla's mill this is where Esther started school. Miss Zeller (Marguerite Titchbourne) was her first grade teacher. The teacher boarded with Mother and Dad till Dad decided to quit his job, and back to Eureka they moved.

They moved into a small house in East Eureka. Esther and Harold went back to school. Esther's teacher was Mrs. Hunsinger, she went to school 3 days. She didn't go to school any more that year. The next move was to the little house Uncle Roe had built for them some time before that. Dad had some more cattle again. Esther and Harold drove a little spring buggy to Iowa Flats school. They had to take hay in the back of the buggy for the horse to eat while they were in school. One day a chicken got in the hay and went to school with them. When they discovered the chicken all the kids chased it till it was caught and Harold tied it by the leg to the buggy with a string, when they started home, Harold found an egg the chicken had laid in the buggy. Well being a boy on the way home the egg found a mailbox. The owner found Dad and Dad found Harold need I say more. This November 27th 1928 I made an appearance on the scene. This place where I was born is where Nuttings now live towards town and across from the cemetery. Harold and Esther were taken to Aunt Myrtle and Uncle Earl Rhodes who lived down on the Tobacco River by the old Pidgeon bridge. I was suppose to be John so guess I disappointed them all they must have thought enough is enough as I was the last one. When they told Harold he had a new baby sister he said "just some more misery". Myrtle was only two years old so she probably didn't pay to much attention, and Esther probably thought another one to help take care of. Dad told me the Dr. told him I had to have a name even if I was not John, so he said oh hell Eva I guess, When my birth certificate came back it was Helen Eva.

The folks left there and moved to what was known as the Gary place. This was a 2 story white house that set on the highway where you turn of to the airport. There was a big tree in the front yard. Also a cellar under the house. Dad said they got the place rent free but could not use the cellar. The owner kept that for himself. That was during the time they were running liquor from Canada and that Cellar and the grainary were drop off and pick up spots. So they did not stay on this place very long.

When we left this place the folks had a big auction they sold cattle farm equipment and all . We moved into town to a house by Grandmother Shenefelt's. It was the house where Opal Kearney now lives. When we lived here there was a lady lived across the road that spanked Myrtle when she would leave the yard. This lady was later admitted to Warm Springs where she spent the rest of her life. Harold, Esther, and Myrtle all had dark eyes like Dads family and I had blue eyes like Mother and I had Mother's curly hair I never wanted to sit still long enough to have it brushed and curled around Mother's finger.

While we lived here Harold was in High School and he played football. Myrtle remembers him coming home from football practice and making onion sandwiches which he shared with her.

They had a forest fire at Whitefish and Columbia Falls. Dad went to work for Columbus Clark who was logging off the burnt timber. So the house in Eureka was closed up and we moved up the North Fork into a very small cabin. We moved from Eureka, taking only what we would absolutely need. Dad had a 1929 car at this time with a hard roof a real nice one, when we got to the cabin he built bunk beds in which Esther, Myrtle and I slept in the bottom one and Harold in the top one.

Mother and Dad had their bed on the other side of the room. We had a table and chairs and a cook stove.

When Mother would put us out to play for the day she said in a half hour we would be covered with black soot from the forest fire.

When she heated water to wash clothes she would fill the wash boiler and put it on the stove, to make it heat faster she would take the round plates from the stove top and put them on the wood floor. Esther jumped out of bed one morning when mom had done this, the cook stove was our only source of heat, she ran over by it to get warm. She was bare footed and stepped on one of the lids. Her foot stuck to it. When Mother pulled her foot loose some tissue from Esther's foot stuck to the lid. She was doctored up with cold water and Soda. In time it healed up with no infection.

Harold was only fourteen years old but he was out working like a man driving a skid horse in the woods. One day he was sick and Dad finally let him come in with the horse. When he got all the soot washed off he was covered with measles. So we all had a siege with the measles. After the job at Columbia Falls was finished we moved back to Eureka. Myrtle had become very thin and was not well. She coughed a lot, the Dr. told the folks to get her out where she could have lots of milk and fresh air.

By now it was 1929 and we all know what happened then. We thought things were tough before now, well this was the great depression. The banks closed things were real bad all over. Dad always said he was glad he had some cattle so his money in them was safe. You couldn't sell them, no one had any money, but you could pay a grocery bill with one or get credit at the grocery store for one. We were never on relief and he never worked for the W.P.A. of which he was proud. He said he let some people take a cow to have milk for their family but he got all the calf's that were born.

This time we moved to the Doxie place, which was on down past Claude Maddens. When we moved they had taken Mothers new linoleum rug and rolled it up tied it with a rope to move it but it was out in the yard waiting to be loaded, Myrtle and Irene Olson proceeded to run full length of it a few times and really cracked it bad. Mother would not live with bed bugs, as some people did at that time. This house was full of them. She put a wash tub with some water in it and a 2# coffee can in the middle, into which they poured something to fumigate for the bed bugs and any other creepy things that might be in there. We left the house for some time. When we came back no bugs but the can and tub had boiled over and there was from then on a big ring on the floor.

This is the first place I can remember , I was between two and three years old. I went out side with an apple and a rooster took it away from me. I can remember the pecking chicken and the flapping wings, I am still scared of anything with feathers that fly around.

After we moved here Dad and Harold had one last big fight Dad thought Harold should work and act like a man and he was only a fifteen year old boy that had to quit school and go to work. Mother had one silver dollar to her name and she gave it to him he walked down the lane, to town and caught a freight train to Bend Oregon he stayed with Uncle Corade and Maimi for a while then he was all over the United States and Canada He came back for a short while a year or so later, he spent some time in the C.C.C's .Mother usually heard from him on Mothers day. Now you see why I never knew my brother very well. This left THE SISTERS THREE. I was still sleeping in the crib here. After the crib Esther, Myrtle and I always slept in the same bed until Esther was married.

On the Doxie place there was an open well. Myrtle was about 5 years old, she liked to lay down and look down the well. Mother kept telling her to stay away from it. Needless to say she didn't, so mother quietly came up behind her and took her by the ankles and dangled her over the well. That put a stop to her well peeping. We also carried water from the well up the hill to water the garden. As Dad was always of some where working mother did the farm work. She would carry two milk pails Esther two ten pound pails, Myrtle lard buckets and me little pails of some kind, full of water trip after trip to water the garden. Then come fall mother would have vegetables to can for winter. When dandelions first came up in the spring after not having any fresh greens all winter every one dug up the small fresh plants washed them good and boiled them and ate them like spinach. They are real good with a little vinegar on them.

This Christmas Myrtle and I each received a doll that had a cloth stuffed body and a painted tin head, there was a place to thread a ribbon through the painted hair on the head so you could tie a bow. Mother made clothes for them. Sharon, Myrtles daughter still has her doll, I don't know what ever happen to mine.

Mother also made all of our clothes coats and all. She even made our under clothes. If she had enough material when she made a dress for us she made bloomers to match, girls wore black sateen bloomers at this time. The catalog had a new color and mother ordered it, we had maize bloomers that year. Everything was washed on the board. Water carried from the well and heated on the stove. Clothes ironed with a sad iron heated on the stove. Mother would put her ironing board on the back of two chairs as it didn't have any legs on it. Also if there was to much company for a meal for the amount of chairs we had the ironing board would be put between two chairs to make more seating space.

But we were always clean, starched and ironed. Also the house was always very clean. There were times in my life I never remember seeing mother in bed she was always up working. If nothing else the treadle sewing machine would be going. She also sang a lot. Little Joe the wrangler, Frogy went a courting, Red wing were some of the songs she sang.

Shoes seemed to be a real big problem. We children usually got one pair of shoes in the fall. They were ordered out of the catalog. When we were older we said they fit even if they were to tight as we didn't want them sent back. After the blisters and sore feet started to appear Mother would put wheat in the shoes and pour water in them the wheat would swell and stretch the shoes, the wheat was left in till the shoes were dry so they didn't curl up. By spring we were cutting cardboard to put in the shoes to cover the holes so we were not walking on the ground it took a good heavy piece of cardboard every day. To this day when I get a new pair of leather work shoes I put them on and stand in a tub of warm water till my feet get wet and wear them till they are dry and they never hurt my feet.

We always went barefoot in the summer time. Mother always wore a crisp starched and ironed dress and apron. The starch was made out of hot water and gloss starch It was stirred while it was cooking so as not to get lumpy, then diluted with water to the strength of starch you wanted. After the last rinse, you put the cloths in the starch rung them out and hung them out to dry. When they were dry you brought them in and sprinkled them with water and rolled them up tightly till you ironed them in a day or so, if left longer they would mildew and before steam irons they had to be sprinkled to get the wrinkles out.

The year I must have been between 3 and 4 we had a chance to move to the Green place, there was a two story house it had a kitchen, front room, and 2 bedroom down stairs with two bed rooms upstairs. Mother and Dad had one of the down stair's bedroom's and we three girls had the other one. There was also a lot of out buildings. Barn, chicken house, pig pen, granary and an ice house. The Ice house has a lot of memory's for me, it had a door on one side that went into a cool room. On one side was shelves that had screen doors on the front that closed with a hook. This is where Mother kept the milk, cream eggs butter and any thing she was taking to town to sell or ship to Spokane.

I was about 3 or so by now and followed Tootsie (Esther) and Tuckie (Myrtle) every where they went. When they wouldn't want me with them they would put me kicking and screaming up in one of these cupboard in the ice house and lock me in. Then go on about their business. From inside this thick walled building into the house or out in the field Mother couldn't hear me yelling. When they got ready they would come turn me loose. The other half of the Ice house was filled with blocks of ice that was cut in the winter and packed very close with sawdust over and between . It would last all summer, we could have cold drinks and Ice cream from it and it was a real good place for hot bare feet in the summer time to play in the cool wet sawdust. Now the granary was a fun place to play also, it had different bins for the grains, wheat, oats, barley and etc. Myrtle and I wore bib overalls to play in part of the time. One day we had cuffs turned up on our overalls and went to the granary to play. We would crawl around and dig in the wheat then the oat and barley, when we were done every thing was mixed up it seems our cuffs were full of one kind when we went to the next. Our parents were not to happy with two playful little girls.

They also had a few Geese I was scared to death of them, when they came at me hissing and flapping their wings, up on a fence post I would go and stay till some one chased them away and rescued me.

Mother had a box on the roller she used in the field up on the hill. She would pull it with a team of horses and let Myrtle and I ride in the box by the seat. Or she would put us in the shade of a tree to play while she worked in the field. She always had 8 to 9 cows to milk morning and night It was Harold or Esther's job to get the cows into the barn in the morning and at night. Also the barn had to be cleaned every day. If Dad was home he helped with this also.

Aunt Marie and Uncle Earl Roose lived over the hill on the Homestead. Also Aunt Blanche and Uncle Dow O'Brien had a place over the hill. We would walk over to visit at both places a lot. We learned to walk on stilts at O'Briens.. At aunt Manes one day Clarence Roose and I dropped big rocks on each others toes at the count of three to see what it would feel like, I remember aunt Marie set us both up on the table, washed our foot in a little wash basin and tore strips of white rag's (before Band-Aids) wrapped our toes and tied a knot to keep them on.

Esther did a lot of the work in the house while Mother was in the field or garden. Another garden to get water by the bucket full. Esther got so she would not answer to the nick name of Tootsie so we had to start calling her Esther. Her name is Esther Lenore one time we called her Esther manore she didn't think it was as funny as we did. Esther set the table one day and didn't give Myrtle a knife, well she decided she needed one and proceeded to get her own. At this time the cupboards were self standing not hooked to the wall. When Myrtle climbed up on it the whole thing came down on top of her broke the glass and most of the dishes, there was a loaded pistol on the top that went flying into the front room. Mother was alone with us so much she kept a loaded pistol handy and she knew how to use it.

Mother and Dad always took the heating stove out of the house in the spring of the year and returned it in the fall. In this house that left a hole in the ceiling of the front room which went upstairs. Jack Stevens stayed with us a lot and he or Harold would take me by the arms and drop me through this hole to the other one down stairs. I can remember trip after trip up those stairs till they called a stop to it for the day.

Mother would brush Myrtle and Esther's short hair and bangs and they could go play. Then I had to sit while she brushed the tangles out of that curly hair I had, then sit while she wet it and curled each curl around her finger. I guess my first experience with scissors came about now. I took mothers scissors and crawled under Mother and Dad's bed and cut each one of those darn curls off right next to my head. When Mother seen me she cried, I was called Bobbie for a while. But it grew back.

For Christmas this year Mother made us doll beds from apple boxes, they were so cute she made doll blankets for them. Some where along the way she made Us stuffed rabbits from flour sacks. With embroidered faces and clothes. Mine is in the Historical Village Store in Eureka. I put it there in 1988 it was very fragile by this time. It is a toy of the depression time.

Mother was out looking for cattle one day, she was horseback, the horse went under a tree and a limb came back and hit her in the face she had a beautiful black eye when she came home. It was one of those that was black then green then yellow a real shiner.

This is where Myrtle started the first grade and also the first year Ruby Stevens Ruby taught school. Esther must have been in the fifth grade.

Mother liked this farm and had worked so very hard on it. Well it was put up for sale and they were a very few dollars short of having enough to buy it, Dad would not borrow what little they needed so we were on the move again.

We moved to the Kearney place on the Black Lake Road, just past Gregors on the next little lake on the left. This place did not have a very good house. It had a kitchen and front room down stairs, and 2 bedrooms upstairs. The upstairs were real smoky and the walls were dirty, so Mother and Esther went to town and got old newspapers and made some flour and water paste and they papered the upstairs. It was clean but if you tried to look at the papers some of the pictures were up side down. I could not read or this might have been a problem. Some of the windows had paines on the top but the bottom half was boarded up. This place did have a barn and chicken house and some land that was under cultivation.

Esther and Myrtle rode a horse to Black Lake school from here. Esther was by her self going to school one day and she had a school bag over her shoulder, when she got off to open the gate the strap on the school bag caught on the saddle horn and strangled her, when it finally broke, she was unconscious, she came to and the horse was grazing along side of the road. Really scared her she could have been hanged if the strap had not broken.

During the time we lived on this place they would go to school to Eureka for a while then back to Black lake I don't know why they switched back and forth. Myrtle has spoke about times she walked to school in Eureka she would carry her shoes except when she was at school as she had blisters on her heals that hurt real bad. This was caused by ill fitting shoes.

We locked up the house and moved to Edna Creek up above Fortine to a mill, Mother took the job as camp cook The girls had to go to school and it was a three mile walk around the road to Curtises house to catch the bus but only two miles through the woods. So on Sunday Dad took Esther through the woods to show her the way. That night there was a snow storm and when the girls started out in the dark through the woods every thing looked different and they got lost, arriving at Curtis's about noon wet to their waist and near frozen. Larry Curtis says he remembers that day as if it were yesterday, What he remembers the most was when they got to their house so cold wet and late was that Esther had on a pair of Dads Orange monkey face work gloves. They were 6 and 11 years old. That was Myrtles only day at school in Fortine, however Esther continued but she walked the three miles in the tie truck tracks to catch the bus. Later on Esther became very ill the Dr.'s didn't know what was the matter with her. She was in the Kalispell Hospital for some time. They thought it could be appendicitis but they didn't do surgery on her. When she was released from the hospital she went to Rose Maddens, as she was very weak but wanted to get back to school. Maddens lived across from the Black Lake School. When school was over for the day Ruby would put her on a sled and she would ride across the road and down to Maddens house and Claude would catch her.

In camp that winter to let Myrtle and I entertain ourselves while she was making pies, mother let us roll can goods down the benches. These cook houses had a real long table with benches on each side for the men to sit while they ate, we were having lots of fun rolling cans to the back side of the table and tearing the labels from them. Well most were gallon cans as that is what the fruit and vegetables came in to feed that many men. The only thing she could tell for sure was can milk. The men ate a lot of mixed fruit and mixed vegetables for a while and we never played with the can goods any more.

Now the job was finished so we moved back to the Kearney place. I have some good memories while others in the family don't. We were very poor at this time but so were most people. No one had any money.

We had a little black and white dog we called Jerry she was some kind of a terrier mixture. Dad poisoned gophers and the dog would get a hold of them and she would get poisoned, when this happened here she would come to Mother. Mother mixed lard and cream I think it was and forced it down her and she would get all right again but she never learned, this happened time and time again. Finally she didn't make it to Mother in time and the poison finally got her.

When dad butchered a pig he would give Myrtle and I the pig's tail wound around in one of his copenhagen boxes, we would carry it around for a long time. It must have gotten pretty rank. When a pig was butchered they would put a 55 gallon barrel over a bon fire in the yard till the water was very hot. Then Dad would kill and bleed the pig and tilt the barrel a little and they would slosh the pig up and down in the hot water. Then it was slid out and they would scrape all the hair from the animal and proceed to gut and cut it up. We would have fried heart and liver for a few days after butchering Mother could not butcher a pig, as this was a two man job. However she did butcher a lot of steers by herself, she would shoot it and bleed it then she would put a single tree between the back legs through the tenants above the feet. To this she attached a rope and put it through a pulley on a tripod. She attached this to a saddle horn on a saddle horse and pulled the steer up from the ground. Some one, usually Esther had to hold the horse steady while Mother would skin and gut the animal, then she would hitch a team of horses to the wagon and back it under the steer she would put a clean sheet on the wagon and let the animal down on it. Then we took it to town to pay the grocery bill or with luck to sell it. When you paid your grocery bill the grocer gave you a little bag of candy, that was the only time we had store bought candy.

Our Dad always worked, but most of the time his paycheck stopped at the bar and never got home. He was not abusive but drank a lot if he had the money. As we got older it was very embarrassing. Our dear hard working Mother kept food on the table and a roof over our heads.

Dad was on a forest service job up on the Sutton Road on Pinkham. We walked up to see him and we stayed overnight. We slept in a tent , he told us if it rained not to touch the tent as it would make it leak . It did we did and it leaked we were in trouble again. We would get tired on these long walks so Mother would go to the side of the road and find us a stick horse, we never got tired riding them. I tasted my first pineapple. I thought it was the nectar of the gods. Myrtle remembers some little cans of cheese and hard tack he had that she really liked.

Myrtle was always going to Aunt Myrtles and Uncle Earl Rhodes and staying over night. Well I wanted to go also, so one time they took me home with them. Aunt Myrtle had a Jar that was made into a vase, it had been covered with plaster of Paris and had all kinds of little things stuck on it. I thought it was so pretty I could sit and look at it for hours, if Mother was in the other room. When I went alone it was not the same. Come bed time I wanted to go home, Mother always rocked me to sleep and sang to me. They lived at the Bottom of sand hill above the Pidgeon bridge. Probably 3 to 4 miles from our place. After Hours of crying Uncle Earl got out the horse and buggy and took me home. I really don't think they were to pleased with me. They never took me home with them again.

In the winter Mother would put Dad's wool sox over our shoes so we could go out and play in the snow as we didn't have over shoes or boots. She made our coats out of adults worn out coats by turning the fabric or using the parts that were not worn. They were nice looking. She did a good job on them. And they were very warm. I got my first store bought coat the year I started High school. It was maroon and had large shoulder pads and it was a princess style, Esther gave it to me and I felt like a princess in it. She made our mittens from the top of wool sox that the feet were to far gone to darn any more. She laid them flat and cut a thumb and the mitt then sewed them and turned them. They were serviceable and warm.

There was a big rock with a sort of flat sloping top up in one field. Myrtle and I would play on it while Mother was working that field. There is now a mobile home parked on top of that hill by our pretty big rock. I hope their children have fun on it as we did.

There is now also a home built on the hill across from where our house once stood. They are friends to our son Dennis and his family.

It is now 60 years since we left this place. In the spring of the year there were a lot of pink bitteroots blooming on the hill tops. Buttercups in the valleys and fields of yellow bells and my favorite purple shooting stars also crocuses. Later in the year sunflowers and white daisies, Yes northwest Montana has beautiful wild flowers. Not many people get a chance to see the beautiful lady slippers that grow in swampy areas. I have seen a few but they are not plentiful and it is against the law to pick or disturb them.

This is the time of the year that all new little things arrived like calves, baby pigs and baby chickens. We always got a lot of chickens so we could have fryers, If we found a dead baby chicken we could have a funeral and put it in a match box and bury it. But when our cemetery started to grow by leaps and bounds Mother started to investigate and she found it was Myrtle and I stepping on them not cows so that put a stop to that.

We were renting from Chili Kearneys Grandmother she had a house up the valley a way from us, she was a frail little lady with white hair. She would come and visit with mother and they would sit and have tea. We girls thought she was very old. I don't remember where Esther was, maybe having tea with the ladies. Meanwhile Myrtle and found a nest of little baby water snakes and we had a bull durum bag, so we filled it with wiggley little snakes and took them into the house and dumped them in Mothers lap. I will never forget seeing Mrs. Kearney going out that kitchen door, across the yard and she was still running as far as we could see her. And we thought she was old! I can tell you we brought no more snakes into the house.

The lake down below the house had turtles in it which we would catch and play with. They also laid their eggs in the mud by the lake. Myrtle and I would dig them up and put them in our mud pies. One day Myrtle told me I was adopted as I had blue eyes and curly hair and didn't look like the rest of them. So I had to eat those mud pies or she would have Mother return me where she got me. Well I guess I got my protein that day as I ate the mud pies turtle eggs and all.

Mother also had a friend Olive Leib who at this time lived at the Flueharty place on twin lakes. That was another one of our outings. Walking up to see Olive. Those lakes really had an odor at that time. But we liked to wade in the mud and the lake. Mother couldn't swim but she was suffering from rheumatoid arthritis at this time and she thought that the water might feel good on her knees and legs so she made herself some water wings out of 10 pound lard pail which she put the lids on tight and put them in a pillow case and fastened the end. She would lay across them and they would keep her afloat. We spent a lot of time in this lake that summer and Mother's leg and knees got better, she never had trouble with them again. We wondered if that stinking mud did it.

When we took our walks we had to be home in time to get the cows in and milk them. We helped to get them in but Mother did the milking usually cows will go into the same stanchion every time. We had one cow named Snorty that was a kicker, she had to have the kickers put on her every time or the one milking ended up across the barn.

One time she went into the wrong stanchion and Mother sometime did not light the lantern, well this time she should have, as she and the pail of milk and all went sailing across the barn. Then we had another cow we named Net Mother would milk her first and turn her out for us to play on, she was so gentle she would let us crawl all over her . One time Snorty was in the coral with a new calf, we wanted to see the baby calf so were looking through the rails on the coral and Snorty came full speed across the coral and hit the rails with her head right were we were looking in. She was just a plain mean cow.

There was an old building down by the road beside the lake I recall some one saying it had been a grainery. One Day Esther decided to play hooky, she went into this building instead of going to school. After while she became scared at what would happen if Mother found out she didn't go to school, so she laid on the floor of this old building all day.

I figured out early if we went to town to get grocery's or visit Grandmother and came home quit late that if you went to sleep or pretended to you would get carried into the house and would not have to walk, Lazy huh!

We visited Mrs. Gregor once in a while they didn't live to far away, she made the best poppy seed cake. But their children were all a lot older than we were.

Mother in the summer time would set on the front porch in her rocking chair, after all chores were done she would hold me, and Myrtle would sit on one side of the chair and Esther on the other and she would rock me and sing to us.

Our Brother Harold had came back to the area and he married a very nice red headed girl from Whitefish her name was Marion Johnson. She had been married before and had a small boy Toby. They came to see us and Mother was canning Bing cherries, she told me not to give the baby any as he would swallow the pit and choke on them. Well I had been the baby a long time and maybe I could get rid of him. There was a day bed on the front porch so I took some cherries and Toby under it and just stuffed the cherries down him and it didn't hurt him at all to swallow those seeds. When we were found all covered with cherry juice, he got coddled and I got swatted.

I got a hold of the scissors again at this time. Mother and Dad had their bed in the front room. Mother had gotten a real pretty bedspread some how, someplace. It had long fringes on it till I remodeled it then it had short stubby fringes where I could reach. Also Mother got Myrtle and I each a little rubber baby doll for Christmas. She had been busy at night making clothes for the dolls, I found them before Christmas in the sewing machine drawer.

Dad always bought a dishpan full of hard candy and a few old fashion chocolates and a dishpan full of mixed nuts this was his contribution to Christmas the candy had a lot of ribbon candy in it you don't see this candy much any more.

The Same Santa
(reprint from a letter to the Editor
in the Western News during the 1950's)

MY FIRST SANTA CLAUS

I was a wee bit of a brat, skinny and scared Dec. 24, 1912, but full of excited anticipation, because friends had invited all of our family to their place for Christmas Eve-with the promise that Santa Clause would come to the party. I'd never seen him.

The only Santa I knew was the pictures I'd seen and what my older brother and sister had told me. I can recall to this day how the goose bumps chased back and forth and I could hardly keep quiet

It seemed forever before we got through supper and dishes were done, but finally - There he was- He had a sorta funny looking Santa suit - but I quickly forgot that when he started handing out toys and candy and was I a proud kid when he even called me by name.

The Santa that brought so much joy to my heart all those years ago, has continued to bring joy to many many youngsters down through the years - Fact is, I happen to know that this same Santa has dug into his own pocket to provide a Happy Christmas for youngsters who would not have had one otherwise - and I'll always have a soft spot in my heart for my Santa and yours - none other than Francis Shenefelt.

Averil Fluharty West

We seemed to have people coming at different times to live with us. Arlie and Florence Stevens were living with us right after they had gotten married. At that time you opened a coffee can with a key, If the top rim came off the can it had a razor sharp top on it. Mother kept milk in these. One day Florence turned around and run her forearm on the top of a can and cut it. I ran to mother for help and told her Florence had cut her arm and it was hanging by a string. Looked that bad to me but guess it wasn't.

Mother went to town and left Esther to watch Myrtle and I. She decided she would finger wave our hair, she had no waving lotion to make it hold. So the next best thing was egg whites, she separated I don't know how many eggs, then we took the yolks and shells way down the hill beyond the root cellar and dumped them out. So Mother would not know we used the eggs. When she came home and took one look at our stiff hair she knew, but all she said was why didn't you save the yolks I could have used them in baking.

Grandmother Shenefelt made a wonderful sunshine sponge cake with egg yolks, it was every ones favorite. Myrtle didn't like carrots so grandmother would set a piece of sunshine cake in front of her plate with carrots on it and tell her she couldn't eat it till the carrots were all gone Myrtle learned to like carrots. But she tried the same thing with me and curds and whey and it didn't work I didn't eat either one.

Aunt Blythe was away at college, Aunt Marie was at Grandmothers with Lloyd, Clarence and Jackie was a tiny baby. Well the boys and Myrtle and I all came down with whooping cough. We were all at grandmothers, where she put us all in a one bedroom house I don't know but we were there for the duration of the whooping cough. Our nose would run we would cough and vomit. They would grab my hands to keep me from rubbing it up in my long curls.

In the spring before time to plant the garden and before school was out. We moved to Sheldon Canyon, where the tobacco river emptied into the backwaters of the Kootani river. The place was owned by Lem Collar. It was later known as Ivan Engrams place and now is under Lake Koocanusa. Esther and Myrtle finished school at the Sheldon Canyon school that year Myrtle was in the third grade and Esther the eight grade. Mr. Ross was their teacher.

We had a nice house here it had a kitchen, pantry, front room and two bedrooms down stairs and two bedrooms up stairs one was not finished. Some one left an old typewriter up there Myrtle and I would play that it was a piano. We would play it and sing and have a real good time with it. We also had a big high barn, a chicken coop, a tool shed and a pig pen. In the tool shed there was a big whet stone with a seat on it and peddles, there was a can with a hole in it for water to keep the stone wet while they were sharpening their tools. Myrtle and I used it like a bicycle we would get on it and peddle and go many places and never move an inch.

I started school here that next fall. Our Teacher was Miss Cruso. I had a little trouble right off the bat with her. Dad told me to ask her if she was Robinson Cruso's sister she did not think it was so funny.

There were two First graders Jim Whitmarsh and myself. Both of us had birthdays in November, he always got his birthday off as it was November 11th veterans day. I did not think that was fair.

This was a typical country school, windows down both sides of the room. A blackboard and roll up maps in the front and a big wood stove with a metal shield all around it in the back of the room. There was a door in the middle of the front that came into a cloak room the boys used one side and the girls used the other. This was where the coats hats and gloves were put also a line of different kind of pails that were used for lunches.

There was a back door that went out to the woodshed— barn and the out houses with well worn paths. In back of the room was a bucket and a dipper for drinking water every one used the same one. The Teachers desk sat in the front of the room with her chair and a metal waste basket beside it. The pencil sharpener was in the front of the room also. There was always a pointer and chalk plus a few erasers in the little shelf at the bottom of the black board. There were four rows of desks of various sizes running the length of the room.

This year Myrtle was a fourth grader and Esther was a freshman in High School. She rode the Rexford bus to Eureka to school. When the High School burned all twelve grades were in the Roosevelt School, till the new High School was built. It was a mighty crowded school.

My first grade to me was real exciting I had wanted to go to school for some time. We only had to walk up over the track and up the hill. If it had not been for one hill we could have seen the school from our house. One day at school the Teacher had trouble with one of the big boys in the eighth grade. She chased him down the road with a pair of overshoes over her head to hit him, she had picked them up on her way through the cloak room, but she never caught him and he never came back to school.

During the year everyone in the school got what they called the seven year itch, including Myrtle and I. Even the Teacher caught it. Mother said it was no crime to get the itch, but it was to keep it. When we went home from school we were greased down with sulfur and lard salve Mother made. We were greased down again before we went to bed. In the morning water was hauled in from the pump in the yard, heated and put in the laundry tub and we were given a bath before we went to school. After the cows were milked the separating done and we three girls were off to school, Mother had to wash all that bedding every day on the board, hang it out to dry to go back on the bed that night. But we did get over the Itch before to long.

I raised my hand one day to go out to the outhouse the Teacher said no I had to get up in front of the room to read. That was a mistake, you guessed it. I was standing in front of the whole room reading and I wet my pants it ran down the isle right towards Myrtles desk she was so embarrassed. The Teacher let me go home. I told Mother I had fell in a mud puddle but she knew different. The Teacher let students go when they raised their hands after that. There was a Christmas party and program at school that year we all had little parts in the program and practiced for a long time as each of us got up to recite in front of our parents and friends we were so proud. Santa also came and gave us each a little bag of candy.

During the year there was a shadow social held at the school house. The lady's brought a lunch. There was a sheet strung up on wires and the ladies would get behind the sheet with a lamp behind them and the men would bid on the shadows and they would eat with whomever they bought their shadow. Their was also a pie social there that year. I am sure Mother took enough for Myrtle and I to eat also. Esther was old enough to be taking her own lunch to be bid on.

I don't remember them having any dances at this school like they had at Black Lake. There was usually a violin and if the school had a piano some one would play it Dad played a mouth harp. The women would bring dishpans full of sandwiches, there would be cakes pies and cookies. About midnight the music would stop and everyone ate. Then the children were put on benches, desks or what was handy, covered with coats and went to sleep. The adults would dance till dawn.

At the end of the school year we went to Tetrault lake for a school picnic. This is when the whole family went. There was potato salad, sandwiches, fried chicken, cake, cookies, pies and home made ice cream. Mother and Dad had a big ice cream freezer, when it was being frozen at home before we went we would put a burlap bag on the top and take turns sitting on it so the handle could be turned some more. Then the dasher was taken out and every one got a taste from the dasher, the top was put back on and it was packed with ice and covered and would be real good at noon. This is the first time of the summer we could go swimming some time it was a little cold in May.

The garden was growing so well, Mother was so proud of it. Her cabbage was doing so good. Someone (Myrtle and I) left the gate open, the cows got in and ate everything. The root vegetables were salvageable but the pretty big cabbages were gone. Mother thought fisherman left the gate open, they went that way to the river. We never told her any different.

The Byers family lived on the Island they had four boys. Laird, Everett, Kenneth and Bob, and one girl Beulah. When we visited back and forth, we walked over the swinging bridge that went over the back water of the Kootani river to the Island. It was maybe a half mile below us towards Rexford. Across from Billy and Stella Parcels place. It was fun to make it rock and jump, when you ran on it or got out in the middle and held on to the cable and swayed back and forth. Beulah had a little toy wood cook stove, it was black cast iron and had little pots and pans. I loved to play with it. Or just sit and look at it. We never had any thing like that at our house.

The closest family that had children our age were the Whitmarshes. They lived about a mile down the tracks toward Gateway, in a small house on the north edge of Livermore lake, they had seven children at home, they were Bob, Don, Jean, Jim, Winifred, Ruth and Joe. We walked the tracks to their house to play. The coal train from Fernie to Rexford went past their house and ours. There was a high trestle in front of our place it went over our road and on over the Tobacco River. Also a smaller one over the west end of Livermore Lake this one was close to the water. This lake had huge big lily pads with pretty big pink blossoms. The frogs would sit on the lily pads. Myrtle and Bob were crossing the trestle which was only inches from the water and she asked him if a person could stand on the lily pads? He told her if you put one foot on each lily pad and stood up real careful you could. So she sat on the trestle and very carefully put one foot on one and the other foot on another and stood up ever so careful and sank like a rock. Bob was laughing so hard he could hardly pull her out. We were there one time playing cops and robbers. Myrtle was a robber and Don was a cop well he caught her and sentenced her to hang. He proceeded to carry out the sentence. We found her in the wood shed with a rope around her neck and only her toes touching the ground. She was really scared and I am the one that cried.

Mrs. Whitmarsh was expecting a baby and in the middle of the night Bob came down the track and was beating on the door for Mother to come and deliver the baby. Mother and Esther went home with him, They brought Phillip into the world he was a big boy eleven pounds. When Mother helped deliver a baby she had the father take the afterbirth out and bury it in the manure pile. That way no animal would dig it up and the heat from the manure would dissolve it and it would go to compost. Besides it gave the father something to do and got him out of the way for a while. As the baby and mother both needed cleaned up and settled down to rest after their ordeal they had just been through.

I tasted my first bananas about this time. Dad had gone to Rexford and Maddens Grocery had a whole stock of bananas that had been frosted in shipping. They were black on the outside but good inside, we really ate bananas and Mother made pies and cakes with them.

Ruby Stevens came to visit one day and she had Jacks niece Loraine Brown, from Whitefish with her, she was about Myrtles age. We went out to play we had made a teeter totter by putting a board across a downed cottonwood tree in the meadow down by the river a ways from the house. Myrtle and Loraine were playing on it for a while and I wanted a turn, Loraine wouldn't get off. Myrtle thumped her end on the ground and Loraine went sailing through the air. She lit on her shoulder, she was crying and told us to go get Ruby, we told her she was a big baby, when she didn't stop we went and got Ruby. She took her to Eureka to Dr. Hunter she had a broken color bone. She still reminds Myrtle of this when she sees her some sixty years later.

Before stores had grocery bags when you bought something at the store it was wrapped in brown paper and tied with string. Every one saved the string so there was always a ball around somewhere. We would tie some string on each corner of our doll blankets and then get up on the barn and tie the string to our bib overalls, this was our parachute. We would jump off, it's a wonder we did not break our necks. One day we were up on the calf shed with our parachutes ready to jump. Myrtle would not go first so I pushed her. She went from the calf shed to the pig pen then the ground, when she hit she also broke her collar bone.

This trestle that run over the road and river had one train each way every day. We would walk over the trestle stepping on the ties. We knew when it was safe as the trains ran the same time every day. We would put apple box nails on the track cross them and when the train ran over them it would mash them together to look like a little pair of open scissors. We kept finding larger nails to try. One day we had some about six inches long and about as big around as a pencil. The train didn't come but a hand car with two section workers on it did. They hit these nails just before the trestle and it derailed them. Boy were we scared, into the house we went and under the bed. It didn't hurt them and I don't think they knew what they hit, these men would sometime stop up on the tracks and come down to the house to buy eggs butter and chickens from Mother when we would see them coming we were under the bed again till they left.

When company would drop in Mother would take a wire hook and catch a couple of chickens by the leg. Then she took them to the chopping block she would hold them with one hand and whack with the ax and the head was gone. They would flop around in the yard while she was pouring boiling water in a pail, she then would take the legs and end of the wings in her hand and douse the chicken up and down in the hot water a few times, then pick off the feathers and take a lid from the cook stove and put paper in the hole and hold the chicken over the flame to singe the fuzzy hair from it . She would then clean it, wash it in salt water, cut it up, roll it in flour and fry it. We always had a lot of lard. When they butchered a hog Mother would render out all the lard in the oven in big pans. Those cracklins that were left when they were all done were so good.

Mother and Dad never made us wait till the adults ate when we had company and maybe not enough room at the table. We were fed first and sent out to play while they ate. Dad would tell a joke at the table a lot, it was. One Sunday the Preacher came to dinner. There was not enough room at the table for the little boy. He wanted his mother to save him a piece of chicken. She told him there was always one piece of chicken left for manors sake. So he watched that platter go around and around the table till only one piece was left. It went around the table again and no one took it. It came to the Preacher and his father said you might as well finish it up. When the Preacher stuck his fork into it the boy said and there goes manors and I ain't had any.

When Myrtle and I would feed the chickens we would put feed close to our feet. When the chickens would eat, we would grab them by the tail feathers. The ones that came out we used to make head dresses when we played Indians.

People came here in the winter time to cut Ice from the river for their ice houses. I remember the horses pulling it up on the banks then the men would load it in the sleigh or wagon to haul it to their ice house. They cut it with long saws that had only one handle on it.

Mother was milking about ten cows at this time. Esther was in High School and had to catch the bus early. But she would get up and go get the cows in the barn. She milked one while Mother milked the rest of them. Then she would come in and bath in the laundry tub (to get the cow smell off). While Mother was setting up the separator. Then she would help Mother get the separator started as it turned hard to start and took two of them. She would then get her lunch packed , eat her oatmeal or boiled wheat and catch the bus to school. This was all repeated in the evening seven days a week. Mother made butter that was sold at the store in town, the cream was shipped out or went to the creamery in Eureka and we used the milk. Mother also made very good cottage cheese which we always ate with sugar on it. When you cook wheat for breakfast, you get a pan of chicken wheat, wash it real good cover it with water and put it on the back of the stove and let it simmer all day and all night. The next morning it is very good with good cream and sugar on it.

One morning when Mother was in the barn yard the neighbors Ram sheep got in there it knocked her down I don't know how many times, she finally crawled into one of the cow stanchions and got away from him. She was all black and blue and really beat up for a while.

I now have a nephew who is six years younger than I am his name is Bobbie this is my brothers boy he had snow white hair and was kind of cute if I had not been so jealous of him.

Our Teacher lived in a little house that was owned by the Ayers family it was on the island side of the swinging bridge. I don't know where she came from she taught there one year and was gone. She was before her time as she was a health nut. She ate fruit nuts and wheat. Heavy dark bread.

We would go down the road towards Rexford about a mile to the Nelson place. It was between the railroad tracks and the road. I remember they carried water from the river across the track and up the hill. Mrs. Nelson would have prayer meetings for the neighbor ladies.

We children would play out side. We always went with Mother. People at this time didn't get baby sitters. If there were an older child they sometime gave Mother a break, but then most of the time they wanted to go along also.

After the prayer meeting there was refreshments. This is the first place Myrtle remembers having peanut butter cookies.

Before school was out and before Christmas this year. Mother went up to Young Creek across the Kootani to cook in a camp for Columbus Clark. She received $25.00 a month and room and board for her and her family if we were there.

We had to go to school, Mother rented two rooms upstairs at Stella and Billy Parcell's. One room had one bed in it, We three always slept together anyway. The other room had a wood cook stove table and chairs.

Esther had turned fourteen that August and she had full responsibility of Myrtle and I. In the mornings she would feed us breakfast, scrub us all up, clean our finger nails, comb our hair and sit us each on a chair and tell us to stay there till it was time to go to school. She had to catch the bus for High School in Eureka and we only had about a half mile to walk. Well we stayed on the chairs about as long as it took her to get out of the house. Then we were down in Mrs. Parcell's kitchen.

We had to carry our wood upstairs for our cook stove and carry our water. It was really a fire trap with that big old wood cook stove.

If I got a tooth ache Mrs. Parcells would take care of me. I would lay on a sofa in her front room with a hot water bottle on my toothache all day, nice warm and cozy. I had a lot of tooth aches that year. Parcell's must have had a lot of apple trees and she made the best apple pies which they shared with us. She also made ground cherry pies they were so different and really good. They raised the ground cherries in their garden.

At Christmas vacation from School we went to camp. That year we got sleds for Christmas. Dad was so excited about them, he gave them to us a day or so early. Those were the fastest sleds in the whole valley, all the time we had them. Myrtle had hers till after her three children were grown and they sold their house in Eureka. She is sorry since that she left it hanging in the garage. I don't know what happen to mine. I probably thought I was to old for a sled somewhere along the way and gave it away.

We moved to Rexford before school was out to our new house. We finished the school year there and then went to camp for the summer. We three girls slept in a tent beside the cook house. Mother and Dad were sleeping in the cook house. There was a long bunk house and Columbus had a little cabin he slept in and used for an office. We were not allowed to go near the bunkhouse, It was a long building with a door in each end. This worked for ventilation in the summer. There was a big barrel stove and rough lumber bunks with mattresses on them, and that was about all. There was no radio's so usually some one had a guitar and in the evening they were outside playing and singing for entertainment.

Columbus's office had a home made table, chair and bed. This is where some one had to take Dad's time sheets to every evening.

The cook house was a long building with a door in each end. The big wood cook stove. A long table with benches on each side There was one long piece of oil cloth full length of the table. Mother had a big wooden box she kept full of baked goods, cake, pies cookies, donuts, and maple bars. She never sat the men down to a meal without some kind of home made dessert.

There was also a server made from rough lumber that she should have had patented as they use them in most all restaurant kitchens to day. It was a table with a shelf under it and one over the top. This is where she did all of her baking and prep work for these big meal three times a day, in the evening before bedtime she would mix her pancake starter for breakfast pancakes then it was covered with a towel and left all night.

While we were in the tent that summer, Mother told all the men if she seen or heard any one around our tent they were dead and they all knew she kept a loaded gun in the house. We had no trouble.

When they moved the mill to another stand of timber they set the mill up and cut enough lumber to build the cook house, bunk house and Columbus's office The barn was usually built from slabs. They took the doors and windows, cook stove and heater. The dishes were put in the big wooden pastry box, the oilcloth rolled up. Our mattresses and bedding what canned food there was and on we went. By that night they would have a rough lumber building up with a tar paper roof and the cracks batted with another board all around and that was our new residence. A table, server and benches were built, Stove set up, oil cloth put on the table and Mother would have dinner that night ready for every one. When we did dishes they were all done by hand and then put back on the table, silverware then plate up side down and cup on top of that.

We didn't have a cupboard but no need for one for the dishes. They did build shelves for the can goods. This summer on Young creek, one day a man asked Myrtle and I if we would go down to the branch and get him that poke hanging on the tree. We looked at him like he was from another planet. He was from North Carolina and he wanted a gunny sack that was down by the creek.

We made a shower there this summer by putting nail holes in the bottom of five gallon square honey can It was then hung up by a rope in a tree down by the creek. To take a shower you put a ladder up in the tree and had a buddy to pour water into the bucket while you stood under it. Of course those showers were mighty cold with the water coming right out of young creek.

When we left Young creek Mother must have sold the cattle as we were now going to move into our very own house. She had bought a house in Rexford for $150.00 from Mr. Weir. It was across the alley from the school.

It had a screened in front porch, front room, dining room one bedroom and a very small kitchen. Out back was a wash house a smoke house and of coarse the path to the back of the lot to the outhouse. We did have water in the house, and electric lights both a first for us, that I could remember. I was in the second grade, Myrtle in the fourth grade and Esther was to be a sophomore.

Our house in Rexford had a lawn in front and under the cloths line. A vegetable garden and flower gardens. Lilac trees in front. I thought it was so pretty. It was white with red trim. I did not realize it was so very small.

We girls had what was called a three quarter bed. (Larger than a twin, smaller than double) it was on the front porch which was screened in. We slept there winter and summer. Mother put canvas roll up curtains up to keep the snow off the bed. She had made them and they were very colorful red and green strip. We would sometimes wrap hot irons in towels and put them at the foot of the bed. When we would all get in bed and cuddle up we would get warm. When Esther would go on a date, she would come home and crawl in between us where it was nice and warm. We lived here in this house for about six years.

We had a front room, this is where the heating stove was. We never had a sofa in our front room. We had a folding day bed. It was a single bed, at times when push came to shove and there were to many people for beds Mother and Dad would sleep on this single bed, both of them. We had a little square table with a drawer in it and a rocking chair. After we had been there a while they got an occasional chair and a Zenith radio and they used it for many years. Either Myrtle or her son Terry still has it. It needs a tube and you can't buy them any more. No pity it is over sixty years old. But the cabinet still looks good. Next in line was the dining room. We had our cupboard in this room. It had glass doors on the top for dishes. The bottom had doors and drawers. The electric meter was on the wall in this room also. We had a water faucet in here with a sink that drained into a pail, after it ran over a couple of times Mother removed the sink. We then had a wash basin on a table under the faucet. From here you went into the bedroom or kitchen. The kitchen was only big enough for a wood cook stove with a few shelves beside it. Also a cupboard base to use for a work area or to do dishes on, there was a medicine cabinet on the wall by the back door, with the only mirror in the house on it. A few years later we got an Ice box that fit in there. And shortly before we moved from here we got a refrigerator and a wringer washing machine. The washer sat on the back porch.

The bedroom was big enough to put two double beds in. There were no closets but shelves built in on both sides of the door. Mother put drapes in front of them.

If you went up a ladder on the out side of the house onto the bedroom roof you could go into a little door which went up into the attic. Myrtle and I would go up there and play but you had to walk on the two by fours or you were apt to go through the ceiling,

When we moved to Rexford it was in the spring of the year and I was still in the first grade, my Teacher was Miss. Montgomery and of coarse I had to ask her if her folks owned Montgomery Ward Catalog Co. One day I was sitting with my foot in the isle, the Teacher tripped over it and WHACK I got hit with the ruler she always carried. She caught me chewing paraffin wax one time and made me stand at the blackboard with my nose in a circle. If you were real ornery you had to sit in the hall on a little chair, I never had to do that. We very seldom had chewing gum but would chew wax that came from a jar of jelly or a gob of pitch from a tree makes a sort of gum to chew also.

Myrtle was in the fourth grade so she was in the same room. Grades one through four in one room and five through eight in the other room Mr. McClure was the teacher in the upper room.

This school had windows on the west side of the school rooms a hall in the middle of the building and a large room down the other side with windows down the east side. We also had steps that went to a landing and around the corner and down another flight of stairs to the bathrooms. The furnace was down here and the woodpile outside a door at the end of the hall. We had a merry go round out in the school yard that we spent lots of hours on. It is now in the Historical Village in Eureka.

When we moved to Rexford so many of the children had bikes, I never wanted anything so bad in my life. Of course that was way out of reach at this time.

We were all out playing soft ball at recess or noon, someone hit the ball over into our yard and hit the house, the kids all said we had lost the ball. One of us went over and got it. They told us the people that did live there kept the balls that came in their yard. So they were real happy the folks didn't do this.

Big thing here in town when there was no school was to go to the Depot and meet the two trains that stopped every day. Number 27 and number 28 one went one way and one went the other. These trains brought the mail so every one would go to the post office and wait while Madge Melvin sorted the mail and put it in boxes. Passengers also came and went on the train. The bread from the bakeries came in on the train. Beside the Depot was the Great Northern Beanery. It had rooms upstairs and a restaurant down stairs. I think the railroad men from the roundhouse and the trains must have used it. I know we had no money to go anywhere like that.

Rexford had a round house, the old steam engine on the freight trains needed a helper engine to get up over the hill at Stryker and would turn around on a Y track there and head back to Rexford some time empty they would really travel, puffing away. We had not been in Rexford long when the trains to Fernie were discontinued.

Hobo's would get off the freight trains at the round house and head straight across the tracks, road and field to our house. Mom always would feed them. They would chop wood, spade the garden or something while she fixed them lunch.

The wash house out back had a place for a stove to heat wash water, benches for the tubs and a big round flat funnel to poor the water out in, it must have just gone onto the ground under the building. Myrtle and I played in this building a lot. There was a light bulb on a long cord with a pull chain over this funnel. We found out if we turned it on, took the bulb out, stood in the metal funnel and stuck your finger in the socket you got quite a jolt. It is a good thing the power from Kutchens power plant was not very strong. The smoke house was claimed for our club house. We also played in there a lot. It was all black from the years of some one smoking meat in it.

We had another dog by now his name was Tippy he was another little wire hair'd terrier of some kind. He was a nice little pet and we had him for many years. Donna Lee LaByer had a bull dog. So ugly he was cute and a nice little dog also.

This spring before school was out we all had a smallpox vaccination. I was scared to have one. Myrtle was a fourth grader so they went first, I was a first grader so was one of the last ones to go. One of the older girls came back in the room and fainted. She slid right under her desk. Myrtle said it didn't hurt but I didn't know what was going on in that room across the hall and I hid behind the door, they found me any way and I had to get vaccinated.

After school was out we went back up Young creek to camp. Esther worked all summer as flunky in camp she and Mother had not drawn any wages all summer so there would be money for school cloths that fall. When Mother went after their wages she found Dad had drawn them all out and they had none coming

We girls moved back to town to start school, with Esther to take care of us. I was a second grader and Myrtle a fifth grader. So we were in separate rooms. Her teacher was Mr. McClure. Mine was Mrs. Griffith. Esther was a sophomore in High School. She went four days and needed an apron and ten cents dues for Home Ec. and shoes real bad. Well there was no money not even the ten cents for dues. So she never went back that year. She went to work for the Man next door his name was Mr. Martin he had a daughter about my age. He gave Esther $35.00 a month and she had to feed them from that and her wages were what she had left. She did all the house work, cooking and laundry and could usually end up with about $10.00 a month for herself. She was only fifteen years old. When the job at camp was finished Mother and Dad came home. It was a very rough winter. Harold and Marion were living across the tracks in Rexford. Bobbie was a baby and he had eczema on his feet so bad they were just raw. No one knew it then but he was probably very allergic to milk. Marion miscarried a baby that winter in Rexford.

I was always a croupy child and Mother would put a few drops of Kerosene on a spoon of sugar and give it to me to cut the phlegm in my throat. I would feel this time I will surely choke to death. Also I would some time have a mustard plaster put on my chest. Ever Had one? No fun HOT! HOT!. They are made from dry mustard that was mixed into a paste with water and I don't know what else. Then spread on flannel and laid on the chest. They will burn if not watched real close. Harold and I both had croup when we were small. Esther and Myrtle didn't.

Things were real tight this winter. Mother was washing cloths on the board and ironing them with sad irons for some of the railroad men we would pick them up and deliver them back to them for fifty cents a wash. Dad was spending all his time at the bar. Rexford water froze up in the winter time where it came across under the bridge so the town would be without water. We could haul water from the well at the Round House. Myrtle and I tied a wash boiler on a sled and hauled water all over town and sold it for five cents a boiler full. We charged groceries and had to watch it real close so we would not get cut off. Our wood pile got so very low there was none left to dig out of the snow. We had to chop up the chopping block, Mother cried when she was doing this. Dad was at the Bar, I would go and try to get him to come home but it usually did no good. We were a proud family and asked for help from no one. And never have.

In the evening all the kids would gather with their sleds and head for The Louis Duchesne hill we would walk quite a ways up toward Black Lake singing and having fun, then whop on our bellies on our sled and down we would go Myrtle usually coming in first and me next. Some times we would go all the way to George Ross's service station. Some times only one ride a night but it was worth it.

In the cold of winter everyone had to drain the water from the car radiator when not using the car. Then fill it with warm water when available, before using it again, it helped to warm the engine but cold water was used also. Antifreeze had not come on the market for sale as yet. There were no snow tires so everyone used chains they were a big bother to keep putting them on and taking them off. To warm up a car you would see people putting a shovel full of hot coals from the stove under the oil pan to warm a car up when they could not get it to start. No electric heaters for the engine then either. Things are so much better and easier now.

Louis Duchesne had a small dairy farm at the foot of the Black Lake road, he delivered milk in a two wheel push cart all over Rexford. Summer and winter. He was a very big man real tall or he looked it to we children. Another family in town that lived on the same street that went up the hill to Black Lake was the Marks Family, they had a daughter Nadine. She and her father played a big gold colored Harp, it was such beautiful music.

The family's that were in school were, Myrtle and I (Shenefelt's) , Whitmarshe's, Marvel's, LaByer's , Knapp's, Smith's, Hammond's, White's, Fagen' s, Toney George, Verna Nelson, Carol Hurst, Webb's, Mason's, Georgie Ross, Art Martin, Alice Martin, Sally Martin, Smith's, Pauline Farr, King's, DeShazer's, Truman's, Birche's, O'Brien's, There were about three different Martin family's lived in Rexford. I am sure I have left some out that I went to school with.

In the winter time when it was real cold we would

get together and play pinochle this is when you all learned young as there was no television and that sort of thing to do.

We would have a couple of tables at some ones house and play till time to go home to bed.

The ice skating rink was across the road from our house. Myrtle and I were given a pair of clamp on skates that you fastened to your shoes with a key and they had a strap that fastened around your instep. We took turns on them. When they would come loose they would crack you in the shins and down you would go. We had fun, but really longed for a pair of white shoe skates like some of the girls had.

Annetta White came to the house one day for Mother to baby sit with Pauline for her, The baby was sitting on the floor crying because her mother was leaving her Mother leaned over to console the baby and her dress tail was drawn into the stove draft that was open. The fire went up Mothers back, Annetta picked up her baby and left. Esther finally threw a bucket of water on Mother. She was burned real bad clear up into her hair. We had a real bad snow storm the day before and the roads were all closed. Esther went to Maddens store and called Dr. Lowell and asked him what she should do. He told her he couldn't get there because of the roads and to buy all the unguentine that they had at the store and put it on the burns. They only had two tubes. She got them and did what she could. Mother was in great pain and laid on her stomach for some time she finally healed up with no infection which is a miracle.

That was one year we were glad to see Spring come. We girls did a lot of hiking over to Sullivan creek. Down to Addie Mae DeShazers, Josephine and Pal Webbs and over the hills, up the toboggan slide hill. Just a lot of fun in the good spring air. We would take our lunch and just take off.

Spring was here so it was time for us to move again it seemed. We moved to Pinkham this time. Dad was working for Columbus again. We moved up Banks Draw to a very old one room cabin. Of course we usually moved before school was out so we finished the second and fifth grades on Pinkham. We walked down Banks draw a very little road, (more like a trail than a road), to the Pinkham school. Mrs. Long was our teacher the remainder of this year.

There were Combs, Workmans, Staceys, Tripplets, Whites, Utters, Kenneys and again more that I can't remember going to school here. We were the new kids once more.

The cabin we lived in was small and one room. We had Bobbie with us and he was in diapers which had to be washed on the board. I don't know where we hauled our water from. I do know we picked up a lot of hewed tie chips for wood. There was a trap door in the floor we could never get open, and imagined there were all kinds of things down there, maybe a still after all we were on Pinkham. And we had heard they had stills up there.

There were a lot of range cattle around there. Myrtle and I would go around with a stick and turn the cow pies over to dry on the other side. She also liked to step in the fresh ones bare foot. Some fun for two little girls who had to make their own entertainment.

Ham and Olive Leib were living up behind Hams folks place, Mother and we three girls and Bobbie would walk over to see her quite a lot that summer. This was a very hot dry summer. Mother and Dad went to Rexford to check the house and the mail and get a few Groceries once in a while.

When fall came they moved the mill to the Cattle Camp which was on the creek a couple of miles above the school. Dad built a small rough lumber cabin by the creek for us. Bobbie disappeared one evening all the men and every one was looking for him. He was a little over two years old. They walked the creek and called and called. It was starting to get dark when someone saw a little foot sticking out from under a scraper that was tipped up against the house. When he seen he had been found he said "get away from me you monkey you". He had filled his diaper and was hiding because of it. Myrtle and I spent a lot of time fishing up and down the creek all summer.

Mrs. Butcher was cooking at the cook house, she quit, so Mother took over, we moved into the cook house. Ham and Olive moved into the little cabin, they had a baby boy.

This cook house was a little larger than most. It had partitions that didn't go all the way to the ceilings, no doors, but it did make two bedrooms of sorts. There must have been a big crew at this camp as Esther was Mothers Flunky and Jim Finch hauled all the water and wood for them. I think the person that did this was called a bull cook.

This summer they took Lunch out to the men in the woods they came into the mill at noon to eat. Esther would do this. She had a go-devil that she pulled with a horse. The dry powder dust was in the ruts about four to six inches deep. They would put the food in cream cans and kettles on this lumber sled, (go devil), dishes and all. She would haul it out to the mill. Then wait while the men ate and bring all the dirty dishes and pans back to the cook house. She was to small to always get the harness off and hung up proper. She could get it off the horse, but it was to heavy to get hung up. So Dad got mad once in a while. When these dirty dishes came back the two dish pans and a bar of soap and towels and hot water that had been heated on the stove all came out and the dishes were done. Then Esther would get the tub out and wash the dirt and dust from herself and get ready to start to help with supper.

The meat was kept in a box in the creek if we were close to one. As there was no electricity, every day the chimneys on the lamps all had to be washed and shined also. There were enough lamps to go the full length of the table and one for the cook. Most were plain kerosene lamps but there were two or three Aladdins which had a mantle in them instead of a wick. At night when you started to blow out lamps you had to remember to turn out the alladins because if you blew them out you broke the mantle this did happen once in a while.

One of Esthers boy friends gave her a box of chocolates. She gave us each one, put the lid on and put them down on the table. She went outside. We had no screens, but lots of flies. And yellow jackets were a problem. I decided I would have another chocolate, I chose a soft center and sucked all the center out. Laid the chocolate shell on the table and went for a drink of water. I seen Esther coming, ran and grabbed the chocolate shell and put it in my mouth. It had a yellow jacket in it. My mouth was full of wings, it stung me on the tongue. I swelled up and thought I was going to choke to death. Esther told me it was because I had stolen some candy.

She also had some dresses hanging in the bedroom she had been hemming. She left the scissors on the bed. Myrtle and I were fighting and I scratched her. Dad reached for the razor strap. He kept it hanging on a nail. I had bent the nail over with the hammer and pounded it in tight. When he got it loose I got it. Then sent to the bed room. There lay those scissors. I cut all the hems from Esthers dresses. I don't know how Mother ever fixed them.

Harold had taken the left over fruit juice and pieces of fruit, he put them in a crock behind the cook stove. He kept adding to it. Well soon he had some pretty good wine. No I did not try it, but Esther did. When Mother went to town. She was acting goofy, Myrtle and I were scared of her. Mother took the wine out and dumped it in the pig trough. We were raising a couple of pig. Some one there had a few Chickens they could have belonged to Olive and Ham Leib or Nina and Gib Street as they had a little cabin there also. The pigs ate the fermented fruit and juice, they were making all kinds of funny noises. The chickens pecked at the fruit and were falling over squawking Every one was out watching them and laughing. That was the end of any wine making.

This is about the time I decided to find out what smoking was all about. Mother had a shelf in the cook house she sold the men gloves, cigarettes, Prince Albert, Velvet, copenhagen and plug tobacco. I never touched any of this. I took some matches, sawdust from the sawdust pile. Went to the outhouse and used catalog paper and sawdust to roll a cigarette. I lit it two or three times and had it going, really burning my tongue, When I heard some one coming. I threw it down the hole, it caught the catalog paper down there on fire and burned down the out house. I guess we needed a new one anyway.

The red mule plug tobacco had a little metal red mule stuck into the plug. When the men would chew it they would throw the little guys away. Myrtle and I would pick them up and play with them for many hour, this was some of our treasures.

When we fished in Pinkham creek. We put our worms in Prince Albert or Velvet cans, they fit in our pockets real easy. Our poles were willows with a piece of fish line and a hook. We caught lots of little brook trout out of Pinkham creek.

Well summer was about over. Esther walked to Eureka to Grandmother Shenefelts. She went to work for Mr. and Mrs. McGlen. She received twenty five cents a day and board and room. She took care of the two children, all of the care of the house. She worked in the store on Saturday and had Sunday off. When she went back on Monday all the dishes were in the sink that had been used while she was gone.

Myrtle and I started school. Myrtle in the sixth grade and I was in the third our Teacher was Mrs. Segar her husband was a border patrol. We walked the two miles to school. We had pretty good lunches coming from camp. Our lunches were packed in five pound lard pails. They made excellent lunch pails and pretty good weapons when swung at the end of the arm. While fighting on the way to and from school. I don't know why but we seemed to fight with the Tripplet kids and we had to go by their house to get to school. There was a family of boys that always had bisquets with lard and salt and pepper on them, I would once in a while trade lunches with them. I usually had a sandwich, donut or cake and an apple. Myrtle wouldn't give me any of hers, she told me to eat what I traded for. When it was still dark early in the morning on the way to school we would hear the Mt. Lions scream up on the hill. We really made tracks then.

We some times would get a ride home with the tie truck if he was making his return trip at this time. This broke into a lot of our after school fights. In the summer some times we would ride the tie truck into Eureka, swim at the bend of the river by riverside park. All the town kids swam there. There use to be a lot of willow bushes you could go into to change your cloths. We would catch a late afternoon truck back to camp. The drivers didn't seem to mind.

Shorty Macy gave Myrtle and I set of China doll dishes for Christmas this year. They were so pretty I turned around and knocked them from the bench and broke all of them except the gravy boat. Myrtle claimed it as I had broke the rest. I think she still has it. At Easter my candy eggs were in a saucer we didn't have baskets. I could not find them, after looking all morning someone finally felt sorry for me and showed me where they were. They were in the speaker of the wind up phonograph. During the summer after six in the evening when the forest service men that were on lookouts had called in and there was no fire danger, they would leave their phones of the hook. We had a forest service phone for a while. Esther would put the phonograph over under the phone and play records for them I remember cranking it for her.

Marion went to take Bobbie out to the outhouse before bed one night and as she opened the door, a lion let out the most blood curdling scream. She slammed the door and no one went out that night. The next morning there were big foot prints right by the front door. A lot of men at this time went lion hunting I don't know if they sold the hides or if there was a bounty on them. No one in our family ever hunted them.

We had a pantry built off from this cook house, we had peanut butter and honey in five gallon cans. After a while the honey would sugar before it all was used up. It was good to eat with a spoon then, Mother had to heat it so the men could use it at the table.

Sometime this winter during our school term on Pinkham. Mrs. Segar had a spelling bee and Math contest for all the school. Their family's and friends were invited to attend. Well I didn't go very far in the spelling part, never could spell to well. But was pretty good in Math, except I couldn't pull out of my head that combinations like 7+6 was 13. I would count the seven and tap out 6 times with the chalk on the black board while I counted. I really embarrassed Myrtle once more, as the whole audience was laughing at me. I mean out loud HA! HA!. But I got it done. By this time I had acquired the nick name of Zippy. Some one said all they seen of me was my dress tail zipping around corners and it stuck. I was Zippy till I was a teenager and with Dad beyond that.

Just before this job was over during spring break I think in 1937. We took our one and only trip. We went to Bend Oregon to visit Uncle Corade, Mamai and Uncle Celos's family. This was before motels. We stayed in homes that rented rooms out along the way. Most of them we were upstairs and of course they had a bathroom. They would have a sign out front and you just stopped of the road. You paid them for your night lodging and went on the next day. When we first arrived in Bend we had a good time. We went to Lava Caves, These were formed by a volcano and real interesting. We also went to wild horse caves. This was a catacomb of caves under ground that the wild horses would break through when they were running over the prairie. I have since tried to find these caves to show my family, we found the lava caves but not the wild horse caves and no one there now seems to know what I am talking about. But we did enjoy ourselves till dad decided to find a bar he liked in Bend and spent most of our traveling money. Not much left to get home on. We ran out of gas between Libby and Rexford, no money. Dad went some where and got a little gas from someone to get home. Not to pleasant a trip on the way back home.

Moving time again, we moved back to our house in Rexford. We swam in the back waters of the Kootenai River about a mile from town. Just below the Kin's bridge that went over to the island. The banks of the river were clay. We would make mud slides on them and have all kinds of fun. All the town kids spent their summers swimming there. Myrtle had a lot of stiff necks, she had a bad one and was laying on the bridge on her stomach. (Not much traffic back then) Douglas Truman came running over the bridge, he ran full length of her. He cracked her neck when he stepped on it and she never had a stiff neck again.

While we were all paddling around in the river, Tony George, who was an only child was never allowed to swim with us. His parents were of Italian decent and did not speak very much English. His father worked for the railroad. After World War II broke out and Tony was old enough, he joined the Navy. When he came home on leave from Boot Camp he went swimming in the river and drowned. His folks left Rexford soon after that.

I went fishing with Fern and Slim Howe a lot this summer. Slim worked on the railroad and they lived at the other end of the block from us. We would go to Tetrault (Carpenter) lake and paddle around on a raft. One day I had a good size fish and when I took it off the hook, it slipped from my hand. I dove in and caught him. Slim had to pull me back on the raft, as I would not let go of my fish.

We were fishing on the bank of the river below the Rexford bridge one time and there I hooked a good size trout and being afraid it would get away, I ran clear up on the shore dragging the fish on the line. Slim told me that fish would be all black and blue by the time I got it home. I looked, it wasn't.

That fall Fern decided we should all go pick huckleberries. She drove a pickup, Mother, we girls, Doris Roberts and Granny White all went. I don't know why Granny White was in the back of the pickup with us kids but she was, sitting in her rocking chair. We planned to stay over night so we had quilts and warm clothes, food, pans, dishes and pails back there with us. We went up by Stryker or Olney some where. It was dark when we made camp. The next morning we woke up right in the middle of a great berry patch. Picked all day and headed home that evening. Tired dirty but full of berries. We took a lot of berries home with us for canning eating and jam.

Fern and Slim had no children of their own. About this time they made two Rexford teenagers very happy. They took Esther and Doris Roberts to Spokane and really showed them a grand time, even had their pictures taken in a studios. This is the kind of people they were.

I contacted the measles this fall and when they were about gone I went swimming, then I got real sick and had an abscess behind my ear. Mother took me to the Dr. we didn't go to the Dr. very often. He said I had scarlet teena and he had to lance the abscess. In no time at all I was better.

One winter while in school in Rexford Myrtle had gotten a new pair of overshoes, they were black and red and had an M on the snap closing. She proudly wore them to school the next day. When she went out in the hall to get them to go home, hers were gone and a pair just like them except worn out were in the same place. There were only two pairs of red and black overshoes in the whole school and both girls had the initial M. The next day she got her new ones back.

Frank Mason and Duane Hammonds one day were tormenting me and calling me Tubby, well maybe I was but—I pushed Duane and he started to fall down the basement stairs. I grabbed the front of his shirt, it tore down the back and came off in my hands. After school that night Mrs. Hammonds, Duane and the shirt came to our house. After Mother talked it over with them they decided the shirt was kind of worn out anyway and he had no business teasing me in that way. After all I had kept him from falling!!

That winter we had acquired a pair of ski's some how. They had leather straps you put your toes in, with a couple of sticks for poles we had fun with them. For Christmas Myrtle and I got pretty dolls with china heads store bought dresses and bonnets. We played with them for a month or so before Christmas, after we found them under Mothers bed. I claimed the blue eyed on and Myrtle the brown eyed one. Christmas eve we opened them and we looked at the dolls and each other and traded dolls. She had mine and I hers.

Mother had a little orange crock dish she kept her change in. It was in the cupboard. One day I was sent to the store for something and she gave me 50¢ to pay for it. We always brought the change home. Well the Heath candy bars had hit the market, they were so good and 5¢. I stopped on the way home at Ross's service station and bought one. I ate it before I got home. When I reached up and put the rest of the change in the little dish. I put my hand and the change in a dish of honey. I had stolen a nickel and gotten caught. So never again, if I wanted something I asked for it, sometimes I got it and sometimes I didn't

Something else I remember at Ross's service station was the big round glass top gas pumps. They had gallon marks on them. Mr. Ross would pump them up by hand then the gas was released into the car's tank. They had a pop machine in the station it was a large red square tub with a lid on it. The water in it was so cold. Pop was .5¢ a bottle, 8 oz. bottles. I only remember coke and orange and it was dripping with cold water when it was taken out. There was a bottle opener on the front with a little container for the lids to fall in.

Georgie and Myrtle were real good friends until the Rosses moved to Washington and we moved to Eureka They finally lost contact for many years.

One Halloween in Rexford we rolled Mr. Arnolds toilet from behind his barber shop out in the middle of the street. We then put his barber pole in the hole and tied a big bow made from toilet paper around it. The same night Bill Fewkes had left a big old truck they used at the store. It was parked beside the store. The others put me in to steer it, good thing they pushed it straight down the street I could not have made it around a corner.

Many years later when I was about in the 8th grade. Kenneth McAllister, Dale Purdy and Delbert Owens came to Rexford on Halloween in McAllisters car. Mr. McAllister didn't know the car was being used. Myrtle, Georgie and I were with them driving across the tracks by Marvels field. All at once we seen a wheel going down the road in front of us. Then we found out it was from the car we were in, when the axial hit the road. Myrtle was scared to death as to what the neighbors would think and what they would tell Mother who was not home, about these three boys being at the house all night. They had the car back together and home before Mr. Mcallister found out it had been used.

As usual spring was here and we moved to a camp above Trego. Esther was either working for another Mr. Martin taking care of his very ill wife, or was working at the Beanery and staying at Marvels.

Betty (Faith) Nelson was Mothers flunky for this summer. Our cook house had a bed room. I remember it because Betty and Mother would take their baths in the wash tub in the bedroom in the middle of the afternoon while the men were all out of camp at the mill. We were at Billy Lloyds Swamp above Trego. Dad dug a lot of wells at this camp, they would fill up then go dry. There was one by the cook house that had dried up but was cool in the bottom, a ladder was put down and a box for perishable items was kept there. It was Myrtles job to go down and get things from the box she was not to happy about this.

We made ourselves hats from strawberry boxes and decorated them with weeds and flowers. Also shoes from boxes and birch bark tied on with strips of fabric. It kept us busy and gave us something to do. We went fishing at Loon Lake, Myrtle fell from the dock and came up through the lily pads, looked like she was growing them on her head.

We had no pigs at this camp to feed food scraps to so they were taken some distance from the cook house and dumped out. It was a real hot summer and the flies were bad, Myrtle and I would go to the dump and watch the maggots every once in a while.. It is a wonder we didn't have bears.

Dad would set up the black smith shop and shoe horses. He had a lot of horses in the woods. Columbus only had two. His were the ones that hauled the loads of slabs to the slab pile, one of them had a big hind leg, in the summer they kept it wrapped with a burlap bag that had been dipped in lysol to keep the flies off. If I handed Dad horse she nails while he was shoeing horses , he would make me a ring from one of the nails. I wish I would have kept one of them. We had a horse we could ride. Myrtle never liked horses. She got on this one and I hit it on the rump. It started to go around in circles. I always said she fell of. She said she jumped off.

A few years before this Harold built a trailer house on a single axle. It must have been heavy. He built it at the folks house in Rexford probably about 14 feet long. It was cute, had a table, bed and wood stove. He pulled it to Texas and back to Montana. Then tried to get it into camp. There was a corduroy road over one part of the swamp and a logging road. He high centered, finally got it off the road and there it sit. I don't know what ever happen to it. By the time school started we had moved camp and were at Swamp Creek. The camp was about where the railroad tunnel takes off through the mountain above Trego. Betty had gone to Libby to work for some Dr. Esther was at the Beanery in Rexford she worked after school and week ends but she did get to go back to school. She had a room at the beanery. She received 50¢ for working four hours after school and $1.00 for working a whole day on week ends. Once in a while living in Rexford she would get a chance to go to one of the Mullegan dances at Gateway, every one took a tin cup and spoon to eat from and they danced all night.

At this camp Clara (Burk) Graves came to work as flunky for Mother. School started and I was in the 4th grade and Myrtle was in the 8th grade. We walked about two miles then caught Fagens bus to Eureka. Trego school had burned and they were busing some of the students to Eureka. We were some of them. Our bus had mostly High School students on it. We left home way before daylight and got home after dark.

We again had pack rat problems in this camp. They would run back and forth on the rafters in the cook house. One morning at breakfast the men started teasing Mother about shooting the rats. Someone said they heard she was suppose to be a crack shot with her pistol. Why don't you shoot that one down there over the end of the table? She said you don't want a rat killed while you are eating breakfast! They all told her they didn't think she could hit it. She got out her pistol and one shot and Mr. Rat lay at the end of the table. They didn't tease her about her pistol anymore.

When we were up young Creek Mother had woke up one night and heard a pack rat she got the flash light and her pistol and shot the pack rat. That emptied the bunk house out in the yard. Guess they thought she had shot Dad.

Dad loaned a horse to a man who needed a work horse for a few days. The Horse died, Dad said the man worked it to death. Anyway the horse was paid for in live chickens. They arrived in burlap bags at camp. They were all butchered that very day. We had no place to keep them. After they were all picked and cleaned, Dad put bailing wire around their feet and hung them up in the wood shed. We had fried, stewed, boiled and baked chicken all winter as they had to be eaten before spring thaw. The men had a lot of chicken but seemed to enjoy it all.

When the roads got real bad and it was very cold, Mother rented a cabin at Diermans for us to stay in so we wouldn't have the long cold ride. The heat on buses was not to hot at this time. Sometimes there was none at all.

Esther quit her job and came to Eureka to stay with us for about a month. Esther came on the train from Rexford to Trego to spend Christmas with us. When the train stopped at Trego on a cold winter evening the conductor told her they could not put her off in a snow bank with no one there to meet her. They held the train for about five minutes or so, till she saw Dad in the old pickup coming down the hill.

After Christmas we left Trego and moved back to Rexford. Clarence Baker was our teacher as we were both in the same room again. Harold had brought an old boys bike to us the fall before. It had no back fender and was pretty bad looking, but we sure did enjoy it. I learned to ride it by coming down Louis Duchesnees hill. I didn't make the corner onto the other road, went across the road and into the bushes. Run the end of the front fender into the calf of my leg. Finally I mastered it. There seemed to be paint around all the time, whenever I knew ahead of time Myrtle would want the bike. I would put on a fresh coat of paint for her. Of coarse it would still be wet when she planned to use it. So it was a bike of many colors. I asked Myrtle a while back what we ever did with that bike. She doesn't know any more than I do. But said maybe it disappeared under to many coats of paint!!

The ice rink was full every night. Esther was a junior in High School and working at the Beanery. There was a B&B Crew from the Great Northern Railroad working in town and a couple of the men came to the Ice Rink.(We all had shoe skates by now). Esther was skating, this is where she met Clyde Paul from Whitefish. He was seven years older than she was. In a couple of weeks she went to Whitefish with him to meet his parents. Before a month and a half was over they went to Missoula and were married. Esther moved to Whitefish to live. Shortly before she was married she found my diary and I had a big crush on a certain boy and had written it all down in my diary. Esther proceeded to tease me one evening and I got her bent over the water faucet and hit her head on it, she was out for a few minutes. Mother really scolded me. She always let us fight if we didn't use weapons, guess she thought the water pipe was a weapon.

Myrtle graduated from the 8th grade this spring. The girls in her class all had Shark Skin dresses made alike but different pastel colors. They were so pretty and had a silky feel to them. Their graduation was real nice. Banquet, flowers and all.

After school was out we went to camp up Dodge Creek on the West Kootenai. We were up above Brocks. Bobbie was with us, he was about 4 or 5 yrs. old. We have a picture of him on the end of a cross cut saw. (He thought he was helping). Jack DeShazer was on the other end. They were at the woodpile in front of the cookhouse. Myrtle went to work for the Ralph Griffith family then the Buster Tiffany family in Rexford, for a while keeping house and taking care of their children. This was her first experience (and probably last of cooking fish with their heads on. With the eyes looking at her from the frypan. She then came to camp to work as Mothers Flunky. She must have hated that job with all those dishes to wash. When we were in Rexford I carried in wood and Esther and Myrtle did dishes. Once in a while at time to do dishes Myrtle would go out to the outhouse. She would stay till the dish water splashed out into the garden. Then in she would come. One night Mother said, I will get that girl in to do dishes. She sent some water splashing out in the garden. Here came Myrtle. Mother said all right young lady now you do the dishes. I think Myrtle was really glad when we finally got a house with a bathroom in it as she always had to go with me if it was dark She would stand outside and say hurry up fraidy cat. And pound on the door.

While we were at camp I had Jaunita Fagen come to spend a week with me. We really had a great week. The Sunday we were taking her home we went by way of DeShazers. Addie Mae, Jaunita and I wanted to go swimming. They told us we could go but go where the DeShazer kids swam, a shallow back water. We swam there a while and decided we were to good to swim where we could touch bottom all-over. So we went to one that was about 12 to 15 feet deep. We started across and were about three fourths of the way across when Jaunita yelled she couldn't make it. She went down and never came up. We swam on across and ran to the house. Only our parents were there and none of them could swim. The women came with us to the pond, the men went up to the road about 1/4- of a mile away. The third car they flagged down was some people that were working on the construction of the new road. The woman said she would get her out. She had been in the water by now the better part of an hour. The woman dove down and finally found her and brought her to shallow water, She said I can't do any more. So our fathers waded out and got her, They carried her in their arms up to the road. We were all around 10 to 11 years old. The coroner came from Libby and took her body to Eureka. We had to go tell her Mother. You can imagine how hard that was.

The 8th grade girls were the pallbearers. They wore their graduation dresses. Her death really put a dark cloud over the whole town for the remainder of the summer and for some time to come.

I did a lot of fishing in Dodge creek that summer, I would take a little of the Hamburger that was in the cooler box over the creek, the fish bit on it real well if you could keep it on the hook. We came home many times with a willow full of small trout. If we caught them we had to clean them. I have a scar on my finger where I closed a jack knife on it. Only once and you learn in a hurry. These little fish are so good rolled in flour and fried real crisp.

We had a lot of chipmunks in the barn eating the horses oats. We would try to catch them, chase them all over in the hay. Once in a while we would grab one by the tail and the tail hide and fur would come off in our hands but the chipmunk would get away. We had so many mosquitoes this summer and no screens in the evenings they would build a bon fire at the door on each end of the cook house and bunk house, put green branches on it when it got going to make a lot of smoke and it seemed to help keep the mosquitoes out of the buildings. I had the job of giving all the horses a half can of oats after they were put in their stalls in the evening. I had a favorite horse and I gave him more, until he got frisky and tore down his stall one night. Then he got the same amount of oats as the other did.

We were in the house one evening and Dad was laying on the cot with his shoes off, he told me to do something and I said no. That was the wrong thing to say I knew as soon as I said it. Up he came I took of running he grabbed the razor strap and came after me. I went out the front door and seen the door to the bunk house I went in one door and out the other then through the cook house and into the bunk house again the men were sitting up in bed yelling run Zippy run. I then headed for the barn and he caught me in the hay mow. I got it not only for saying no but for running and for going into the bunk house not one time but two.

When school started Myrtle, I think Bobbie and I all went to Rexford to go to school. Bobbie 1st grade I was in the 6th grade and Myrtle was a freshman in High School. Mother hired a Mrs. Pomeroy to come and stay with us I don't know who she was for sure. I do know she did not stay very long.

Myrtle, Bobbie and I were alone one day. We were eating dinner Bobbie wanted some water, when I got it for him, I threw it in his face I don't know why. Myrtle picked up her fork and threw it at me. It pierced my arm just below the elbow. The fight was on. I calmed down in the front room sitting on Myrtle choking her when I seen blood from my arm on her face. It scared me, I could have killed her.

When Mrs. Pomeroy left, Bobbie must have went with his folks as I know Myrtle and I went to stay with Olive Fagen. I didn't like it there. I don't know if it was because it reminded me every day of Jaunita or what. I know I didn't like the food. We had a lot of baked hubbard squash and cream of pepper soup. Now I like peppers and love baked squash. Any way I guess I was such a brat and complained so much, Esther came up from Whitefish to opened up the house and stayed with us during the week for a while. We went to camp on week ends and she went home. She had been married now for about 7-8 months. Clyde worked out of town on a crew so she was alone all week. While she was there she was cleaning things out that had been packed for a while, she reached into a box and grabbed a dead mouse, that shook her up. She was now pregnant and sick an awful lot. She delivered a beautiful baby boy the following April, Richard, Who is now Senior Vice President and general counsel of Xerox Corporation. He and his wife Beth now live in Connecticut. They have two sons, Christopher who is an Attorney with a firm in Buffalo New York and Matthew who will be entering Law School next fall. Christopher married a girl he went to law school with. They were married Sept. 30th 1995. Her name is Stephonie.

After Esther left, Maimi who had returned from Oregon and was living in a small house at Black Lake by Aunt Blanch and Uncle Dow O'Brians came to Rexford to stay with us.

This spring Mother was not working as they had no cook house at the next mill. It was close to Eureka and the men stayed there. We moved to a very little shack dad threw up at the north end of Glen Lake. He had built a barn for his horses, it was like most camp barns very open. With a roof to keep the horses and hay dry.

We did a lot of swimming and really had a nice summer that year. We still got our mail in Rexford so about once a week Mother, Myrtle and I would go to Rexford to get the mail and check the house. Dad had a Model A coup Myrtle drove it even though she wasn't old enough and had no drivers license. When we came to Douglas hill Mother and I got out and walked down Myrtle, drove down Mother was scared to ride down the hill with her. She would ride up it on the way back. Myrtle never hit anything. Myrtle and Esther both got their drivers license when you sent your name and address and fifty cents into the court house, they sent them to you in the mail. Neither one of them has ever let them expire. So have never taken a driving test.

Harold and Marion were there part of the time. One day Harold seen a child out in the water splashing and yelling for help down the lake from us. He took of running through the brush and undergrowth when he got to where the child was, there was a man and woman sitting on the bank. He went in the lake clothes and all and pulled the little boy to shore. He set him down in front of his parents and told them to never let him play like that again and not to yell for help unless he really needed it. They apologized and said they were not thinking and it wouldn't happen again.

Our cabin was at the edge of a field and some ones garden. I think Laird Byers, they had real sweet turnips we pulled and ate a few. Bobbie said he remembers when we lived there and he was out in the field and a deer came bounding along and jumped right over his head.

Myrtle and Marion decided one day to swim across the lake. I just knew they wouldn't make it. I was in the row boat following them. Crying all the way. When they walked out on the other side, by the old dance pavilion, I was so mad at them. I don't know if it was because they swam across or because they made it. They wanted a ride back across the lake and I wouldn't let them in the boat. I made them walk barefoot around the lake through a stubble field and in wet bathing suits. I went back across the lake in the boat by myself.

We moved back to Rexford for the school year. Myrtle was a Sophomore and I was in the 7th grade. Myrtle said if you were lucky enough to have a quarter you could go to Davises Cafe and get a Hamburger and coke for your lunch. I don't imagine she got to do that very often. One day while we were home alone. Myrtle and I decided those long drop cords on our lights were real old fashion. We proceeded to unscrew all the white porcelain rosettes at the ceiling. We laid them all on the table and took the scissors to them, we cut them off short so the bulb would be up by the ceiling. Then we rewired them and put them back up, with a long pull string on each one to turn them on. I don't know of any one redoing them or even checking our work. The house didn't burn down and the lights all worked.

We had a Preacher come to Rexford for Bible School. It was held in the multi purpose room at the school. It was for a week, the first two days most of the children from town were there all cleaned up and sparkling. The second day the Preacher told us if we did not let him save us he would pray that lighting would strike us. The next three days there was only three or four children.

One highlight of our school year was when the Canadian Mounted Police in his Red Jacket would show up. He showed us movies and gave a talk to all of us. He passed out pamphlets and it was always a thrill when he came.

About this time Lifeboy soap came out and we each were given a bar in our hygiene class. We were also given charts to keep on our personal care. That soap was red and had a good smell.

On Sunday December 7th 1941 when Japan bombed Pearl Harbor, I was so frightened, I was 13 years old and knew that the next target must be North West Montana. They would be here anytime.

We had no one in our family go into the service. Dad got drunk and tried to join the Navy then was scared they would take him he can't swim. He was to old. Harold was a beat up wrestler, with broken ear drums and a lot more so they wouldn't take him either. A lot of Esthers old boy friends, and men working in the mill left and some never came back.

It was a frightening time. Then rationing came. Gas, tires, shoes, sugar, meat and butter. You had to have a ration stamp to buy any of these things. Candy and gum were no longer on the shelves for sale. And cigarettes were doled out by the package you couldn't buy a carton. People were buying rolling machines and tobacco and rolling their own.

Silk stockings were no longer available and nylons were not on the market just yet.

One year for Mothers birthday I wanted to get her something special from the store. I had no money. I spotted a brown and green tea pot made of pottery at Fewkes store. I finally went and charged it on Mothers grocery bill. She told me I should not have done that. It was set up only for groceries. But she really liked her tea pot, she used it for many years. Mother drank green tea. Finally the lid was broken, she planted an ivy in it. Long after Mother passed away the Ivy in the teapot was on Myrtles refrigerator in her kitchen in Eureka. Myrtle used ivy from it to put in her daughter Sharon and her daughter in—law Jane's wedding bouquets. It was living till after Sharon's daughter Eva was born. It finally just died.

Myrtle and Georgie got some short fuzzy jackets one year, I think they first wore them to the prom over their formals. Myrtles was turquoise and Georgies was light blue. They were so soft and fuzzy and pretty. I got home from school before Myrtle. I would put hers on and prance all over the house in it. When I would see the school bus stop down in front of the service station I would put it back as if it had never been moved. I think that is one thing I got away with.

Esthers friends in Rexford had by this time mostly all moved away. Nadine Marks, Marion Thompson, Gwenith Ross, Patty Marvel Doris Roberts. And all the young men were in the service strung all over the world.

Myrtle and Georgie had pals in Rexford. Paul Marvel Eldin Butts Art Martin but they had boy friends in High school in Eureka. Dale Purdy and Delbert Owens.

After Myrtles Sophomore year and my 7th grade we spent the summer in the Yaak. Mother was cooking again I think this was her last camp job. Dad had gotten a battery radio that ran on a car battery, the only time they listen to it was the evening news and it was mostly all war news. One day Mother was frying donuts all at once she told me to go get Dad at the mill, she was going to lay down. I took the grease of the stove and I went and got Dad. When we got back she was hemorrhaging real bad he went some where and called Dr. Clark in Eureka. The Dr. came and got her and took her to the Hospital in Eureka. Mrs. Speed came over and took over the cooking. I finished cooking the donuts before she got there. When it was time for her to get out of the Hospital Esther and Myrtle came and brought her home. Myrtle had been staying in Whitefish with Esther when Mother got sick. Mother finished up her job in the Yaak and I think that was her last job at a mill cook house.

Esther and Clyde took me to visit with them in Whitefish in the summer time for a week now and then. Dick was a baby and Esther would put him in his buggy, it was a beautiful wicker one with tan corduroy lining in it. It had big wheels and was so easy to push. I could push the baby to the corner of second street and Spokane avenue but had to turn around then and go back. One day Esther gave me a dime and told me to go to Haines Drug store to the fountain and order a chocolate soda she was sure I would like it. I sure did I had never tasted anything like that before. You can't get them like that any more.

A lot of family's were now moving out of Rexford. The Clyde Smith family moved to Alaska. I wrote to Flossie for many years. Donna Lee's family moved to Edmonds, Washington. Whitmarshes moved to the Seattle area. Ross's moved to Spokane. Myrtle was a Junior in High School and I was in the 8th grade. Clarence Baker was still my teacher. In April of 1943 Mother sold our house in Rexford to Alden White who lived next door. Then she bought Grandmother Shenefelts house in Eureka for $450.00 from the people that had bought it from Aunt Blythe. It was not the house she really wanted but she didn't have the $700.00 they wanted for the other one. After we moved to Eureka I didn't go to school the last 6 weeks but got my 8th grade diploma any way.

Mother and Dad had Mr. Schuck build a second bedroom on the house. It even had a closet. Mother, Myrtle, and I put up the celotex the ceiling was a little crooked. Maybe the room was.

Every spring after the wood heater was taken out it was time for spring house cleaning. We would kalsomine the walls. This was a powder (what ever color you would choose). It was mixed with water and put on the walls with a big brush. Made everything clean and fresh smelling. Just like I can remember coming home from school and Mother had just finished scrubbing and waxing the floor. When they had an auction of Professor Prices house, after he passed away. Mother bought a square dining room table and side board . It was pink and turquoise color and looked real nice in our dining room.

This is the first house I can remember with a bathroom. We had kitchen, dining room, front room, two bedroom, cement cellar and a bathroom. Mother always did a lot of canning and there was a big crock just inside the door with sauerkraut in it When I went down for something I always took the rock and towel and dish from the top and had some cold kraut to eat it was so good.

We had an old barn on the back of the lot. It had been Grandfathers horse barn. It had a wood shed in the bottom now and storage in the hay mow. I had sold a punch board shortly before we had left Rexford an for doing so I received a big Shirley Temple doll. I stored the doll still in her original box in the top of the wood shed. After one winter I went up to check her out when I opened the box her face legs and arms were all pealed up and ruined so she went into the trash.

The first summer in Eureka, Myrtle went to Portland Oregon as soon as school was out. Clyde had been injured in the ship yards. He was working as a carpenter and got his hand into a saw and nearly lost his hand. They lived at Vanport which was a housing project between Portland and Vancouver that had been put up to house all the people that were coming to work in the war effort on the coast. Myrtle lived with them that summer. She and Esther went to work in the Oregon Ship Yards as sweepers. They soon became welders. And both worked at this till the war was over. When Clyde got out of the Hospital he went back to work in the ship yards again.

Mother told me we would both have to find a job. She would keep a roof over our heads and food on the table. If I wanted to go to High School I would have to buy my own cloths to do so. Dad was working but we didn't see to much of him. Mother was doing housework for Mrs. Gibbons who was teaching school. Mr. Gibbons had a garage. She also worked for Dr. Dickenson's family. He was a dentist. I know she worked for others but can't remember who. She worked in the Christmas trees that winter and for a few more years. She would come home with red hands where the tags faded when they were wet. She must have gotten awful cold. She would be so wet when she came in.

Right after we arrived in Eureka I went to work for Jack and Ruby Stevens. I worked six days a week with Sunday off. I made five dollars a week. Hey that was enough for school cloths. They at that time had five children. Jackie, Willy, Billy, Roy and Anita was a tiny baby. In the afternoon between lunch dishes and Dinner when Anita was napping and the three older boys were out playing. Sometimes I would take Roy and we would walk over the hill past the community hall and down town. There were no houses on the hill at this time. I helped teach him to talk that summer. The twins were taking piano lessens. One would practice for a half hour and I would send him out to play, telling him to send his brother in to practice. Little did I know one practiced for an hour and the other not at all. However the one doing all the practicing ended up owning all the rabbits. He was getting paid off in rabbits to practice for his brother.

Mother raised ground cherries in her garden. They made the best pies. They looked like tiny green tomatoes with a point on one end. You never hear of them any more.

Myrtle and I had dates with a couple of local boys when we first moved from Rexford. When they came to the house we told Mother to tell them we were not there to see what they would do, as they were late. So she did, she went to the door and said the girls said to tell you they are not here. So we came walking out looking sheepish

The drug store seemed to hold a fascination for me, when we moved to Eureka. The only times I had been in a store that had a fountain were two times in Whitefish once when Esther gave me the money for a chocolate soda and another time for a chocolate sundae, both really dreamy.

So I really didn't know what anything was or how much it cost. But soon learned. One night after school had started, I was a freshman and Myrtle was a Senior (we never even walked to school together). I got ready for my walk to the drug store, Myrtle asked me where I was going? When I told her she made a remark that I probably would survive one night if I didn't go to the Drug Store. or something to that effect. So I gave her a push out of my way. She went backwards across the room and set down in Mothers platform rocker, kind of hard. She went over backwards. I took one look back as I went out the door. She was yelling help me up! Not me no way. Her feet were up over the seat. Well needless to say I kept going. I later ended up working in the Drug Store for Whithecombs. I worked week ends and some evenings mostly at the fountain it had about six stools and I think four booths. I was working for twenty five cents an hour. Cokes were 5¢ Phosphates were 5¢ comic books were 5¢ mud balls were 10¢ They were a lot of tiny scoops of vanilla ice cream with chocolate syrup in a coke glass. You can still get mud balls in Eureka at Lynn's Cafe. Made different, price different, but the same ingredients. Mud balls sound more exciting than chocolate sundae.

One day Mother for some reason could not go to work at Mrs. Gibbons. I went in her place. I had never cleaned out a fire place before and Jim tormented me all day. I did get the ironing done but don't think I accomplished much more.

There were 39 Freshman in our class and it was a real new experience for me. Mr. Day was our Principle it was his last year before he retired. Other than the half year we were bused from Trego to Eureka, I had always been in much smaller schools.

My job at home was keeping the wood box full. I chopped the slab wood (have a few scares on my feet to show for it). Then I would carry it in. As our wood shed was on the back of the lot and up a hill I had steps from the wood shed to the garden and from the garden down to the back yard. When there was no garden growing in the fall and winter I would throw the wood as far as I could from the wood shed and then into the yard by the back porch where the wood box was and carry it the rest of the way. One day in the wood shed I ran a nail in my foot it came through the top of my foot between the little toe and the next one. I pulled it back out and Mother poured Iodine in the hole, then I really did some dancing.

One night I came home and no supper. The kitchen stove was cold. Mother said she must have used a lot of wood that day as the wood box was empty. Well—the night before I was in a hurry so I stood a few pieces on end and then lay wood on top to make it look full. Mother knew this and so did I. After that I filled the wood box the way I was suppose to.

Myrtle played a coronet in the band and I played a clarinet. But I never set the world on fire with my music. My junior year I played an Oboe, I had a solo in our spring concert and a man in the front row thought it was a clarinet off key and he laughed all way through my solo. Myrtle did much better with her music. She doesn't know what ever happen to her horn. Mother gave mine to the neighbor's children so they could play in the band.

That winter we skated at the little pond by Roosevelt school, where the Sr. Citizens housing now stands. Would build a big fire and have a ball.

I had a boy friend who delivered hand bills for the theatre so he got into the shows free, It cost a quarter for me to get in. We went to a lot of dances at the community hall he played in the orchestra but that was all right there were lots of others to dance with. Mother could see the hall from our house. I had a half hour to get home from the time the lights went out at the hall. Of course we all walked no one had a car or gas or tires.

Myrtle Graduated in May of 1944. She went back to Oregon to work in the ship yards. She still has her welding card and her last check stub. She was making a lot more than Dad was in the woods. I think she was making like $1.50 an hour. He was making $3.00 a day. She was living with Irene Olson at this time. Esther and Clyde had bought a home in Troutdale Oregon.

They all went to Clydes cousin s for Thanksgiving. Myrtle and Lena made pumpkin pies. Sugar was rationed, but they scrounged around and got enough for the pies. Lena had chickens where they lived. The pies were put on the back porch to cool. When they went to get them the chickens had walked across the pies. So they spooned the tops off and no one was the wiser. They still had pumpkin pies for desert.

I went to work as a waitress for George Davis for a while. Twenty five cents and hour and tips were not heard of at this time. He had the railroad contract so we fed a lot of railroad men. One Saturday I spilled a cup of hot coffee down a man's neck. No one was to happy with me about that time. Mother had a chance to go to work there as a cook and we didn't think it was to good of an idea for us to work at the same place so I got on at the grocery store for George McGlen and I worked for him until his death. He was a great man to work for. I worked with Albina Johnson and Mrs. Patrick they were all very patient with me. I also made 25¢ an hour working here.

George taught me how to clean a whole chicken. I made such a mess of it he told me to wrap it up and take it home. He said it was so hacked up he could not sell it. He probably knew we could use it anyway. He would delight in bringing out a half of a hog head and laying it in front of me on the cutting block. We had to cut the meat from the jowls to go in sausage. I told him that the thing was looking at me, he would always laugh at that.

Mr. McGlenn was a very kind man, he had a red and white bird dog of some kind. It slept in the back room of the store. The old dog would come up to him and if he picked up the broom the dog would roll over on its back with all four feet in the air then he would take the broom and scratch her tummy and she would get up shake and go back to her bed and lay down.

He got a kick out of telling people about when he had a batch of kittens running around the back room. Tommy Price was delivering groceries for him. So when he was leaving the store, George said you have a delivery across the tracks. Would you put those kittens in a potato sack and throw them from the bridge. Could you do that ? Tom said sure he could. So he left with the kittens and the deliveries. Well when he came back George asked him if he threw the sack from the bridge. Didn't ask if he threw the kittens from the bridge. He said sure did. George said those are the best darn swimmers I ever seen. He turned around and looked at the kittens all curled up in the corner with their mother sound asleep and walked out to the front of the store and we had a mouse free store with all those cats in the back room.

There were probably not over 300 items in the whole store. Every one charged their grocery's by the month and they all had their own little books. The cookies were sold in the bulk by the dozen. We kind of had to guard the cookie boxes when people came in with lots of children. This was not a self service store or supermarket. You waited on people and got what they wanted and if they were walking the grocery's would be delivered to their house. The bread came in on the train and there were no preservatives so each loaf had to be gone over and checked for mold before it was put on the shelf. We sold Cigarettes one pack at a time. Wings, Spuds, Lucky Strike, Camels and a few more brands. I had started smoking and thought Mother didn't know. She always put my cloths on the bed and I put them away. So I had my cigarettes in my drawer. I came home from school one day to get ready for work. Mother had put the wash away. She asked me if I was smoking ? I said no. She wanted to know about the cigarettes in my drawer. I told her they were for my friends as they couldn't always find them for sale, she said the open package to ? That was all that was said but I didn't smoke in front of her till after I was married. Cigarettes were 12¢ a package then. After 32 years I stopped smoking.

One day Steve McCullough brought back some skinless wieners, he said they were slimy. He didn't want to spend money and ration stamps for something he couldn't eat. George asked him what he wanted in place of them He said he was going to the Post Office and would get something on the way back. I was in the back room washing wieners in vinegar water to get the slime from them, they came in that way. George brought that pound to me and said to wash them and put them on the top of the new box I was working on. So I did, you guessed it Steve came in and wanted to know if those were fresh wieners. He took the same pound home he had just returned.

About this time we received some new Items in the store that sold real well. It was Arid and Mum deodorant. Both were in white jars with red tops the Mum was in a short squat jar and Arid in a taller and smaller around one. From that day on body powder didn't sell so well but I am sure the town smelled better.

Myrtle and Esther sent me a light blue pleated skirt and a brown cardigan sweater for my birthday. I just loved them. At that time we wore our sweaters backwards and buttoned down the back part of the time with a dickey collar under them. We also wore broom stick skirts that were very easy to make and not to expensive as they only took a couple of yards of fabric and a button.

For Christmas I was sent a bottle of Cotton Blossom Cologne. I really liked it, till our little kitten did what kittens do. We could smell it but not find it. Myrtle was home and she had company coming. So we poured some of my cologne on top of the wood heating stove. Never liked it much after that. After her company left we found the little pile behind the sofa.

On our way to school some of us girls would stop at a friends house and we would go up to her bedroom and have a Cigarette. Their house had at one time had heat registers in the bedrooms. They had been taken out and left a hole in the floor. We had to get rid of the cigarette butts so when they got cold we would dump them down this hole. We felt pretty safe as this girls mother was not suppose to climb stairs. We stopped after school one day and the lady of the house asked if we would clean out the top shelf of the cupboard for her as somehow they were filling up with cigarette butts. We cleaned it all up and that ended our early morning cigarettes.

Our folks had built a little house (one room) out back for Maimi, she used the bathroom in the house and the water from the house. She helped weed the garden and take care of the chickens. Dad decided he had to have some chickens, he put up a coop and fence by the woodshed. I hated those chickens. Go into feed them and they would pick at your feet if you had sandal on. One of them kept falling over. Mother would set her up and she would be all right till next time. She had a miss shaped body, with a large stomach. When they butchered them that fall for the freezer. That chicken was thrown away. She had a huge liver and it was bright yellow. Dad won a turkey at a raffle, he was told to hang it up by the feet and stick it in the roof of the mouth with a sharp object and it would kill it and the feathers could be picked off with no hot water real easy. So he hung it up in the woodshed and stuck it as told Mother started picking it. WOOPS It came back to life and flapped its wings, knocked Mothers glasses off and really did some moving around Mother took it down and chopped its head of and picked it same as a chicken.

I rushed home from school one day to change cloths to go to work. I opened the closet and could not believe my eyes. Maimi had worked over all my dresses while I was at school and Mother was at work. We did wear our clothes kinda short during W.W. II. She had sewn a strip of black sateen about 8 inches wide around the bottom of every thing in the closet. I wore my school clothes to work that day. She was about 92 years old at this time. She was a very sweet old French woman she always dressed in black and had since Grandfather had died in 1925. She would sit in the dark and knit her long black stockings she wore. I never said any thing about the dresses just got busy and put the hems back in them. She never mentioned them either.

We were raised on French Crepes and didn't really know what they were. We called them French pancakes or Maimi Pancakes. Mother would make them for breakfast and we would eat them with syrup and butter on them while they were hot. Those left over we would put sugar on them when we came home from school and roll them and ate them that way. Maimi also made a stew that was real thick like it had a gravy on it. I liked that real well also. Or she might cook nothing but a big pot of corn on the cob for a meal. She didn't like to cook.

Mother was hanging out the wash one day. Mrs. Moulder the next door neighbor was talking to her over the fence. She said Eva do you know you just hung up 32 pair of women's panties ? Mother said well I guess you know we all wear them then don't you ?
End of conversation.

We had a Humbug Circus at school my Sophomore year. Each class had a candidate. I was the one from the Sophomore class. The Queen was chosen by the one that sold the most tickets to the games. This is the only event I remember Dad going to when I was in school. When it came time to announce the winner, they had us all lined up on the stage. They called the name of #4 first then #3 and #2 and then said and the Queen was Helen Shenefelt. I was watching Dad's face it was funny as every name they called off his face got a little longer. But it lit up when I won. After it was over it would have been nice if he would have came home with us instead of going down to the bar.

I was a cheer leader this year. Come tournament time, Johnny McKenzy took a load of us down to Whitefish in the back of his pick up. He had a box built on it and hay in the bed of the truck to ride on. There was a bus went but I was not allowed to ride in it. Reason-Mr. Korn our Principle had gone on down to the tournament and left Mr. Gordon our band teacher in charge. He decided that girls and boys should not ride on the same bus. There was only one bus available for the pep Club. We were telling him the Pep Club always went together on the same bus. He said well not while he was in charge. So I opened my big mouth and stuck my foot in it. I told him he was a narrow minded old so and so. So I got sent home till Mr. Korn came back to school. Then I got back in. Well the bus did go and the whole pep club got to go on it, but me . So Johnny took some of us in his pickup. The cheer leaders stayed at the Hori Hotel (Remington Now) We were walking down the hall and seen 3 girls walking towards us. We stepped over, they stepped over. Then it dawned on us there was a long mirror at the end of the hall and that was us. We got quite a laugh out of that. At that time we could go to the tournament eat out and stay in the hotel for the whole week end on $5.00 and felt lucky to have it. Our Cheer Leading outfits were home made the skirts were reversible they were black satin on one side and white satin on the other we had black sweaters and black an white saddle shoes. The Cheer Leaders this year were. Helen Alavana Alene Voorhees, Beverly Titchbourne, Ramona Peltier, Evelyn Vlasak and myself. On the way home the pickup had a flat tire. With tires being rationed no one seemed to have a spare well he didn't have one. We were right at the highway shed at Stryker. He worked for the Highway Department and had a key, he opened up the building and got a roaring fire going in the big old wood heater. We were told to stay there till he got back for us it was very cold. He got a ride into Eureka, got a tire, went and told all our folks where we were. Not many of them had phones. By the time we all got in town it was 6 a.m. We were a tired bunch of kids.

We were now allowed to wear blue jeans to school we rolled them up half way to our knees and wore white shirts with them with the tails out. And if we had our hair up in pin curl's we wore a tea towel tied turban style around our head. Also wooden soled shoes were popular as they didn't take a ration stamp. They were sure noisy on the stairs at school. We also wore huaraches they were leather and squeaked when you walked of coarse we wore bobby socks.

The next summer I was still working at the store. We did a lot of swimming at second dam in the tobacco river. It was a dam left from the big mill days in Eureka. It was down over the hill from Wetzels house on riverside. It was a wooden dam and had a shoot you could go through there was also a diving board. I guess they must have fished there also as I have a picture of John Finch and Olaf Erie fishing off the diving board.

Mother was cooking for Margarett and Bud Tichbourn their Cafe was a couple of doors south of the Drug Store in later years it burned down. She cooked on a wood stove that had been converted to oil. Washed dishes in old laundry tubs made from cement. The bottom was real ruff as the cement had worn away and there was rocks that had come through. You had to use bleach in the rinse water to disinfect the dishes so this job in this cafe was hard on the hands. She use to come home so very tired and lots of time with a tooth ache, her teeth had gone real bad. She started to have them pulled and kept on working. She lost a lot of weight during this time. We had a real good summer though it was only Mother and I. Dad had gone to work on a carnival with Harold for the summer. Some of us got together a couple of times and walked to Glen Lake during the summer , we would go out one way and come back the other.

One night after work I went and joined some of the other kids up by the High School. They were eating carrots they had pulled from a garden, they asked if I wanted one well sure. We were going along when Mr. Salters came from an alley at us, every one took off but me. He grabbed me by the back of the head and said I will teach you to rob my garden. I didn't know what he was talking about. He took me up the hill to Livengoods. Mr. Livengood was the city policeman. Mr. Salter knocked on the door. He said here is one of your girls and I just caught her stealing carrots from my garden. Mr. Livengood said she is not one of mine but you had better let loose of her. Then he asked me about it I told him I had just got off work and met some other kids eating carrots and I did eat one. He didn't even ask me who the others were. He just told Salter he had better be darn sure before he ever touched or accused any one else.

On the day the Japanese surrendered, I was working at the drug store and was wrapping women's unmentionables in brown wrapping paper, we could not put them on the shelf till they were wrapped. After work we were all celebrating and a few of us decided to go to Glen Lake to a cabin one of the boys folks owned. We went to Hank Leonards chicken house and swiped two chickens the boys went in the chicken house and handed the chickens over the fence to us girls. We went to the lake started a fire to get hot water to pick the chickens. The boys killed them and picked then , cleaned them then we girls fried them. Had a feast and did some swimming and just had fun. Thinking we had got away with something. The next week the boy who's folks owned the cabin went into the barber shop to get a hair cut. Hank was asking him how he celebrated V.J. day ? And were the chickens any good ? Then he started to laugh and said he had followed us to see what we were going to do with his two chickens and they smelled so good he nearly joined us for supper. So we didn't get away with anything.

I was going home from a dance one Saturday night and seen a bunch of men and cars around the Mortuary which was on the way to our house. We stopped and asked who had died and they said they had found George McGlenn in the back room of the store. He had hung himself on the banana hook. I had worked with him till six o'clock. It really hit me hard. He was such a good man to work for. I worked in the store for Mrs. McGlenn for two weeks and every time I walked in to the back room I would cry so Mother told me I could quit and I did.

Went to work full time in the Drug store. School would be starting now before to long. I was engaged to a young man who was in the Navy. We were both to young. I ended up sending his ring back to him in a letter I guess he got it as he stopped writing as did I.

I decided to take a trip to Portland to see my two sisters before school started. I went by train. They met me at the Depot. Myrtle lived in Vanport We went to Jantzen Beach Amusement Park. That was really something for me. Then we ended up working a couple of days in a hamburger stand. You stood at the counter and yelled "They are already ready and already hot onions in the middle and relish on top hamburgers 25¢ While you were working you could ride the rides free during your break and lunch half hour. I went on the octopus one day and got deathly sick and vomited all over a soldier that was in the same seat as I was, I was so embarrassed I never have ridden another one of those to this day.

After my stay in Portland I was put on the train and went to Seattle. Decided I would go see Donna Lee LaByer. I only had a box number for them in Edmonds. When I got off the train in Seattle, I asked and found a city bus for Edmonds. I now realized I was in an awful big city. I was becoming pretty frightened. I got off the bus in Edmonds at a grocery store. I went in and asked if any one there could tell me where LaByers lived. No one knew them, they asked me the address and I told them I only had a box number. One man asked me what they looked like, if they had any children, what age they were and if they had any pets. I described what they looked like a couple or three years ago. Also their little bull dog. He said he might know the area they lived in. So dumb me I went in the car with him. He was a nice man. We found their house. They were not home but the dog was in the yard. When they came home the dog and I were sitting on the front steps. Mr. LaByer really scolded me and said it was sheer luck I had found them. I intended to stay a couple of days. After my two days Donna Lee and her Dad took me to the train depot. Well the Depot was full of service men and they were taking service men and their family's only first before civilians "and dumb girls from Montana". This happened for three days in a row. The fourth day I got in a line with a bunch of sailors and got swished on the train. So finally got home. When I thought of that trip in later years I thought how dumb. Anything could have happen to me and no one would have even known where to start looking for me. I was between 15 and 16 years old.

Well back home and back to school. But first thing first I had to have a job for after school and weekends. Also one that would let me have time off for the ball games. I went to work at Titchbourns cafe, Mother and I worked opposite shifts. It was getting pretty busy there as all the boys coming home from the service. Milkshakes with a raw egg in them and raw hamburgers with raw onions in them, were all the rage. YUCK!!

Mr. Korn had gone to Deer Lodge as Principle. So now 3 years into High School and three Principles. Mr. Boslaugh was our new Principle this year and he would end up teaching in this capacity until he retired. I think he must have been in the Eureka school system for about 30 years.

Our Junior year started with 31 students in the class. There were three cheer leaders this year they were Evelyn Vlasak, Helen Alavana, and Helen Shenefelt (Me). We had new uniforms this year. We had black flared wool skirts, white blouses and Orange Letter sweaters. Myrtle had moved to Seattle and was working at the Port of Embarkation. She worked there for a while. Then decided she could make more in a restaurant so went to work at a fountain she at least got one meal a day. She lived with Mary Livengood for a while and Gloria Kline. Myrtle is the one that found a Orange Letter sweater for me. She ordered it at the Octonic Knitting Mill. I had it till about 1965, then my children wore it out for me.

I was home one night and Mother was at work. I had scrubbed the whole house. I waxed my room then proceeded to wax the rest of the house. By then my room would be dry and I could wax myself in there.

When I finished and stood up I turned around and looked at the window for, some reason. It was dark outside, pressed up against the window was a man's face. When he knew I had seen him he turned and left. I knew who he was. When Mother came home I told her. The next day he came into the Cafe. She went out of the kitchen and right out to where he was sitting and told him we knew he was a peeping Tom and he just might get himself shot if it didn't stop NOW. We never had any more trouble with him.

Things were getting better at home we now had Ipana tooth paste in the bathroom instead of baking soda. Mother had now gotten her teeth pulled and had dentures so she had no more tooth aches but coughed a lot. If I polished my nails that made her cough. So I would go in another room from her to do it. I didn't know it but she had asthma.

I took Home Ec. this year. We made a full meal one day and had to make biscuit My group made hockey pucks. We hid them till the Teacher asked where they were, then we had to show her you couldn't even cut them. For my sewing project I made a pair of flannel pajamas the top turned out fine then I started on the bottoms. They turned out like a long skirt with a point in front and one in back that was suppose to be the crotch. I couldn't figure out what I did wrong. The Teacher told me I had to read the pattern and figure it out. I ripped and ripped and finally figured how to get legs in those pants, I never did like those pajamas after I got them finished.

Miss Morrison was our Gym teacher, we had horrible green gym suits with bloomers, they would pull clear down nearly to your knees. That is where she wanted you to wear them. We played basket ball in them. Just before going on the floor we would pull them up and she would not call us on it then. We were going to Fernie to a game and I wanted to be sure my sox were white, I bleached them real good in the morning and hung them on a hanger. (No one had dryers I don't know if they were around then) When I came home to get ready to go back and catch the bus I put my white sox on and my boots and took off. At the gym in Fernie when I took my boots off I had a few pieces of round elastic around my ankle The sox had to much bleach and had disappeared so I played with out any sox. When we went up there we played boys rules, in Eureka we played girls rules, they always really trounced us but we had two games a year one up there and one down home. There were no girls sports at that time. We were up there one time and stayed in different homes. Donald Morgan was so pleased that he had been chosen to stay in the Mayors home. Sunday morning he found out why, he had his catholic metal on when he was playing and he had to get up and go to church with the family. We all went to a show in Fernie one trip and when it was over we all started out of the theater like we did at home and noticed every one were just standing at their seats while God Save The King was being played then they left. We were half way down the isle just standing there feeling foolish.

You could now get anything that was available without ration stamps. You could also put your name on a waiting list for a new car there was none made during the war. Also a washing machine (wringer type no automatic's yet). Toasters were also something you could put your name on a list for, they were not automatic, you had to watch them to see when to open the doors and turn them over and watch them close or you had black toast.

Titchbourne's Cafe had high backed wooden booths the seats were also wood no padding, it had a horseshoe counter with stools. There was a small room in back with a juke box. We did a lot of dancing there during the week. Margaret and Bud had an apartment in back behind the Cafe.

There were still dances at the community hall on Saturday night. Mrs. Harvey played the piano, Duane Meuli the drums and John Finch the accordion once in a while some one else but that was the main ones.

This year come tournament time all the basketball players had to get in the Pythagorean Theorem in to the Geometry teacher before they could go. I helped some of them and nearly got in trouble again. We stayed at the old Whitefish Hotel this time for $1 .00 a night, there were four of us so it only cost us 254 each. We were all laying across the bed one afternoon, all at once one leg of the bed went through the floor. We just moved it over a little so all four legs were solid. After that we could hear music coming from down stairs.

I stopped at Prices one morning to pick Phyllis up on the way to school wearing the latest thing in clothing, Peddle Pushers. Mr. Price started to laugh and ask me if I knew I had grown out of my pants. So I went into detail to tell him what they were he still laughed.

We put on the play of Dear Daffodil for our Junior production. I wanted the part of Daffodil but Jeanne Peltier got it, but I did get a part in the play. We had so much fun at play practice and were very proud of the job we had done.

This was a great year in school. I left my Junior year really looking forward to my Senior year. Myrtle was the only one in our family to Graduate from High School. And I left my Junior Year thinking I would be the second one.

You could now buy Nylons stockings in the stores. I never wore to many of them as that meant wearing a girdle.

Just before school was out three of us decided we would play hookey, never had before. We jumped out of the reference room window just as the coach walked around the building. He asked what we were doing ? We told him," going around to the front", door and that is what we did. That year Mr. Buckley said the only body contact the foot ball team had was when Bunkie Hobson tripped over the water pail.

We were still having lots of dances at the community hall. With all the young men who had come back from the service there was Beer, Wine and some hard liquor now at the dances. I never found any I liked and didn't like what it did to people so never partook of much of it. This was going to be a great summer the war was over and every one was coming home and no worries.

Esther and Clyde had come back from Portland they went into the tie mill business with Dad, big mistake with his drinking. They bought an old house on the way to east Eureka. After completely redoing it inside it was a nice little place.

I had been going out with a lot of the young men who had come home from the service. Bud Mikelson and I were out for a Sunday drive down by Rexford. Allen Darling was riding a bike along the highway. When we got even with him he turned into the front fender, he turned to see where the car was and in doing so turned his front wheel. It threw him against the side of the car and the open car handle tore a hole in his back. Bud put him in the back seat took his own white T shirt off and had me get in the seat with him and hold the shirt against the wound. We took him to Eureka to Dr. Clarks Hospital. They had to send someone out to Glenn Lake to find Dr. Clark to come in and take care of him.

About this time Tommy Price came home from the navy. We started going together and the 8th of June 1946 we went to Kalispell with both sets of parents and Sisters to get married, 17 and 19 years old. When we went to the Court House we went into the place where you got hunting license. They told us to go across the hall. Tommy's Dad said I told you that you weren't old enough you don't even know where to get a marriage License. We both needed our parents to sign for us as we were minors. We were married by a preacher at a parsonage on Main Street in Kalispell. Then all went to Laurence Park for a picnic. Esther and Clyde rode back to Eureka with Phyllis and Jim Harris. They let us use their car. We stayed in the Kalispell Hotel, so did Charles and Vivian Purdy they were married the same day. We went home the next day and moved into our apartment over the Soil Conservation Office. In the Old Bank building (Browns Pottery now).

Mrs. Price had a little reception for us when we got home. She had made a filled Angel food cake. It had fruit nuts and whip cream mixed into the crumbled cake from the middle . It was then put back in and frosted with whip cream. Very good as I remember. Esther's son Dick was about five years old. He had a piece of cake then went to Mrs. Price and said, that sure is tough but can I please have another piece ? Mrs. Price brought that up quite a few times she got a kick out of it.

Tommy worked for Vick Peltier at the Creamery. Esther and Clyde gave us a building lot. We started to build on it. We had two rooms up over the Bank building. The bathroom was in the hall. We cooked on a wood cook stove. Had an Ice Box, we got ice for it at the creamery a couple of times I forgot to empty the water pan, the office girl down stairs would go out in the street and yell up to me that I was dripping through the ceiling We had to carry our wood up stairs also. When we got married Tommy had a bed and a chest of drawers that had a desk on the top of it. When we moved to Spokane, in later years I sold the chest to Esther she used it in her sons room for a long time and it is still in use at the Paul cabin at Bitterroot Lake.

We bought a table and chairs, wood cook stove and some cardboard closets (that kept falling down). That is what we set up house keeping with. I was a lousy cook. Within a month I was pregnant and had morning sickness so bad. We were trying to get the house up so we could move into it. Material was not to plentiful nor money to build it. I could not work much as I was sick all the time.

I took Dick who was about six years old, over to 2nd Dam fishing. We did catch fish and he remembers we put them in a small white cloth sack (flour sack) he got to carry them home. He was so proud of them. When he comes from Connecticut to his cabin on Bitteroot lake he still likes to fish for trout.

We also talked Esther ,Clyde and Dick into going camping with us that summer. Of coarse they drove as we had no car. I don't remember where we went but during the night Esther had something chewing on the foot of her sleeping bag. She thought it was a porcupine or something like that so she picked up the hatchet and was going to run it of. When Tommy shined the light on the varmint she stopped in a hurry, It was the prettiest little skunk you ever saw. Next morning we packed up and went home in a hurry. No more camping.

We did work on the house all we could it had two rooms and a path out back. We never did get the water in. There was a stand pipe by the back door. We moved in when it was just a shell no walls up inside. As I remember there was no insulation either. One day I was trying to wax the linoleum and the wax would freeze as I poured it on the floor, before I could spread it out. I would sit on the floor beside the frozen wax and cry. I was really trying to make a home where there was only a shell to live in. I got so very large before Butch was born I had Toxemia or pre-clampsia the Dr. put me in the Hospital at 7 1/2 months for a week. Then on a very strict diet. No salt, no eggs, very little protein, mostly cooked cereal. I went home for a month. I was a very sick young girl. At 81/2 months Mother and I went to Whitefish and rented a room and stayed there till I delivered my baby. He was a big 10 lb. healthy baby. He was born in the old-old Whitefish Hospital that is now Reeds Apartment's. I had the mumps in the last stages of my pregnancy The Dr. told me the baby would have them also. So would probably never have them as a child. He had them harder than the other children.

Rayola Banning had married a Young Man from up in Canada she also had Toxiemia when she became pregnant when her baby boy was born in Eureka she went into convulsions her baby lived but she died in child birth.

I went back to school for a short time so I could turn over some offices I held to others. At this time you did not go back to school if you were married it was not allowed. When my class graduated in May of 1947. I was sitting in the audience with a beautiful baby boy about 2 months old my first born Butch. I did later get my Diploma from the Spokane Continuation High School. We didn't have a car so we bought a baby buggy. There is one in the log cabin at the Historical Village in Eureka just like it. Barbara and Glenny Roose had one for Shirley just like it. Shirley was born the same day as Butch. Shirley was a very tiny little girl with lots of hair. Butch was a big bald baby boy, when his hair started to come in it was a mass of curles all over his head and still is curley now.

I had the baby in the buggy all clean and sparkling, I proudly took him to town. He was now old enough to hold things in his hand and chew on everything. I went in the Drug Store for a minute and could see some of my school mates looking at him in the buggy. They were all laughing. When I went out they had given him a black licorice sucker. He had gotten it in his mouth and then rubbed it all over his face. They thought it was real funny. There was my beautiful baby boy down town and a royal mess. I didn't think it was very funny at all and took him home.

Myrtle came home from Seattle and went to work for Titchbourn' s in the Cafe. She had her upper teeth pulled and lost a lot of weight. She looked so nice. She had started going out with Wayne Richmond. They were to get married. She and I were making her a wedding dress. When I became sick before Butch was born we gave up on that and they came to Kalispell and were married while Mother and I were in Whitefish waiting for me to have my baby. They were married February 24 1947. They moved into a very little one room house across the street from Esther and I. So there we were again THE SISTERS THREE.

We were putting up the walls in the bedroom and Butch was about 5-6 months old. He was sitting in his crib and wanted my class ring so I gave it to him to play with, I never seen it again. I feel it is in between the walls in the house. Has been for 48 years.

Myrtle came over one day and wanted to know how to make cream puffs. (by now I had learned to make a few things). I gave her the recipe . The next day she came over with what looked like a small pancake. I asked her what it was she said my version of a cream puff I don't know what she did it just didn't raise. Another time she came over this time she pulled a little hard thing out of her pocket. We asked her what it was she said a parker house roll. She had killed the yeast with hot water this time. She could make good spaghetti Harold had taught her, but it was real spicy and Wayne couldn't tolerate spices. But she also learned and is now a wonderful cook. So is Sharon their daughter. Sharon is the same age as Butch for two days out of the year. She was born March 8th 1948 two days before Butch's first birthday. Myrtle and Wayne now moved into a larger house. It had three rooms all in one row. It was on the other side of me. The heating stove had a problem the black tar soot would run down the stove pipe and puddle on the floor. Myrtle had made a skirt for Sharon's basket, the cold air blowing in around the doors and windows would make the skirt blow in the breeze. They survived, I guess that was a case of they had their love to keep them warm.

I went to the grocery store one day and walking home with grocery bag and baby I put my wallet in the grocery sack. When I emptied the sack I threw it in the wood cook stove. Put the lid on and went on about my business. Then it dawned on me, the wallet. I opened the lid and all that was left was the snap and a few coins. That wallet contained all the money we had to our names, which was not much. But we had no more.

That spring I was sitting rocking and feeding the baby when a gust of wind came up. It blew the front door open and scared me so bad. I grabbed my baby and run to Esthers house crying my head off. Leaving the door wide open. I have always been afraid of the wind and still don't like it.

Esther and Clyde had their name in for a long time for a new car. It finally came up, They sold the car they had driven all during the war to Johnny Holder he drove it for a long time.

They always had a dance at Grasmere on the Canadian Thanksgiving. We went up to one and they sold some extra turkeys that they had cooked and didn't use.

We bought one and brought it home I had no refrigeration and put it in the cupboard. A couple of days later I fixed dinner with it and talk about a rotten turkey we really had one. We had Esther and Clyde over for dinner one day and Clyde said I was the only woman he knew that could take perfectly good food and ruin it.

Before Butch was two years old, we sold our house and all our household belongings and moved to Spokane on the train. I was down town in Spokane one day with the baby he was pretty good sized for a two year old. The buses were not running as President Truman was in town and all traffic was stopped till his motorcade got through to where they were going. By the time I could get on a bus all the seats were full. After about four buses I got on one and said I would stand and hold the baby. The bus driver closed the door and said "I am not moving this bus till someone gets up and gives this woman with the baby a seat". I felt so dumb and embarrassed I told the driver to open the door and I would wait for another bus. He wouldn't Finally an older woman got up and gave me her seat she said she only had about four more blocks to go anyway.

We were in Spokane no car no job, A BIG MISTAKE. We moved into an apartment which was three rooms and a bath up stairs in a house. I got a job as a car hop in the Tip Top drive in. The lady down stair's took care of Butch for me. I had to ride a bus to and from work it was a long bus ride. Wash cloths diapers and all in the bath tub and hang them all over the apartment to dry. We had a coal cook stove in the kitchen. I spent the better part of one day trying to get a fire going. I didn't know you had to start a coal fire with wood then add coal. I had a terrible time there. We had a Tailor Tot stroller for Butch, I walked to the store one day and had a bag of grocery's in the back and had put my purse on top of it. I didn't notice it fall off the sack but when I got back to the house there was a man sitting on the step and he handed me my purse. He said he had found it and looked inside for an address and name. Then he said and there is a picture of the baby so I know it is yours. There were some honest people in Spokane at that time.

This is where our marriage started to fall apart. I don't remember where Tommy worked, but I do know he stayed at McClures and didn't come home night after night. We finally moved back to Eureka and moved into Robin and Joyce Clarks house up on top of the East Eureka hill. I went to work for Norman Clark in the grocery store, Myrtle baby sat for me. We had a very cold winter. Tommy brought home a venison and I didn't know what to do with the meat. Some one said can it, now how do you do that ? I cut it up in small pieces and fried the whole deer. Put it in quart jars and poured the grease from the skillets in on it, but didn't process it any further. Guess the grease sealed it as we ate it and it didn't poison any of us. It was real good ground up with onions and mixed with mayonnaise for sandwiches. Or put in a skillet and heated up.

Butch had the croup real bad one night I could see Mothers lights in her house across town, but had no way to get there. I kept waiting for Tommy to come home but this was another night he had interest else where. I sat up all night holding the baby over a steam teakettle on a hot plate on the floor. I put the hot plate and teakettle under the rocking chair. I thought if I went to sleep I would not burn either one of us that way. Then I put a sheet over the top of the chair and us to make a steam tent. Once during the night he started to cough and he turned blue and went limp. I run my finger in his mouth and there was a big gob of phlegm which I got out and he then caught his breath again. By this time I was mad frightened and very hurt that I should have to go through this by myself. The croup usually lasts three nights and the child feels better during the day.

The stroller had small wheels on it so the next spring it didn't do much good when we lived up on top of the hill and a gravel road all the way up. Butch was a little over two years old now, he would walk down that hill when I went to town, but come time to go back up he would sit down and hold his arms up to me and I would end up with him and groceries to carry up the hill.

Esther and Clyde had sold the mill by now and moved to Half Moon. Then later to Whitefish when Clyde went back to work for the railroad.

Myrtle and Wayne lived on Central Avenue now. They had Sharon on a sled going over to Mothers. Somehow she was tipped out of the box. She hit her head on the ice and cut her forehead open. When they got to Mothers she was all bloody and her parents were upset. When it was all cleaned up it wasn't to bad. Sharon was bald for ever so long. Myrtle would fasten a bow in her hair somehow once in a while. Someone said if they would cut the baby fuzz off, her hair would grow. So Wayne cut it and it did start to grow. When her hair did come in it was real thick and curly. She took a streak of biting. She ran up to Clyde when he was sitting in a chair and bit him on the inside of his leg. She would bite Butch on his back and he could not shake her lose she would draw blood.

When she wanted something she would say u-huh. For the longest time that was her name. You ask her what her name was and she would say u-huh. Butch would go to the kitchen sink and pant when he wanted a drink. Myrtle said that was silly he could ask for a drink pretty soon Sharon was panting for a drink also. She did everything Butch did even down to standing in front of the potty to go. It did not work so well for little girls.

Myrtle and Wayne made some root beer. They awoke one night to breaking glass, it was root beer blowing up, what a mess.

I planted two apple trees in Mothers garden when Butch was a baby. Last time I seen them they were very big and had apples a plenty on them.

Tommy and I moved to a house a block north of his folks. It was beside the Burges Drake home. Phyllis had come home from Pennsylvania She had separated from her second husband and brought her baby Lenny. She was living with her parents. I took care of the baby for her when she went to Kalispell with Tommy and Bernard and Lois Benson. He was such a sick baby. I kept steam on him all day and into the night when they got home. I think hehad pneumonia.

While we lived here we both seemed to be going our separate ways. Two silly young kids with no business being married. I was working again. Seemed we never did anything together or as a family. The plumbing in this house was real bad and kept backing up. We moved to the other side of town to Birleys house.

While here I had two different women come tell me they were having babies that belong to my husband. He was working for the forest service at Murphy Lake. I didn't even confront him with it I knew it was over for both of us. I moved to my folks filed for a Divorce sold my furniture to pay for it, it was not contested and was over in twenty days. I was given custody of my son and was awarded $40.00 a month child support. I received the $40.00 the first month and never again.

I worked at Gamble store for a while. Then left Butch with Mother and went to Kalispell to work. I rented a room on the East side in a big private home. I worked in a Cafe and small store on Main street across from Montgomery Ward. Then I met Joyce and we rented a small apartment on the west side on second avenue. I then went to work at Woolworths. I was at the sox counter. The gals there told me no one goes to the basement to get stock by them self, go with one of the other girls as the Manager liked to chase lone girls around the basement. So we would go in two's or three's load our baskets with stock and then pull them up the stairs with a rope handle on the basket. I made $12.00 a week and paid $18.00 a month for rent. While trying to help with my sons needs also.

We did a lot of partying in the evenings, but never missed a days work. We went to the Appleway, Stardust, Hennesys Steak house and the V.F.W.

I met a very nice young man from Oklahoma who was working on Construction in Polson. He was such a sweet gentle man. I knew he would be going back to Washington before to long. When he left we thought we would write. But I never heard from him. About a month after he left I discovered I was pregnant. I moved home and told my folks. The hardest thing I ever had to do.

I then asked them if they would keep Butch for me while I went to Spokane. Of coarse they did. After being in Spokane for six weeks, Esther got me a job housekeeping for a man in Whitefish. He had two small boys. I could keep Butch with me there. This man's wife had left him and he had two little boys about the age of Butch. I did the house work, cooking and took care of the three boys.

In February 1950 Myrtle and Wayne had a baby boy, Terry. He was a very good baby, such a husky little guy. Myrtle had him at home. One Day Sharon disappeared and Myrtle couldn't find her she looked all over for her and finally found her in the baby's basket.

I went to Esthers a week before my baby was due and went a week over. Finally I went into the Hospital at noon and they gave me shots to induce labor. At six that evening I delivered my beautiful dark haired baby girl July 29th, 1950. This was Virginia Reneé De Long.

When I went into the Hospital I had to give them $75.00 deposit. I had been making $40.00 a month housekeeping and had saved the $75.00. I went back to Esthers the next morning after she was born and was given a $49.00 refund at the Hospital. I owed the Dr. $50.00. I borrowed $1.00 and paid him off. So here I was broke with two children to support. When Virginia was four days old I took her up to a camp Mother and Dad were in up by Stryker. They were living in a cook house tent. Mother had Butch there with them. One night there was something rubbing against the tent and Dad went to see what it was and it was a bear. Myrtle an Wayne were also up there in a tent with their two small children. They had built floors in these tents and were quite comfortable. I didn't stay there to long but went back to Mothers house in town.

Esther gave me Dick's pretty wicker buggy for the baby. This is another blank spot. I don't know what I ever did with-it. But someone in Eureka must have ended up with it. I went to work in a Cafe and also at the Grocery store part time. I was working with a bottle of oil of cloves in my apron pocket all the time as I had a constant tooth ache some where all the time. Mother soon came home. Otherwise I could never had made it. I had no help from anyone. I was making 50¢ an hour. I went to a Dentist in Kalispell. Myrtle and Esther took me down . I ended up in the Hospital in Kalispell that night and had my teeth pulled. Myrtle came and got me the next day. I was home with no teeth for six weeks. The day I was given my new dentures I could not shut my mouth over them but went back to work in the cafe that night.

I went after the mail one day and Glenny Roose asked me if I knew where I could get a hold of Wayne, I told him he was in camp. He said he has a letter here that has to get to him, I think he took it up that evening. It was a draft notice from the Army to go to Korea. He had about a week or ten days before he had to report.

Maimi had passed away the year before and her little room was still standing at the back door. They got busy and built a little bedroom on to it and Myrtle and the children moved in there before he left. So Mother had two daughters and four grandchildren under four years old living with them.

Mother had Maimi living with her a good many years every time someone would die she would say I wish it had been me. She finally knew it was her time and she went to bed and within a week she was gone. Now I wish we would have tried to understand her better and gotten some answers from her about the family but we didn't. And every thing went with her when she died. She became very wrinkled and I may be someday also. In fact all three of us could.

Towards the end of October, these construction men who were working for Smith and White out of Seattle came to town to start on the R.E.A. power lines being put in. Who should walk into the Cafe with a big smile but my guy from Oklahoma. I introduced him the next day to his daughter and his future son. Mother told him he could not afford a family the way he ate. Myrtle made some cookies to send to Wayne at Christmas time and she made a mistake of bringing them into the house we all had coffee and she had to bake more cookies to send to Wayne. Jim knew he would be done with the job there in the spring some time. On week ends I usually had one day of. We would take the children and go to Kalispell for dinner. Jim was renting a room from Mr. and Mrs. Llyons one street over from the folks. When he was not at work he usually was at the house. His friend that he had came out from Oklahoma with told him not to get involved with a divorced women with children he was getting taken for a ride.

Since he had started going with me he had stopped all the drinking he was doing. One Friday night before he even went home and got cleaned up, he was still in his bibbed overalls covered with creosote. He came in the Cafe lit to the gills. He started teasing me by untying my apron and such. Then I thought he had left and I went to the Kitchen to get a glass of Milk. There he stood talking to my boss. He picked up a chef knife and was poking it at me. I had a glass of milk in my hand and I let fly with it, Milk went in Jims face and all over the Boss. I went right on out front and went on working. That night the Boss told me I had better take a few days off. I went home and told Mother what I had done, she said well you will probably never see him again. The next day was Saturday and about ten o'clock the front door opened and he said, any milk in here ?

Sharon called her baby brother Pretty Buba, after she started talking. She really missed her Daddy when he had to go into the service. Terry was not old enough to really have the attachment that Sharon had. He very quickly became a Mama s boy. When Wayne finally came home it took Terry a while before he decided there should be a man in the house. Terry took a streak of standing in the toilet and stamping his feet in the water. It took some doing for Myrtle to put a stop to that. Waynes Army picture, Sharon said her Daddy had a boat hat on. I guess the army hat looked like a boat to her.

Jim and I went to the local Dr. to get blood tests taken for our marriage license. This was a new law that had just been passed. The Dr. rummaged around on a window ledge and found a syringe, then said who is first ? So I went first he then wiped the needle of on his shirt sleeve and drew my blood and put it in a little bottle. Then looked at the needle and wiped it on his sleeve again and took Jims with the same needle and vile. Put it in a bottle and it came back in a week O.K.

We went to Kalispell and got our license, We were Married on a Friday evening by a Minister in the parsonage, (he had forgotten to heat the church) in Whitefish February 16 1951. My sister Esther and Jims friend Billy Wallace stood up for us. The Minister had a son in bed in the front room who was ill with rheumatic fever. As soon as the ceremony was over he said Dad are you done yet. Esther gave him her corsage before we left. During the ceremony there was a dog and a cat came in the room the Ministers wife caught the dog and put it out but this big old black cat came between Jim, Billy and the Minister and wound around my legs as cats will do, and purred and purred.

We went from the Church back to Esthers house she had baked one of her very good white nut cakes and decorated it up as a wedding cake. We had cake and coffee took pictures and etc. Then Jim and I came to Kalispell we stayed at the Blue and White Motel on Idaho street. Forty four years later it is still in operation.

We went back to Eureka the next day and went to Mothers. Myrtle had baked us a beautiful two tiered wedding cake and made a big dinner for us at mothers I don't know what we had to eat but we did have shrimp cocktails. We then collected our two children and moved into an apartment that was behind Hank Leonards barber shop. We rented from Kate Clark, paid $40.00 a month. It was two rooms and a small room with no window where the toilet was that was all the bathroom consisted of. The other two room were a bedroom big enough for a chest of drawers, a double bed, Butches crib and Virginias baby basket. I don't even remember a closet in there. I know it had one window. The other room had a double window over an open kitchen sink and the only door. There was a Kerosene cook stove, Hoosier cabinet complete with flour sifter in it. Table and two chairs. That is about all. The Men Jim worked with gave us toaster, electric blanket, and a rolling pin. The note attached said the toaster was so I would get up and fix his breakfast, the electric blanket was to keep me warm as they knew he couldn't and the rolling pin was to hit him over the head with because he didn't keep me warm. We are still using the General Electric pop up toaster it has lasted 44 years and raising four children.

I had never driven a car in my life my only mode of transportation had been shankes mare. Jim told me when the job was done I would have to take the car to the next job as he would have to drive company equipment He had a brand new Chevrolet car it did have an automatic transmission. So my driving lessons started. I drove it up to the store one day while he was at work. Put the groceries and the children in and put the key in and nothing it would not start. So I left it and walked home. When he got home he asked me where the car was So I told him the whole story, he said did you put it in park or neutral ? I didn't know so he walked up town and brought it back to the apartment. I had left it in gear when I stopped. Another time I had gone to the store and when I backed out there was a pick up with a bent bumper sticking out. I scraped the back fender on the car, went home and parked it thinking I would tell Jim after dinner. Butch seen him coming down the alley from the shop and he started bouncing on one foot then the other and when Jim got there Butch was yelling Daddy Jim Mamma ruined your car she hit a pickup with it. Then showed him the little scratch. I really think he was relieved that was all I had done.

The Cafe where I had been working had punch boards lining the counter. There was one that had a pair of ladies black panties and bra. on it. It was about sold out and the man that owned the place had gotten his profit from it. Jim went over there for coffee and to shoot the breeze with the guys one night. They took the panties and bra. and slipped them in Jims coat pocket to play a joke on him. The next time they all got together for coffee he told them I said thanks they fit fine. So it kind of backfired on them.

We went to Whitefish for me to take my driving test. At that time they gave them at the city hall in Whitefish certain days of the month. Here I was I had never driven in a town that had stop lights or stop signs, never parallel parked in my life. I made it through the written test with flying colors. Then we went for a ride. Did pretty well till we came back and he told me to parallel park in the front of the building. I told him I never had and that my husband was standing there and would really laugh at me. He asked me if Jim had to take a test and I told him no. He said I was going to fix him just drive around behind the building and park in the parking lot. I then told him I had to drive the car the next month to Seattle he shook his head and said drive as much as you can between now and then. I told him I would and I got my license. This was in March and we left for Lynnwood Washington in May. I had still only driven around Eureka, Lynnwood was not even on the map at this time. We knew it was north of Seattle and south of Everett. The whole town consisted of the Lynwood Tavern and a Motel.

Mother wouldn't let me get in that car with my two children by myself and leave for Washington so she decided to go with us and come home on the train. Now one of THE SISTERS THREE was leaving Montana once more. To enter into the journey of life.

The day before we were to leave we hooked a luggage trailer on behind the car. I was going to pull that with our belongings in it. We took Butches crib and could not get in the baby basket.

Next morning bright and early we headed out, Jim in a big old company truck and us following him in the car pulling the trailer. He had a case of break fluid in the truck as it had a leak in the breaks somewhere. This is still when you went down that beautiful old road along the Kootani River and past Troy down to the bottom of Moise Canyon and back up. When we were going down the canyon all at once he run into the bank. I stopped behind him and wanted to know what was wrong, he said I ran out of breaks and had to stop to put some brake fluid in that is all. He fixed it and we went on. I don't remember where we stopped along the way. I do know when we got in Spokane I was scared stiff. At that time there were no freeways all the roads went through the towns usually right down town. As long as I could see the truck I felt pretty safe. All at once he started to go through caution lights so I went through on red. I didn't get hit or stopped. In later years I told someone about it and they said well they saw those Montana license plates and knew you didn't know any better. At one point out in the flat lands in Washington I went ahead for a while and all at once he was not behind me so we pulled over and stopped I could not turn around as I couldn't back up that silly trailer. We waited and waited and finally a car stopped and Jim got out. He was broken down and would be delayed for a while. He turned the car around and we went back to where the truck was till it was fixed and then we took off again. We went over the pass into Seattle I don't remember which one, probably Snoqualmie as we went through Seattle I remember the world globe on top of the Seattle P.I. building. We found Lynnwood and rented a small two room cabin for a week till we could find something else. Found the Depot in Everett and put Mother on the train for Montana. The next day he went to work. I did a lot of hand washing that day and hung them every where to dry. We were wishing we had brought the baby basket by now. We finally took a drawer out of the chest of drawers put a pillow in it for the baby to sleep in. We did get the crib put up even though it came out about eight inches in the doorway. After dinner that night Jim said lets go down the road a little way to where one of the men I work with has his trailer parked. On the way down there Jim told me there was always a lot or gossip on construction. Don't repeat anything you hear and half of what you see. I don't want to send you home to your Mother. Mom told him if I didn't behave he could come home to her. She also told me I had a good husband and stay with him and be a good wife. That was her parting words for me at the depot when we put her on the train for Montana.

We went down to Harold and Doris Wrights they are the ones that lived a little way down the road. They had about a 14 foot trailer. It had a dinette that they had taken one seat out at the table and put in a crib for their baby girl Wendy. There was a small kitchen and a bedroom big enough for a bed. It was cute and cozy. There was no bathrooms in trailers at this time. Trailer courts had bathrooms and shower rooms in the wash house. The wash house had wringer washers and they would run for a half hour for a dime. There was a meter box on one of the legs of the washers.

They were parked at an old motel in north Everett. It had a row of cabins and about six trailer spots. Doris told us there was a two bedroom cabin for rent. We looked at it and decided to rent it. We moved in over the week end. (I now had access to a laundry to wash cloths in). The cabin looked clean other than a stale old building smell. There was a chest in one bedroom that smelled like urine (we put it out in the garage). I put the baby down on the floor as she was now crawling. When I picked her up she was black. I scrubbed the whole cabin with S.O.S. pads to get the floor clean. Virginia now went into the crib and Butch in the bed in the second bedroom. The cabin was nice enough but it didn't have a refrigerator. There was a screened in box that extended into the garage. You could get into it through a door on the kitchen wall. It was cool but not cold so I had to get milk for the children every day as it wouldn't keep any longer than that. Jim told me he had $1000.00 in Oklahoma in the bank. He had sent it home when he was in the service. His mother wouldn't send it to him when he bought his car. Now that he was married (even tho she did not approve of him marrying some one who had been married before and with children) maybe she would send it and we could start looking for a trailer. She did send it and after looking for a couple of week ends we found a real nice 28 ft. 1948 Schultz. It was $1000.00 so we bought it. We parked it right there where we had been living in the cabin. In a trailer spot. The trailer had a bedroom with a small closet and a built in vanity. In the kitchen there was only enough room to get between the stove and the bar to stand at the sink. Across from that was a refrigerator the first one I had since I was married. There was a closet beside the frig. and cupboards over the stove and sink also cupboards under the sink. The front room had a built in china cabinet, table and four folding wooden chairs and a davenport which was across the front. Also the oil heating stove was in the front room by the front door. No room for the crib. We would tip the davenport seat up and leave it up and put Butch on one end and Virginia on the other end of the back , worked fine and they couldn't fall out of bed. This trailer had beautiful wood in it. I made new curtains for it and we were very proud of it.

Now we had to get rid of the crib and the luggage trailer. Jim hooked the trailer up for me and told me to take it to a second hand store down the way. I did and they took the crib no problem but only gave me five dollars for the trailer, as the tubes were showing out of the tires. A wonder we ever made it.

A GYPSY FROM MONTANA

TO MY HUSBAND JAMES DELONG
AND MY FOUR CHILDREN.
TOM, VIRGINIA, DENNIS,AND KEVIN
WHO TRAVELED THIS ROAD WITH ME

We had a great summer. On Friday night we would go to a drive in restaurant and get the best fish and chips ever to go. Then off to the drive in theater. We would eat our fish and chips while waiting for the movie to start. After the cartoons were over Butch would curl up in the back seat with a pillow and a blanket. Our baby girl would go to sleep with her bottle and lay between us in the front seat. She had so much dark hair and beautiful expressive eyes. She was an angel and so good. They moved the shop from Lynnwood to Marysville so one day Jim brought home a company truck and moved the trailer to Marysville. We parked in the California Trailer Park. We were beside Harold and Doris Wright.

I had to find a Dr. as I was pregnant. One day Virginia had a fever and broke out in a rash. I called two different Dr.'s offices for an appointment and they said it is probably the measles so don't bring her into the office and expose others. She was a very sick baby so I bundled up the two of them and went to another Dr. She didn't have the measles she had ear infection.

On Sunday we usually went for a ride some where. We went to Aberdeen to visit Aunt Marie one Sunday. Another Sunday we went up to New Westminister in Canada for Sunday dinner.

Marg and Jim StPeter from Eureka left the Montana job with Smith and White they had been in Coulee City and now showed up in Marysville they lived in a cabin there in the California court. They had two children Peggy Ann and Mike, Butch was in-between them in age and played with them all the time.

Virginia was such a good baby and took her naps so good I didn't even think about the fact nothing seemed to wake her up. One day I kept Wendy for Doris while she went to town. When she returned she had a sucker for each of the children she came in the front door and the two girls were sitting on the floor playing. Wendy heard her and she crawled over to get her sucker. Doris kept saying Ginger (nick name) look what I have for you. She had her back to Doris and paid no attention. Finally Doris touched her shoulder and she turned and smiled and crawled over to her. Doris got a funny look on her face and she said Helen I don't think Ginger can hear.

We tried all kinds of calling and everything all afternoon so when Jim came home I told him and the next day I took her to a Dr. in Everett. He confirmed our suspicion our beautiful lovable baby was deaf. He also recommended if we could go to Spokane to take her to a certain Dr. there he said if anyone could do anything for her he could.

I next went to a Dr. in Seattle he told me the same thing and also recommended this same Dr. in Spokane.

We took Butch and Virginia to a fireworks display at a ball park in Everett when Virginia was not quite a year old. She was so fascinated by the flashing lights we all watched her as much as the fireworks. The children really did enjoy that. About this time I wanted a feather weight Singer sewing machine I needed to make baby clothes and hem diapers. I found one in Everett it was $80.00, then Jim seen an add in a paper for one of another make for $50.00 so I told him to go get it if I could not have what I wanted. He went to town and found a good salesman and paid $250.00 for a Pfaff which I had for many years and made an awful lot of clothes for the children and myself on it. I never got my Singer.

Mother was going to come stay with us when the baby was born. She didn't make it. One Sunday we had some old friends of Jim's for dinner I didn't know them very well. I went into labor while getting dinner I kept thinking to myself they would never leave. When they finally left I told Jim he had better find someone to watch the kids and take me to the Hospital. Marg took Virginia she was 14 months old and not walking she could get everything she wanted by walking around the walls in the trailer. She learned to walk in Marge's cabin while I was in the Hospital. Mary Ann Bergseth Jim's Bosses wife took Butch. And we took off for the Hospital. I sent Jim home as he had to work the next day. At eleven o'clock I delivered a perfect handsome little 8 lb. baby boy. I had them call Mary Ann, Leonard went over and told Jim but didn't get him clear awake and he said yes and went back to sleep. The nurse finally came in about 12:30 and told me I had better go to sleep as she didn't think my husband was coming in. The next morning Jim went over and asked Bergseths if they had heard anything yet. So he then came into the hospital with a big bouquet of flowers to see me and his new son. I had wanted to name the baby Mike if it was a boy but Jim said all the Mikes in the trailer court were to darn ornery So we named him Dennis James. While I was in the Hospital Jim sent Mother a telegram and she came on the next train and got there the day after I got home. One day in the Hospital a lady came in my room with a gift all wrapped up, the nurse pointed to me and the women shook her head no then came over and asked me if I was Mrs. James DeLong from Marysville that had a baby boy the day before. I told her I was and she said wrong one. I knew who she was looking for. A month or so before that one day a very pregnant woman knocked on my door and wanted to know if I was Mrs. James DeLong she had some letters in her hand. I told her I was and she said so am I. That was startling, Then she said we live down the road and seem to be on the same mail route I think this mail belongs to you. So that is the one the lady with the gift was looking for.

I went home from the hospital and we had gotten a baby basket on legs there was room for it in the bedroom in front of the back door so we lucked out there. When Mother walked into the trailer she looked around and said I will take care of the children and such but you take care of the house, she didn't know what to do in such a small space.

When I sent out the baby's birth announcements I spelled his name wrong and so he was a boy with a girls name. Instead of Dennis James I had put Dennis James. After the comment Jim had made about the name Mike, Marg came over one day with a cartoon of Dennis the Menace. She had it all folded and handed it to Jim.

Some one told me if I would get a playtex girdle and wear it I would lose some of the fat on my stomach after the baby was born. So I bought one, they were all the rage then and were made out of rubber and you had to powder your body to get them on. Mother was still with us. She slept on the davenport with Butch and Virginia. We had no bathroom in the trailer we used the one in the middle of the court as everyone did. I went out to the bathroom and that darn girdle rolled up around my knees. I couldn't get it up or down I stood up and my dress covered it so I took off for the trailer. I was walking very funny as this thing had my legs tied together at the knees. When I got to the trailer I couldn't step up into the door. I sat in the door and was laughing till I cried, Mother and Jim both wanted to know what was wrong with me. I finally scooted into the front room and pulled up my dress and showed them. When they got done laughing with me and at me we decided how we would get it off. They pulled and tugged and twisted, it would not budge. Mother finally got my sewing scissors and cut it off. There went my expensive girdle I had worn about two hours.

When the baby was born Virginia still had her bottle and was still in diapers so we had a double shot there. Mother went out to the wash house to do the washing and I gave her some dimes for the machine. She had never used a pay machine before and was out there for some time and came in. She said I can't get that machine to start, she said she put the dime in the box on the machine leg as I had told her to and it just wouldn't go. I went back out with her and found she had not turned the knob to let the dime drop down in the box. She thought that was an awful contraption.

Mother stayed with us for a week then she had to get home so we took her down and put her on the train for home. I always waited for Jim to get home and after dinner I would go out and do the washing. That way I didn't have to worry about three little ones, I spent the day with them. One evening I was hanging this never ending line after line of diapers out and there was a little girl watching me, she came over and looked up at me and said "You sure have a lot of dish towels."

When Dennis was about a month old I wanted to have an evening away from the children, we never left them or got a baby sitter just always went where we could take them with us. Jim said why don't you go to the show I will be all right with them for a couple of hours.

So I did, after I had them all bathed and ready for

bed. When I got home the baby had been changed from hide out basket and all. I asked Jim why he had done that ? He said I didn't. I went and got Marg she did it for me. When I asked why he said the baby had messed his diaper and it was all over everything and he couldn't leave him that way and he couldn't clean it up. So he got her to do it for him.

It was now October and it can get a little cold even on the coast in the winter. Harold and Doris Wright had their trailer parked beside us one morning the water was frozen up. Jim said as soon as it warmed up it would thaw out as the hose was laying on top of the ground. He went of to work. About eight o'clock Doris went out and scrambled up newspaper and put it under her copper tubing and lit it on fire and thawed out her water. Well smart me I scrambled up newspaper and put it under our rubber hose and burned it to pieces so that night we had to go to town and get a new hose.

All this time we were saving for a new bigger trailer. I had paid the Doctor every week and when the baby was born we had him paid for. Jim came home one night and told me he had sold the trailer. I asked him who bought it as no one had even came and looked at it. So he said a guy that picked him up to go to work. He was going to bring his wife out after dinner that night to look at it and they were giving us $1000.00 just what we had paid for it. Dick and Marion Harrison and their baby girl Julie came out, liked it and bought it. We told them they could have it in a month. Saturday we went into Seattle and were going to look at trailers. We found and American Trailer 32 feet long and eight feet wide. In 1952 that was as big as they made them. We ordered a two bedroom and it had a bath. It would cost us $3200.00 set up in Marysville. I went to the bank on Monday to get the savings out to pay on it and the girl at the bank said you only have $32.00 in savings. I was really shook up as I knew we had nearly enough to pay for the new trailer.

I went home and got all of our deposit slips and back to the bank I went. They agreed that I had deposited this money but didn't have any record of it in our account. It took them three days to find it. Some one had put it in the other James DeLongs account. We finally got that straitened out.

While we were waiting for delivery on our new home we decided to take our new baby and the other children to see some people we had met that really thought Butch and Virginia were something special they were an older couple and had never had any children. I dressed the kids all up and we took off it was raining, we had to stop at the drug store for some reason and I laid the baby in the front seat to run in, Jim and the kids stayed in the car. When I came out and opened the car door I don't know how but the baby rolled out blankets and all into the gutter full of dirty rain water. Thank God he didn't hit his head on the curb. We went home and I never could get those blankets and clothes clean again.

Seems every time we drove down Broadway in Everett Jim would think one of the baby's had messy pants but what we were smelling was the paper mill or Pea silage every time. Twice when Virginia was tiny I put her in on our bed for her nap, everything was quiet and when I went in to check on her she was sitting in the middle of the bed with the clock taken completely apart with nothing but her little fingers she could get all the screws out. I then learned to put the clock in the kitchen at nap time. Another time I went in and she had gotten my lipstick and she was wearing it. There was none on the bed or any where except on her mouth but she had made a big mouth. When I went in there she was smiling at me so proud like she had really done something great. Butch was a real good little boy. He had such a beautiful head of curly hair and never gave us any trouble. He would try to help me any way he could. He was only four years old.

Virginia was a sweet little doll but wouldn't let you cuddle her very much she was a leave me alone baby. Always small, when she was four years old she was still wearing a baby's size two dress.

We finally got delivery on our new trailer. When we bought the other one it had chair's to go with the table so we assumed the new one would have also, we let the other ones go with the trailer. Well needless to say our new one had no chairs, we had to do some scrounging and finally bought metal folding ones not nearly as nice as the ones we gave away. Here we had a bathroom and no sewer hook up. The Landlord let Jim bury a septic tank which he made out of two 55 gallon barrels that he chopped holes in with an ax. It worked and we used it for a long time. Now the Kids had their own bedroom it had bunk beds in it. We gave Butch the top bunk he loved to climb the ladder. Jim put a board across the front of the bottom bunk so the baby's couldn't fall out of bed and we put Virginia at one end and Dennis at the other it worked great. We had a shower in the bathroom it had about a six inch raise around the bottom. I would put a rubber sink plug over the drain and put water in it to bath the children it worked fine as a shallow bath tub.

One day I made lemon pudding as I didn't trust myself to try pie crust. It was in dessert bowl's and Butch wanted to know if he could have some. I handed it to him and in between us we dropped it. It came out of the bowl and bounced across the floor like a rubber ball. Tough! oh boy.

Butch was only four years old but one evening Jim started out with a sack of trash and Butch wanted to take it out to the trash barrel that was not far behind our house. Jim gave it to him and in a matter of few minutes he heard a slap and Butch started to cry. There was a Boy about 12 years old that lived with his father across and down a few trailers from us. Well this boy ran home and Butch said when he took the trash out this boy was out there and he just slapped Butches face and ran home. He left his hand print on Butches face. Jim was over to that trailer in nothing flat and told this father what had happened. Also said if that kid ever touched one of his kids again he would beat the crap out of him. The father of the other kid said if Jim ever touched one of his kids he had a gun and he knew how to use it and he would kill him. Our Landlord heard this conversation and he went over and told the man to hook onto his trailer and take his son. He had one half hour to clear the premises or he would call the sheriff. In twenty minutes the man pulled out. We never saw them again.

On this job Jim had worked up a long way north of Marysville now they were getting really to far to drive every day. They were way up the Skaget river above Concrete Washington. At this time there wasn't much of a road up there and they had to go over a couple of railroad bridges with all the equipment They weren't going to be there very long so the Kids and I just stayed in Marysville and Jim came home on week ends there were five or six of the couples had their trailers there where we were. One day one of the women invited all of us over for coffee. She proceeded to tell us she had gone up and caught her husband stepping out on her and they were all doing it. She looked at Marg and Me and said the two Jim's also. She really was having a bad time and they soon got a divorce but she wanted us all to be in the same boat I guess. As she was the only one that had a problem. And was a little jealous.

We were in Everett shopping in a super market one day. I was carrying the baby we had Virginia in the infant seat in the shopping cart. The carts were small in the fifty's not like they are today. Butch jumped up on the back of the cart and he and the cart came over backwards, Virginia hit the cement floor face first. The blood was coming out of the pores in her fore head We left groceries and cart and all on the floor. Jim picked Virginia up and we took the kids and took of for a Dr.s office. They told us there was nothing wrong with her to let her go to sleep and she would be all right when she woke up. She was real bruised but had no bad effects from it.

Jim wanted some black eyed peas. I had never heard of them and I told him they didn't have any in the store. He went and bought some. I told him they weren't peas they were beans and I had no Idea what to do with them. He said his mother just boiled them, so I put them on and proceeded to over cook them they were a little mushy. He told me they were no good. I had some I had not cooked left and thought well I won't try that again so I proceeded to put them in a quart jar some of them spilled in the sink and I just washed them down. They went as far as an elbow in the drain and stopped. Well the water made them swell up and they plugged up the drain real good. Jim had to take the pipes out to dig them out and get things working again. I have never cooked dry black-eyed peas again. The can ones are not to bad, just heat and serve.

Next was Okra, I never heard of it but he would like some. I found some in a can, bought it and heated it up like any other can vegetables. It was so slimy but I thought that was the way it was suppose to be. He wanted fresh Okra fried. It was years later I tasted okra at his Mothers in Oklahoma. It is real good and not slimy. So when I find fresh Okra or fresh frozen we have it rolled in corn meal and fried and it is so good.

Come Christmas time I had never spent a Christmas away from home and I was homesick any way. So we decided I would take the three children (4 months, 18 months and four years old) on the train and Jim would come just before Christmas. That way I could stay for a week. He took me to the train in Everett and all I could get was two seats. I had all night and most of the next day facing me. I put Butch in one seat and pulled the foot rest down and put blankets on it and put the baby there. I held Virginia. I had two babies with bottles and in diapers and a small child to entertain. When he had to go to the bathroom I had to load all of them up to take him. Finally the next day out of Spokane there was a women on the train that took Virginia and entertained her which helped a lot. When I arrived in Eureka I was so exhausted and ended up being sick most of the week

I had looked forward to. Jim came for Christmas so I had help on the return trip.

Jim came home one day and said we are moving to Plains, Montana on a job. We will be moving in two days this was in the spring of the year of 1952. He would pull the trailer with a company truck and I would have to drive the car. With a lot of advice from neighbors (some of which we took and some not) we got the trailer all taped with masking tape put the toys all in the front room and bright and early one morning we took off for Montana. There was still snow on Stevens pass out of Snohomish and Jim was behind me with the trailer. The road was covered with ice and snow. Part way up the pass the car ahead of me slid into a spin and into the ditch. I put my brakes on and I went right in behind them. I kept thinking Jim will be here soon to help me. He soon came and went whizzing on by. Well a wrecker finally came and after unloading the trunk I found the chains and they put them on for me and I took off so mad at Jim I could have choked him. When I got to the top of the pass there sat the trailer and truck. I got out of the car and Jim came out of the cafe across the road I let the children out of the car and Virginia seen her father and ran towards him there was a car coming and Jim dashed out and grabbed her before she was hit. When I gave him the devil for leaving me in the ditch he said if I would have stopped I would have been in the ditch with the trailer and I knew the wrecker would come and get you out. Guess he was right but It still made me mad. Then on to Montana. We put Butch and Virginia in the back seat and the baby in the front with me. There were no car seats for baby's then so they were all over the car. He would get on the floor and over by the gas and brake so I would have to stop and get him back on the seat. When we needed a diaper changed I would pass Jim and drive faster till I found a place to pull out and change the diaper and get it in the trunk before Jim caught up with us. We made the trip to Montana fine and were set up in a trailer court where some of the other couples were parked and there were some cabins there where some of the family's lived that had no trailer. My family were coming down from Eureka and Whitefish to spend Easter with us I had planned Easter Dinner and had every thing under control. Saturday night I had put the children to bed and gotten the house all cleaned up made three Easter baskets. Had just decided that was it when there came a knock on the door, when I opened the door there stood this women from the cabins she had blood on her face, and was a mess I could tell she had been drinking. She said come stop him he is beating me and will kill the kids. Jim shot out the door and she followed him. He said when he went into their cabin the man was sitting on the bed playing with the kids. He said she had been drinking and wanted to go party and leave the kids alone. He told her no and she started in and the only way he could shut her up was to slap her. Well here came Jim with these two children about 3 and 4 years old to keep for the night so their folks could go up town. I was so mad, had to make out the sofa for them and tear three Easter baskets apart and make five out of them. By the time the folks got there the next day we had taken the extra children home and every thing was under control.

ESTHER and Clyde took Virginia home with them for a week. While they had her Esther would put her hair up in pin curl's when she put her down for her nap and Virginia would take all the pins out and throw them on the floor. She also took her to the Dr. there to see about her hearing and they told her the same thing I had been told.

I made an appointment with the Dr. in Spokane every one recommended. Left the boys with one of the women on the crew and Sis and I went to Spokane. The Dr. told me she had no nerves in her middle ear and there was nothing they could do for her. He recommended that I give her the John Tracey corespondent course as he could tell she was very intelligent and we should get her learning as soon as possible. He also said to treat her just like the other children. And not to bother with a day school. Put her in a state deaf school where she will learn every minute she is awake and get her in there as soon as possible. He said the one in Salem Oregon took them at four years old where the other states didn't take them till they were six. I got the correspondent coarse and gave that to her. She whizzed through that it was matching a toy horse with a picture of one and etc.

Jim came home one day and said we move to Clarksfork Idaho tomorrow. How I always seemed to have the money to move on I don't know. We parked in a field in Clarksfork the town was full of trailers and construction workers. They were putting in Cabinet Gorge Dam, a new Highway and a Power Line. We were parked beside Bob and Opel Peterson, StPeters, Wrights ,Fennels and Kanutsons were in the park we were in. The rest of the crew were strung all over town there were even some trailers parked in the school yard. Boy did prices go sky high there. We would go into Sandpoint about every two weeks for groceries.

I put my children to bed right after their baths at about seven o'clock at night so I could get my washing done or ironing while Jim was there with them. One night I was out hanging out clothes and I thought I heard some one yell for help down across the field towards the river. I went and had Jim come out of the trailer and told the kids in the yard to be quiet and then we heard it again. Some of the men were in the yard also. They all took off across the field and there was a man in the river. He had been fishing and a big rock had fallen on him and had his foot pinned in the river. They got him out and the sole of his boot and the bottom of his foot was sliced of. Jim came and got the car and took him into Sand Point to the hospital. Good thing I was out washing that evening.

We really had a great summer here. It was a beautiful place for the children to play and I was not working. Some days it was so hot we would all put our dinner in the trunk of the car and take off to the lake as soon as the men came in from work , they would take a bar of soap and a towel and take their bath in the lake. We would start a fire in one of the firepits and keep the food warm then have a big pot luck. We all enjoyed a cool swim in Lake Pend Oreille. Any one that has lived in a small mobile home knows how hot they can get and you must realize this was before air conditioning. The Ranger over the camp ground told us if someone had a fire going that they weren't using to go ahead and use it instead of starting another one. So we did. One evening a man came over to our table and told us to get our things off the fire he had started. In no uncertain words. Not a nice man at all. So they explained to him what we had been told and he said he would throw our stuff out if we didn't remove

it. So Andy Kanutson stood up he was a huge man. This other man looked up at him and said lets forget the whole thing. Want a beer. We had a big blue granite coffee pot. It had a bail on the top with a wooden handle. From the bon fires and fire pits the wood had gotten very charred and was ready to fall off. One night it finally caught on fire. Another camper came over and told us our coffee pot was on fire we told him thanks but we knew it. He gave us a funny look and walked off shaking his head.

The men baited a little black bear by putting some bacon in a man haul and leaving the door open. They caught the bear but the joke was on them. The bear messed all over the man haul and they had to clean it up so they could ride home in it. Jim came in one night from work and put his lunch pail on the cupboard. We sat down and ate supper. I was doing the dishes before I bathed the kids. Jim and the kids were in the front room. I opened the lunch pail to wash it and a huge frog jumped out of it. It jumped into the front room and nearly scared me to death. Jim and Butch caught it and put it out side. I was so mad I thought Jim had put it in there, even though he said he didn't. Another women opened her husbands Thermos and a snake swam out into the dishwater. That was enough, so a stop was put to the jokes!

We had our trailer parked with the back of it up against the fence at the side of the road. It was so hot and no one had air conditioning. I kept the doors open all the time. Our bathroom door was right across from the back door. One day I was sitting on the toilet watching the cars go by and it dawned on me they could probably see me as well as I could see them so I closed the bathroom door from then on. Our bathroom was very small and we had a plastic sink. I would put Dennis on the training seat and he cut teeth on the sink it had little bite marks all along the front.

Dennis became very sick one day he was listless and running a fever. Then started to throw up. Opal Peterson told me we had better take him to the Hospital. When Jim got home she kept Sis and Butch and we went into Sandpoint. We didn't have a Dr. but the one on call at the hospital took care of him he had Pneumonia. We had to leave him in the Hospital for a week. When I went into see him he would be sitting in a crib playing with everything they could find to give him. They spoiled him royally. With in a week we could bring him home and he was fine. Not long after that the kids were all out playing in the field by the cloths line. There was a spike tooth harrow leaning against a tree, no one thought anything of it. Well every one started yelling and I looked out and seen Sis on the ground. I ran out and the harrow had fallen on her and one spike had gone on each side of her head and one in her chin and mouth. I lifted it from her and she was really bleeding. Marg took the boys and I put Sis in the car and took off for Sand Point. Driving out of the court I saw I had an empty gas tank and I had no money. I drove up to a station and told them I had to get to the Dr. and needed gas that I could not pay for till Friday. He filled my tank and said go. I took her to the Dr. that had taken care of Dennis. (By now he was Denny Jim) when we walked in both covered with blood they took us both in a room in a hurry. The spike had run in her chin just below the lower lip and knocked her two front teeth clear up in the gums They mummified her in a sheet and put 19 stitches in her chin. When they got done the nurse gave her a sucker, she looked at it and threw it at her. I said maybe now I could get her bottle away from her and the Dr. said no that would pull those teeth down. We went back in a couple of weeks to have the stitches out and she didn't have much of a scar.

Denny Jim would get on all fours in bed and rock back and fourth till he would knock spice cans down in the kitchen cupboard on the other side of the wall. Some one would have to go and pull him báck down in bed. He also would sit on the sofa when he was tired and rock back and forth. The only one of four that did this. Hazel Kanutson would sometimes come and get Dennis and keep him all day. She had no children of her own. In later years they adopted two.

While we lived here in Clarksfork we did get to come see the folks a couple of times in Eureka. We knew our time there was coming to and end as the job was about done. And this contractor had nothing in sight for another job. And we had nothing to pull the trailer with.

By now Butch was five years old and a perfect little man he tried to help me all he could. He could be a little devil but most of the time was a loving little boy. Virginia had her second birthday here in Clarksfork we had a party for her in the afternoon, she would not open her presents or let anyone else do so. We took them all in the house still wrapped up. When her Daddy came home from work she showed them all to him and then sat down and open them.

A lady on the crew that lived in the court we did came over one morning after she had gotten back from a trip back east to see her folks. She asked me if I would take her into Sandpoint to the Dr. Well nosy me I asked her what was wrong with her ? Was she pregnant ? She said no much worse, I seemed to have gotten crabs from a toilet on the train and must get rid of them. I have given them to my husband. We all knew what her husband had done when she was gone back east and knew who had given them to whom. I took her into the Dr. and he told her they can't live only so long off the body so he didn't think that is where she got them but she was convinced she had. Anyway she got some medication for them and they got rid of them. End of the story of the crabs.

By now we knew the job was about over, we had nothing to pull the trailer with. Jim had a new Chevrolet car when we were married. We put a hitch on it one time and found it was not heavy enough to pull that steel American trailer we had. We looked around and found an old Dodge Van. Jim thought it was in pretty good shape so we bought it put a hitch on it and heard there was work on the coast so we took off. We headed first to Portland. We went down the Washington side of the Columbia River for some reason.

When we arrived at North Bonniville the Van was real sick. We pulled into a garage and the man said it had to have a new motor. We talked it over and had no money for a new motor. So decided we would try pulling it with the car. Told the man we would get back to him. Don't know what he ever done with it as we never got back there again. We took off with the car even though some time the front wheels didn't want to stay on the ground. Jim went to the union hall in Portland and they told him to try Seattle as they seen nothing in the future. We took off for Seattle and got just north of Vancouver and started blowing tires. We finally put the trailer in a park and went to Marysville. We rented a cabin there and a man we knew went back down and got our trailer for us.

The week we were in the cabin Jim got a short job. He had to take the car to work so I was out there with no car. One day I had no milk for the baby so I sent my five year old down the road about a fourth of a mile with a note for a quart of milk. It was foggy and by the time he got to the store he was scared. The store owner called the police and they brought him home and I got bawled out real good for sending him. We owed one car payment on the car. I had written in and asked what the last payment would be to pay it off about four months early. It was the full amount so Jim said they don't get it till it is due. One evening here came two men to get the car. From the finance company. They were going to take it right then so I paid them the last payment. The next weekend we went into Seattle and found a Chevrolet Suburban that pulled the trailer like a dream, we had it for a long time. Marg and Jim St Peter were there also they were in the same trailer park we were. Denny Jim had his first birthday here we were all so very broke by this time I did bake him a cake and Marg and I pooled our food and I think we had wieners and kraut and fried potatoes for his first birthday.

Now the job was again over and we were told they were hiring out of the Union hall in Pasco. St Peters and us took of for Kennewick. No work there but we were down to very little money and could not go any farther. Jim was getting a dollar an hour working for

Welches grape juice there in Kennewick. That doesn't go very far with three children and car payments, trailer payment and parking. I was washing diapers in the bath tub as I had no money for the laundry. I hung them on the line one day and when I went to get them they were all gone. Someone stole them. I had two baby's wearing towels torn up sheets old tee shirts and every thing else for diapers. But they were all happy. I had been buying hamburger at a store down the street. It was cheap I went to get some one day and there was a sign on the door" CLOSED FOR ILLEGAL SALE OF HORSE MEAT". Jim walked to work so we would not have to use the little bit of gas in the car. We got down to two dollars and some change. When Jim came home from work I said this is silly I am going to go to work. I took the car with our little bit of gas in it and I found a job at Berts Dinner at the Richland Y . I was a waitress at night so Jim was home with the Kids. The first night I made $7.00 in tips that looked like a million to us just then. I bought groceries, in a week I had enough to buy a few diapers. Jim got called out on a job in Cle Elum ,this must have been about the first of November as it was a little chilly by now at night. He came and told me while I was at work that we had to leave that night. He would get the trailer all ready to go and pick me up when I finished my shift. My boss lady told me she would give me my pay check at the end of my shift. Jim came a few minutes before I was ready the children were asleep in the car and there was no cars out front so he pulled the trailer across the front of the building and came in and had a cup of coffee with me while we were waiting for Bert to make out my check. When we got in the car I could see Virginia in the first seat so I asked where the boys were. By now we were going down the road. Jim said Butch was in the back seat and Denny Jim was on a pallet on the floor behind my seat. I reached back to see if he was covered NO BABY. I let a yell out of me as I went over the back of the seat. Jim slammed the brakes on and helped me over the seat on my head. Denny Jim had woke up while Jim was in the Cafe and had crawled back and gotten on the back seat with Butch, they were all snuggled up together. So we were on our way to Cle Elum so Jim could report to work the next morning. Construction work was not all fun.

We arrived at Cle Elum in the wee hours of the morning it was very cold. We found the trailer court and he parked out front very lopsided. We all finished the night in one bed to keep warm as there was no heat in the trailer without electricity We had set the wind up alarm and Jim went to work with the rest of the men that morning. He had a lunch no coffee and cold cereal for breakfast. Here sat the kids and I in a lopsided trailer with no heat no water and no bathroom. When every one got up and around I recognized our old trailer we had sold to Harrisons. So the kids and I spent the day with Marion till Jim got ours parked and set up after work.

About this time Butch started waking up in the night with a fever and he would vomit and was real sick when I would take him to the Dr. come morning they could not find any thing wrong with him. He lost weight and became real thin he had dark circles under his eyes. This went on for a long time. I sat up many nights just holding him. Whatever it was he finally got over it.

When Jim got his first pay check he had rec. in months he stopped in at the Sunshine Tavern and Cafe in Cle Elum to cash it and have a drink with his old cronies that were on the job. He had not been doing any drinking since we had gotten married. Well he had one too many and tried to hit his foreman who he didn't like and didn't like the comments he was making. He broke the leg from a table and all the dishes on it, and a mirror behind the bar. Well the men brought him home and he wouldn't give them the keys to our car. The city police had been called and they said if he went home they would not put him in jail. Kenny McBride asked me for my keys so he could go get our car. I couldn't find them, finally Jim took both sets out of his pocket and said he would go get his own car. He started walking to town we were about two miles from town. They had brought Dick Harrison home and opened the front door and he fell full length of the front room on his face. Marrion just left him there, she didn't even cover him up. Kenny went and picked Jim up and took him to town to get the car. By the time all the drunks were home and the cars home. Every one was in bed about 4 a.m.

The next morning the kids and I were up but Jim was in bed and mighty sick. A city police car pulled up in front of our house. Knock, Knock on the door I went to the door and they wanted to know if James DeLong lived there. I wanted to say no but told them yes he was still in bed. This police said that did not surprise him he said Jim even wanted to fight with him the night before. He said I have a matter of a damage bill here that has to be paid by four o'clock or we will have to come and put him in jail. When they left I got Jim up and it took the rest of his pay check to pay the damage bill which he went and paid. That was the last time my husband did any drinking. We were to go out for my birthday that night. I did go with the other two couples but Jim was still sitting on the bathroom floor by the toilet very ill. I left the kids with the neighbors kids and a baby sitter.

One day a bunch of us women decided that we were going to get our ears pierced. There were six of us, we went to town and bought ear rings I got posts that has a red stone in the middle surrounded by rhinestones. They are still in my jewelry box today. The backs screwed on them. Then we all sat with cloths pins clipped on our ears to numb them, while soaking a needle with white thread in it in a saucer of rubbing alcohol Then this gal that did the piercing cut a potato in half. She held the flat side of the potato behind the ear and stuck the needle through into it. Then tied some knots in the thread and pulled the knots back and forth through, then soaked the ear ring in alcohol and put them in. It is a wonder someone didn't get infection but no one had any trouble. We sure surprised a bunch of Husbands when they came home from work. Every morning and evening we cleaned our ears and ear rings with alcohol till they were all healed up.

Next thing our landlord told us we would all have to move as he had to shut the water off for the winter. We found a place to park down across the river. Come Thanksgiving I had ordered a turkey from Safeway and was waiting till pay day to get it. When Jim came home from work the evening before Thanksgiving I jumped in the car to go get things for dinner the next day. When I got to the store I discovered they were closing early and the door was locked and they would not let me in. There was a butcher shop in town I went there and they had one turkey left it was twenty five pounds, I bought it and went to a small store in town and got a can of cranberries one of sweet potatoes and a can of pumpkin. Went home with Thanksgiving dinner for my family any way. Then it dawned on me no way would that Turkey fit in my little blue roaster. I went to the land lady and told her my problem. She said there is an old tin dish pan in the garage use it. I told her it wouldn't fit in my oven so she suggested I bend it to fit. Come morning the turkey was ready but I didn't have a pan big enough to mix dressing in. I scoured out the sink and mixed it in that worked fine. We had our dinner after all. And with only two adults and three little kids we had Thanksgiving dinner for a week or more. And many turkey sandwiches after that. There were still no dryers in the wash rooms, this court had a old garage with a coal heating stove in it there were lines in there to hang cloths on. They dried fine but were stiff, this was before fabric softeners, and they smelled like the coal smoke. They were dry they were clean and they smelled funny but we wore them.

Christmas was coming and we had very little money. This would be my first Christmas away from home. I made the kids all night cloths and I made Virginia a very homely rag doll she was scared of. Knitted sox for Jim. And I cried all day Christmas I was homesick and the only thing I rec. for Christmas was an alarm clock Mother sent to us. Well got through that fine anyway. We were going on a job in Mitchell Oregon they told us there was a trailer court there. The rest of the crew left Christmas day, I wouldn't move on Christmas so we left the next day, it was so cold and a lot of snow. We Stopped at a station for gas and couldn't get under the overhang so they took the nozzle through the front seat to get to the tank which was by the passenger's door. When he took it back through he turned the nozzle and dumped gas in the seat so we had that smell for a few days and it was to cold to drive with the windows open. We stayed over night at Bigs Junction just where you turn from the Columbia River to go south. The next morning when we reached Madras we caught up with the rest of the crew that is as far as they had gotten. They were just pulling out on the road. We were behind them till we got to the pass out of Prineville Jim passed them all going up Ochico pass. We were the first trailer into Mitchel, Stopped at a station and asked them where the trailer court was and were told the closest one was in Prineville Now Mitchell is a very small town built in a canyon with only main street running through. Jim told them there were nine trailers behind him and where could he turn around to stop them before they all got in town. This guy didn't seem to excited and he said well... .you can go ten miles up to the other end of the canyon and turn around at spoos mill. We turned around in main street it took about a half hour and no one got through but we got turned around. By this time there was a man had came out to watch all the goings on with every one else. He had a big handle bar mustache and cowboy hat. He came over and asked if we were with the power line crew coming in. By now the rest of the trailers were at the edge of town. They told him we were and he said he owned a farm at the edge of town and if they wanted to put in the power he had water and we could put in our own septic tanks and out houses for those that didn't have modern trailers. He would give us our first months rent free for doing the work to get settled . After that first month was over we were all wondering how much the rent would be we had paid as high as thirty five dollars at some places most courts at that time were twenty to twenty five. One day we women all got brave and took all our kids and went to this man's office. He was the man that owned the local power plant that would be out of business when the R.E.A. was completed. We told him we had come to pay our rent and how much was it ? He started off with this well... .1 am furnishing the water and the lights so do you think twelve dollars a month would be fair ? We all agreed and paid our rent took our kids and went home had a cup of coffee and celebrated. The barn yard was on a hill side and all mud. The man came out and parked the trailers with a little tractor he had as we could not get the cars down through all that mud. He had a cow out there but he thought someone might decide to milk it so he took it to town somewhere. I don't think anyone on the crew knew how to milk a cow. There was an old chicken house with a few chickens and a pig pen with a couple good sized pigs in it. We told the kids to stay away from the pig pen. They kept wanting to go peak at the pigs so we told them if they fell in the pigs would eat them just like they ate the left over food and potato peelings we fed them. One night after Dinner the kids were out playing and all at once We heard Butch screaming, We went running out and Bob Groves was standing by the pig pen just doubled over laughing. The top board was broken on the pen and Butch was laying in the muck in the bottom of the pen scared to death. He had crawled up the pen and leaned on the top board and it went in with him. That kept the kids away from the pen.

Jim came home one day and I was out in the yard talking to some of the women and he got out of the suburban and went around back and said I bought you a washing machine. Needless to say everyone was wanting to see. He hauled out a #2 tub and wash board and cloths line rope. Every one used them along with me. The closest laundry was sixty five miles away in Prineville.

While living here Butch did something one day that upset me I don't even know what it was but I spanked him and slapped him till I left my hand prints all over him. I was so sorry and so ashamed I never did touch my children very much after that. I decided if I could not control my self any better than that leave them alone. I swatted butts a few times but never again lost my temper like that and I am so ashamed of it yet to this day.

This trailer court/barn yard had a creek running down in back of it actually only a clear water trickle over rocks. Denny Jim all at once decided he didn't like cloths, so he would take them off and throw them in the creek shoes and all. I would look out and he would be standing naked, Virginia would point to the creek and there would be the cloths. Four years after we lived there this same trickle came raging down this canyon and took the back from the post office and took the safe and all. If we had been there at that time we would have all been washed away. We had gone to the local cemetery while we lived there and had seen on some very old grave markers where people had drowned in a flood and could not imagine a flood in that area when the only water was this tiny creek. Some more people came in and parked in a meadow down below where we were they were Dough and Charlotte Kelly they had two boys Assa and Bub. Butch enjoyed them. Real nice people.

Years later they were on a job in Wyoming and Bub their youngest boy was killed in a hunting accident. We were never on another job with them again. We stopped to see them in Umatilla Oregon one time when going through to Oklahoma. He decided I should cut his hair. All he had was a pair of hand clippers and her sewing scissors. Needless to say I would forget to squeeze the handles and pulled out more hair than I cut. We never seen them again until we stopped in North Las Vegas when going through in 1966. Asa was married and also lived there . We visited them that evening and never seen or heard of them again.

I had been corresponding with the Deaf School in Salem. They had a weekend retreat for parents and small deaf children under four years old. I set up an appointment for Sis and I to go. It was all set up and we were to leave early Saturday morning. We got up real early our suitcase was packed and set beside the door the night before. Sis and I kept real quiet so as not to wake Jim and the boys up. It was way before daylight. We took off went to Prineville, Bend and over the Mountains. When we reached Lebanon I stopped for gas and went into a store to get some snacks. I had Sis all dressed up like a little doll and so decided to put something over her dress so she could eat something and not take a chance on getting dirty. Reaching in back of the suburban for the suitcase—not there. I knew I had not stopped anywhere that any one could have taken it. It had to be sitting by the door at home.

Here I am miles from home for three days with a

three year old that I was so proud of and no clothes for her. This was way before credit cards so the clothes had to come out of what money I had with me. No checking account. We stopped in Eugene at a Sears store, We got a night gown, three pairs of underpants, a couple pairs of sox and three dresses for Sis and one slip. One cotton dress for me and two pair of underpants. So we arrived at the school not with a suitcase but paper bags. All the cute cloths I had made for Sis were home.

We had no phones where we lived so I could not call Jim. When he got up and seen our suitcase, he had no car I had it. Jess and Kathleen were going to Prineville that morning. Jim sent our suitcase with them. They put it on the bus for Salem being assured that it would be there the next day. It arrived just before we left the school on Monday.

While we were there I saw the whole school it was very nice and the children there seemed so advanced. They ran all kinds of tests on Sis and observed her play. They told me we had a very smart girl she should get in school that fall. Also get her a hearing aid it might do her some good. We made an appointment with an audiologist in The Dalles we took her in and they tested her and fit her with a hearing aid. Then we went in two weeks later and picked it up. We bought a lot of hearing aids through the next few years but none seemed to work for her. She finally just stopped wearing them.

One nice sunshiny morning Jim left for work. The children were still asleep so I decided it would be a good time to get some wash out. I proceeded to get the wash tub (my washing machine) set up on two chairs in the front room and got one load all scrubbed and rinsed (in the kitchen sink). While I was out hanging them up I heard some running and laughing in the trailer so I stopped and went to investigate. When I went in here was Dennis and Virginia, they had gotten up and taken a box of sugar crisps and sprinkled them in my wash water. So I set them down to eat and went out to finish hanging the one load I had gotten washed. When I went back in they had taken coffee cups and poured wash water all over the front room. I gave up that day and cleaned up the mess got Butch up and got them all bathed and ready for the day, so much for my wash day.

While here in the heat of summer the Children came down with the measles. They were all pretty sick and had an awful odor. I would put them all in our bed and air out the front room then put them all on the sofa and air out the bed room. This went on for about a week.

There was one boy in the court that was somewhat older than the other children and he put a rope around Butches neck one evening and tried to hang him from a tree. Jim seen this and rescued his son. Gave the other boy hell but it really did not help much but he did leave Butch alone. Dennis and I were siting on the steps one day and this Kid came up riding his bike and stopped by us. Dennis was not two yet and he put his hand on the sprocket of the bike and the kid took of and ran one of the points on the sprocket through Dennises finger. He still has a terrible scar from it.

Kathleen Hall and Betty Wright lived up the hill from us. Halls beside us and Wright$_5$ beside them. One day Kathleen went to the store. She came home and took her groceries out of the car, Betty was in the yard and said something to her. Kathleen set her groceries down and Pow!! she decked Betty right there in the yard. I was out hanging out diapers. She then picked up her groceries and Betty went in the house. That evening the two husbands had a little discussion and that was the end of that.

Mother came to see us from Montana she didn't think very much of Mitchell Oregon it was about 250 people and all the windows in town were dirty and there were two prices on every thing in the stores and the construction people paid the high price and we were 65 miles from the nearest other store. But we had a nice visit and we took her to Bend Oregon to visit her Brothers.

While we were on this job Jim broke his arm. One of the levers on the machine he was running had a faulty weld on it. When he put pressure on it it broke and threw him off the truck on to the ground He broke his arm and the boss fired him. They failed to come tell me he had broke his arm and was in the Prineville Hospital When the men came home from work I asked the man next door where Jim was and he said in the Hospital. I didn't believe him. So went to his foreman and he said didn't any one come and tell you. He broke his arm and you will have to go get him in the morning.

So here we set in Mitchell Jim had no job, He could not pull the trailer so we sat. He had a cast over his elbow and down over his fingers. He hit me with it in bed one night under the chin boy did I see stars. I had to find a job in a town of 250? I did I went to work in a Cafe that had 8 stools and you did it all

Cook, waitress, dishwasher and I even washed the windows. It put food on the table anyway. Jim was home with the children. His Mother came to visit us at this time. The first time I had ever met her and here we were in this mess in this god forsaken place. The day we were to take her to the Bus. Jim Locked the trailer door and locked my purse and the house keys inside. At that time the trailer doors had a number on them and you could buy a key for the doors. We drove to Bend and found a trailer sales that had one and when we got home we found Jim had slipped his in his pocket with his fingers that he could not get his hand in so we had one all the time.

We were sitting having coffee one morning and one of the men from the job came and told Jim to grab a lunch and come to work. Jim told him he had no job and the man said there was a sit down strike in the shop yards the men refused to go out without him so the boss said to come and get him. It seemed he had hired a man with only one arm and this really made every one mad.

One week end Jim decided to take Butch fishing so he was all legal and went and got the only fishing license he has ever had. He was fishing and the game warden came by and checked his license and asked him when he moved into Oregon. Jim told him and then he got a ticket as he was less than a week short of having been in the state 6 months. During all the time we were in construction we were never allowed to vote, hunt or fish as we were never in one place long enough to even register to vote.

We had a party one night there in town and Kathleen had about 50 records the old 78 kind. When we got home she said I will take those records in the house tomorrow. The sun came up the next morning and with it shining through the window it proceeded to melt all the records together and ruined every one of them.

That summer the kids had a turtle. I came in the house from outside one day and Denny Jim had his tooth brush and he was really scrubbing that poor turtles head. I asked him what he was doing He so unconcerned said" aushing his teeth." Poor turtle did not stick his head out for hours.

Butch came into our bedroom one morning and he was just black except around his mouth and eyes as if some one had painted him. I looked at Jim and so was he. We all were and so was the whole house. The oil stove had sooted up and ran soot down the outside of the trailer just like a water falls and also gone all over inside what a mess to clean up, all that oily soot on the walls curtains and furniture even in the closets and cupboards.

We would have people come over at night after the children were all in bed to play cards. We would see Virginia get out of bed and sneak along the wall and into the kitchen then she would peek around the corner of the cupboard till some one motioned for her and she would come all smiles and set on your lap so quiet for a long time then would get down and go to bed.

We had been here a while with our little home made septic tanks, Jim and Jess decided one evening that they must have a lot of grease in them that needed shook down. They put a dynamite cap in one and set it off some way. It really went KERBANG and felt like the trailers went straight up and back down. They had every one out in the yard in a hurry.

By now the land lord had built a wash house and put an old wringer type washer out there. None of the wash houses had dryers as yet so we dried outside and on drying racks set up in the bathtub in the trailer.

One day shortly before we moved from Mitchell I had to run to town for something. It was on a Saturday so Jim was home , the two little ones wanted to go with me Butch was doing something in the yard and didn't want to go. I had just got up on the road and was not going very fast. (before child seats) They were both standing up in the front seat beside me. Sis by the open window and Denny Jim in the middle. All at once he yelled MaMa and threw himself across my arms in play. Knocking my hands from the steering wheel. We were on the shoulder of the road by now and it gave way and we started to go over side ways. All I could think of was the baby's going out that open window and the suburban rolling on them. I took my arm and threw them both on the floor and by the time we lit in the garden down about six feet below the road, I was on top of them. All I could think of was getting turned around to get the keys turned off. In case of fire. Butch seen us go over, He yelled at his Dad , MaMa had a wreck. They ran down through this women's garden I handed the kids out the drivers window to him and then he helped me out. Jim ran around the car and opened the back door, starting to throw spare tires out. I asked him what he was doing and he said going in after you. Then he realized he had already helped me out the window.

No one was really hurt, I was hit in the back by the tire Jack when it came out from under the seat.

Jim went to town to get our Landlord with his cat to pull the car out. No wreckers in Mitchell. By the time they got there the women in the house was out there puffing on a big black cigar yelling at me for ruining two hills of corn. Our Landlord didn't like her and he drove the cat so very careful to the car and then pulled the car through her garden. Thank God this was before every one was suing every one or we would have been in a law suit. The car had the right side pushed in about six inches but no broken windows. He told me I had to drive it that way. And it was a while before we got to a place to get it fixed.

By now the job in Mitchell was winding down and they had 1 small job at Rufus Oregon at that time Rufus had a service station/store and about four trailer spots out back. Now it is a real nice little town. We were there in the spring of the year and the Misquotes were so thick you could cut them with a knife. One afternoon after the door had been opened dozens of times and the house was full of them I decided to spray. So I took the children out sprayed the trailer real good and we went for a walk. When we came back the misquotes were all dead but so was the turtle. That was the end of pet turtles. We were not in Rufus long and we moved on down the line to The Dalles. Quimbys lived across the road from us and I don't remember who else was there. I know there was a huge Parrot in the office and there was always a mess of seed hulls around his cage.

The Indians at this time were still dipping for fish at Sililo Falls. They would bring in these nice big Salmons to town and go from door to door and sell them. They caught me one day when I had some money, so I bought one. I took newspaper and cleaned the fish cut his head off and wrapped it all up in the newspaper nice and tidy and put it out in the trash. Then I proceeded to slice up the salmon it went real well till I came to the tail. I had forgotten to cut it off. Well lazy me I didn't want another trip to the garbage can. I looked at the tail and thought that should go down the toilet, so I flushed. It went down but not out. When Jim came home from work I told him the sewer was plugged up. He wanted to know what I had put in it. I told him and he said so go take it out. He would not budge. I had to disconnect the sewer hose from the trailer and I could see the fish tail in the elbow where the sewer came from the trailer but it was slippery and I could not get it out. Finally with a stick and a meat fork I got it out. End of Fish tail!!

About this time Jim thought I should be saving more money than I could. I told him to pay the bills and just give me grocery money, that would be fine with me. Came time for the car payment and he was a little short, it was a week late. Trailer payment same thing. He gave me back the check book and said you at least get the payments in on time. This was over forty three years ago and I have never heard any more about it.

When we left The Dalles this time we decided to go to Seattle to get on the books at the union hall. I don't know why but this time I decided to get the trailer all ready to go before he came home from work so it was all disconnected and unblocked when he got home so after supper we put all the toys and Oil barrel and awning in the front room and took off. There was suppose to be some jobs coming up in that area. I don't know why but we went from The Dalles over the ferry and up Maryhill across Washington to Ellinburg and then across Bluit Pass. I had never been across there before I guess it was a good thing it was night. So black you couldn't see a thing. Finally Jim said I think that was the last curve how about a cup of coffee? We always traveled with a Thermos. I poured him a nice hot cup and handed it to him. About then a hair pin curve came up. He dropped the coffee in his lap. We made it around the corner fine then he stopped and we had a cup of coffee. We went on to Wenatchee then over Stevens pass into Seattle. We parked the trailer out north on Aroura. Jim put his name on the books no work right now. It was the first of September and time for School to start. We had a first grader. Butch had turned six in March. There was a school about four blocks straight down Aroura from the trailer court. This is where my first—born started his rounds of many schools. The other Kids and I would walk out to the sidewalk and watch him coming home at night. We were here about a month and Jim got a short job in Cle Elum On the Move again. We parked behind the Hill Top Cafe. Butch started school here then. First grade two schools in two months. We found this to be normal school conditions for construction children.

While here this time we parked behind the Hill Top Cafe. There was a small bus that picked Butch up right behind our trailer at the Ranger Station. He came home one day with a note from his Teacher. She said they were having a party in his room and even though she knew we lived in a trailer did I suppose I could furnish some cookies? If I had no way to bake them maybe I could send some boughten ones. I felt like writing her a note and telling her beings as I cooked over a bon fire in the yard I couldn't send anything. I went out of my way to make cookies and decorate them real pretty so Butch would be proud of them.

The Job here did not last very long so here we were sitting again no work. Decided to hole up here until he got called on another job. If you went looking for a job and the union found out you got fined. You set and waited till your name came up on the books at the union hall then you got called out. Sometimes if it was a company you had worked for before they could request you.

I went to work for Ann and Lowel Cook at the Hill Top Cafe in front of where we were parked. They were a real nice couple. They had moved to Washington from Michigan. She didn't want to move but Lowel said you at least didn't have to shovel the rain!! And they picked Cle Elum. That winter we had so much snow you could not believe it. Every time Lowel was out shoveling snow Ann would open the door and tell him in" Washington you at least didn't have to shovel it".

This Cafe was a truck stop and a turn around for Trailway freight trucks out of Seattle and Spokane. The drivers would drive that far out of those two places and then stay in the bunk house till a truck came in from the other direction then take it on.

We had truckers from all over the united states stop there. We had a cup rack behind the counter it had 250 + cups on it each one had a name on it. Lowel told me if I didn't give the truckers their own mug I had to pay for the coffee. Most of them came in quite regular. We had one cup that I would take down and wash every so often as no one claimed it. It said Vick Gods gift to Women. I wanted to take it down but they said he would be in again. One cold snowy day an oil tanker stopped out front. A tall skinny dirty man with no teeth literally poured out of the cab. He staggered across the parking lot. I asked Lowel who it was every one was laughing. When he came in the door Lowel said well hello Vick where have you been so long.

One morning a trucker came running down the road he had just left the Cafe headed to Seattle. He came busting in and said I gotta use the phone I just laid that semi of eggs on its side. Everyone was telling us we could have scrambled eggs all winter. When they got the truck unloaded and loaded on another truck they had one case of eggs leaking. That was a big soft snow bank he laid it over in. Ann and Lowel were so good to us. As long as I worked for them we had free rent and if there were left over from the special they would give them to me to take home.

In November on my birthday I had to work. It wasn't busy that afternoon so they told me to go on home an hour early. When I opened the front door, Jim said to the children get your toys picked up your Mom is home. Usually when I came home the house was all neat and clean. This day you could not get in the front door. They gave me a birthday gift that night it was in a candy box but wasn't a box of candy. I unwrapped pkg. after pkg. in that box till I came to a tube of lipstick. I treasured that gift, as we were so broke yet I did get a gift.

One cold crisp Saturday the children wanted to go down a half block to a play ground. So we dressed them all up in warm clothes and let them go. They hadn't been gone long when Ann came running up from the Cafe and told me I was wanted on the phone. There was a women on the phone who said Dennis had fell from the slide and could not stand up they thought both legs were broke. I ran to the play ground and there he lay with all these people around him talking Italian and he was scared to death of them. Butch and Sis were beside him. When he seen me he jumped up and came running he was not hurt at all.

Come Christmas they let me have time off to drive to Montana and spend Christmas with my family. We had a grand time I don't know if my sisters did, with my three running all over their houses. I had gotten Denny Jim a stick horse with a horse head on it for Christmas. We had packed every thing in the Suburban when we left home. The next spring I found the horse under the back seat all wrapped for Christmas.

We came back home I went back to work Butch back to school and we settled for the winter and what a winter it was. I awoke one night and could hear a muffled cry. It was Sis I could not figure out where she could be. I got up she was not in bed then It dawned on me it was coming from out side. She had gotten up gone out the front door (trailer doors could be open from inside even when they were locked) She could not get back in. Here was this baby standing in the snow bare footed and in her night gown. She was so cold and frightened and so was I. I took her to bed with us and finally got her warmed up. It still frightens me when I think of it she could have wandered of or froze right there on our step. I think the good Lord watched over us. The next morning Jim went to town and got two screen door hooks and put them on the doors up high where the children could not reach them and they were hooked every night before we went to bed.

Finally in the very early spring a phone call came for Jim at the Cafe. He got called out on a job at Kennewick. I would not quit my job with no notice they had been so good to us. Jim went to Kennewick and stayed for a week, got a place at the Mad Turks trailer park for us to put the trailer and the day before he came after us we got the biggest snow of the season. He spent all day Saturday chopping Ice from the roof the ice sickles were hanging from the roof clear down over the windows to the snow. He had it all ready to hook onto snow shoveled out ready for departure the next morning. We woke up to two feet of new snow. The forest ranger came over with a cat and dug us out and helped get us out to the road. Jim had buried the water hose and he could not get it out so he chopped it of and left it in the ground. We did get to Kennewick by dark. We did some slipping and sliding but arrived OK. Jim went back to work and I put Butch in his third school for the first grade. That year.

I met people on this Job I had never met before. Some of them we still hear from yet today. Forty two years later. In the same court we were in were Rosenbocks, Nortons, Taylors, Robinsons, Dillons and us. Maybe others that I can't remember

Spring came very welcome to us this year. It had been a hard winter . There is a lot of wild asparagus (or there was then) growing along the Columbia River. Jim would go down about every other evening and pick a lot, the next day I would can it. He got just the tips that came up that day they were so good. We also fenced our yard and built a sand box for the children. We went down by the Snake River to get the sand. We took the back seat out of the suburban and shoveled the sand in to it. We loaded it to full and it was sitting on the axial. We had to unload some of it before the vehicle would move. But had a nice sand box at the back of our trailer. One day I had the children down for a nap and I was laying on our bed reading the windows were open. We were parked by a walk way through the court. I heard someone crunching in the gravel as they walked by. Then I heard a small voice say hello you old s— b—. It was coming from our sand box. Out the door I go and here is a kid laying in the sand box in the shade of our trailer. This elderly man said is that one of yours? I told him no mine were all down for a nap. He told this kid he better go home and tell his mom to wash his mouth out with soap and take a nap also. The Kid said O.K.
and took off.

John Robinson had two Weimaraner dogs, they were in Seattle at Obedience school. John had lost his drivers license for two many D.U.I's. It was time to go get his dogs he hired Jim to go get them. I was not to thrilled about having those two big dogs in our car but he did it anyway. They had a very small trailer and two very large dogs. She was a women from England that had married John when he was over there in the service. They had no children. Shortly after the dogs came home they got a new trailer. One night they had it packed wall to wall people watching home movies. Butch was sitting on the floor by my feet. He said Mom what is that behind my ear it itches. I looked and told him it was a little pimple just leave it alone. The next morning he was covered with little pimples. Chicken Pox and we had exposed every one of them.

One day a bunch of us women decided we would go swimming with the children where the Snake emptied into the Columbia it was a nice wide sandy beach with trees for shade. We packed our lunches and went early in the day so as to be home by four o'clock when our husbands arrived home from work. It was a beautiful day. After we ate we were all lying in the sand and I went to sleep. So the other gals watched my three and let me rest. I got hot on one side and turned over on the other. When I woke up I was so burned, even the bottom of my feet. For days I could wear nothing but a cotton duster and that hurt where it hung from my shoulders. I had to take care of the children and house. I was out in the wash house doing the laundry and a women came in. She wanted to know what I was doing for that burn? I told her I was putting vinegar on it. She went home and got some Stanley foot lotion called Kool A Ped. She said you go home and rub that on everywhere that burn is. It was great it was cool and it pulled the burn right out. As long as I could get it I kept that in the house for sun burns for all of us. I cant find it any more. Maybe Stanley Home Products went out of Business. I sold for them when Sis was a baby for a short time.

Lavonne Dillon decided she wanted a dotted swiss sun dress for the fourth of July dance. She knew how she wanted it but did not sew. I volunteered. Believe it or not with no pattern it turned out real nice. We all went up to the social club in Kennewick for the dance on the third of July. They came and took drink orders five minutes before you had to stop drinking. Before they came to take away the drinks one of the gals dumped the contents of her purse on the table and they put the drinks in the purse with the straws sticking out. Said they paid for them and they were going to drink them and they did. The dance went on for another hour or so. They would come back to the table from dancing and look like they were smelling the purse on the table. They were getting a drink till all the glasses were empty.

When the other two kids had chicken pox Denny Jim had two and Sis had three and Butch had been covered when he had them.

Madaline Robbins came over one day and wanted to know how to make Macaroni and cheese. I told her to put the macaroni milk and cheese with some thickening in a baking dish then bake it till the cheese was melted through it. I thought anyone would know to cook the macaroni first Not Madaline She came back over later that afternoon with this casserole dish. She said it is hard as a rock what did I do wrong? She had put all of it in the dish and put it in the oven. What a mess.

While living here a little boy came to our door one morning wanting Tom?? I told him there was no Tom there Butch piped up and said Mom he wants me. I felt real foolish but to me he had always been Butch.

Helen and Ike Norton's had a beautiful baby girl. She was a real active little girl. One day they were bathing her she was about a year old. They noticed a lump on her shoulder, the next day Helen took her into the Dr. He ran tests and took X-Rays and they found out she had cancer. One lung was gone part of her ribs and a collar bone. They were told she had about a month to live. She never cried but pulled most of the hair out of one side of her head and she died in her Mothers arms while she was feeding her one morning. They had little Johnnie who was about our Denny Jims age and they could have no more children. Real sad and a shock to the whole crew.

I decided I wanted to go visit in Montana. Jim took me to Pasco and put me and three little ones on the train at 12:30 A.M. Most of the passengers were all cuddled down for the night. Well they all were woke up before I got mine settled down for the night. While we were in Whitefish at Esther and Clydes house. Butch threw a baseball through the kitchen window. Virginia pulled the chain on the coo-coo clock and broke it. Dick popped some pop corn and the kids strung it all over the front room. I told Esther I would vacuum it up, but she said no, we will after you are gone. Dick said, "Oh yes we will vacuum it!" He was about 12 years old.

Where we lived in Kennewick we were by an irrigation canal. We would be woke up at night with something gnawing in between the floors in the bathroom. If the children left any marbles on the floor we would hear them rolling around during the night. One of us would get up and stomp on the floor and the noise would stop for a while. When I would get up in the morning there would be dirt dug out of the planter I had sitting in the middle of the table. Real spooky till I found where they were leaving their calling cards and they were to large to be a mouse. I would set mouse traps and they would spring them and eat the bait but be gone. I went to the hardware store and bought a rat trap. The first night we heard it spring, we got up and could see the trap sticking out in front of the divan. Jim pulled it out and we had a big wharf rat caught by the nose. Jim opened the door and threw him out in the yard and took him out of the trap and into the garbage can the next morning. We now knew what we had to contend with. They were coming up the water hose and in the air duct under the oil furnace. Between the floors and out the cold air ducts behind the divan. Jim plugged the holes up one at a time with steel wool. It took a long time to get rid of them. I got some rat poison in a tube like tooth paste. I spread it on bread cubes it just smoked and smoldered when I did this. Then I dropped it down between the floors. The next day while vacuuming I felt something under the kids bunk beds thinking it was a shoe I pulled it out with the vacuum wand. Thank god I didn't grab it with my hand. Yes it was grandpa rat about a 10 inch body covered with shaggy hair and a tail about that long with no hair on it. Butch took it out to the garbage can and yelled and showed it to any one within hearing distance. Look what we killed in our trailer?? We never got rid of all of them till after we moved to Umatilla. They said they lived around that irrigation canal. When we moved to Umatilla there was a irrigation canal above the trailer court there also, but no rats.

Spring was here again it was 1953. Time to be on the move again. This time we were moving to Umatilla Oregon school was not out yet so Butch finished his 1st grade in Umatilla only 4 schools that year not to bad. We were in Oregon now so Sis could start the Oregon Deaf school this fall. At this time there was no bridge over the river at Umatilla so you went across on the ferry. Jim moved a few trailers other than ours. The only one I remember was Rosenbacks. Dolly and Rosie had a chow dog. During their stay in Kennewick the dog had chewed some of the electrical cords under their trailer to the clearance and tail lights. After work one night Jim and Rosie decided to move their trailer. They got it all hooked up but no lights. Seemed they just wouldn't work no matter what they did to them. It was getting late so they just took off with no lights. The kids and I were in the car with Dolly and Rosie was in the suburban with Jim. We pulled on the ferry first and then got out of the car to see them pull the trailer on. When they bumped onto the ferry all the lights came on. We were all clapping and cheering. The man on the ferry said didn't you think it would fit? We told him about the lights and I think he thought we were a little odd. We continued on across and got it parked before dark.

Having gone to town one day to get the mail, we had a letter from an insurance company I had never heard of. At a stop light I opened it and it was a check as a settlement on Jims arm he had broken when we were in Mitchel I glanced at it and thought it was $80.00. I threw it on the seat and continued on down the road. Came to a stop sign and was slowing down when I looked at the check again and it was for $800.00. I ran that stop sign. Good thing no one was coming. We put the money away to take a trip to Oklahoma when we could.

Coming home from town another time we found out how they kept the grass so green in the court with out watering it. There was water running down through the court about 6 inches deep. We had to take our shoes off to get from the car to the trailer. The children thought that was great fun. They plugged up the irrigation ditch at the top of the court and let it run. You left nothing under your trailer water would hurt.

There was a pot and pan salesman came to our trailer and Jim bought Rena wear pans for me they were surgical steel. We really did not need them I had some revere wear which were real good pans. He gave them to a neighbor. These have been beautiful pans for 43 years I am still using them and they look like new.

There was a butcher shop over in Herminston some one found that had real good meat at a great price. Dolly and I would go over there about once a week to get meat. Dolly had no children and Dennis had kinda adopted them as his own property. We would put the children in the back seat and the two little ones would stand up. No seat belts then. Dolly had a Cadillac and it had power windows. When going for meat one day Dennis was standing by the window he found out he could push a button and open the window. He would stick his head out. I would tell him to get his head in and Dolly would close the window by her controls. He decided it was a game and stuck his head out again while the window was closing. Got his head stuck in the window. It didn't hurt him but he stopped the game anyway. I was trying to wash one day and Dennis and Sis kept taking a trike away from a little boy. There was a sidewalk all around the wash house and he was riding on it. After so many times of correcting them, and my money had ran out on the meter on the washer. I collected my three and put them in the car and went to town and bought two red trikes. We went home and I finished my wash and the kids rode around and around the wash house all day. Butch had a small bike at this time.

One of the women in the court was pregnant with her first baby. She had never been around children. One day she wanted me to go with her to Pasco to buy baby clothes. We went on a Saturday so Jim could take care of the children. Every thing I told her she would need she would buy a dozen of them. She ended up with enough clothes for six babes. When I told her she didn't need that many she said she didn't want to run out of anything. I am sure she never did. This was Helen and Danny Laurnch. They had a trailer with an upstairs in it. We seen her in 1994 she is living in Eugene Oregon. Danny died quite a few years ago and she is still living in the same trailer. It must be about 40 years old.

Guess what fall is coming on and so it is moving time again. This time we move down the river a little way to Arrlington Oregon it is situated right where the John Day river runs into the Columbia a real pretty little town up a canyon. The day we went down to find a place to park the trailer we visited Dough and Charlotte Kelly. Sis was three years old she went into their bathroom in their trailer and shut and locked the door. When she wanted out she could not get the door open and was crying and we could not tell her how to unlock it. The only window was a very small vent and the door had a Piano hinge on it. Jim and Dough had all kinds of tools out trying to figure out how we could get her out. Everyone was upset as there was no way we could even console her as she could not hear us. Finally after about ten minutes she figured it out herself and came walking out.

We got a space to park our trailer that day and moved the next. Right after we moved Sis had her birthday I remember she got some puzzles at her party and immediately showed us all to dump them out and put them together they were A.B.C.'s and numbers. She had never been to school but was a very smart little girl.

After Dillons and Rosenbachs moved the men were finishing up in Umatilla. Jim came home one night and had been there quite a while. Dolly came over and wanted to know if he knew where Rosie and Shotgun were. He said he didn't. Then she wanted to know if they were drinking. He told her a little bit. She went home and very soon the land lord came and told her she was wanted on the phone. (no one had phones at this time in trailers) It was Rosie he and Shotgun were in jail in Arlington. They got picked up for D.U.I. coming home. Dillon was driving down the middle line in the highway. When he got stopped Rosie got out and told them they could not arrest his friend so he got hauled in right along with him. Dolly told him he could rot in jail but she and Lavone went down later and bailed them out. Lavone came out of her trailer with a pint of whiskey and said this is my husband or might as well be. She had found this one floating in the tank of the toilet. She had found them in shoe boxes in hats in the top of the closet and all over the house.

The trailer court here you came up kind of a steep hill then it leveled off. There was one man lived in the back of the court and he came in real fast. We knew when he came up that hill you could not see over the hood of the car, if a child were in the road you would not see them. Sis could not hear the cars but was real alert. This man came roaring in one day and Jim jumped in front of his car and hit the hood with his hand. The guy slammed his breaks on and said what in the hell do you think you are doing. Jim told him If I had been a child you would not have seen me and they would be dead, now how about slowing down around here. The man agreed with him and came in very careful after that. We were coming home from The Dalles one day and Sis was standing up in the front seat between Jim and I . She had taken her shoes off (black paten leather slippers) The car windows were open all at once a shoe went sailing past Dad's nose he reached out the window and caught it.

We had a registered letter at the Post Office one day I got it out and it was from the State of Idaho it seemed they had state income tax which we had not filed when we worked in Idaho and they had caught up with us and we had to pay a lot of interest. We were innocent we did not know we had to pay it. We got that straightened out and paid. Some of the people after finding out what it was did not get their letters out. I don't know if they ever paid it or not.

We had Sis all registered for school She had to have two complete weeks of clothing with her number sewed in every item. I was busy making her dresses blouses skirts and all things I could make and buying the rest. We had her all ready to go. Kellys said they would keep the boys while we took her down to Salem. Going down was not bad, coming home without her was murder. Jim did not say a word all the way home. When we arrived at the school they took us to her room and we unpacked her clothes. They told us we could not see her for three weeks, and had to tell her goodby. We could not sneak out on her. Here was our baby girl who we could not tell we would be back. She knew no sign language. She clamped her little arms around her Daddy's neck and they had to pry her loose. We were all in tears when we left. The hardest thing we ever did. We know now if we had not put her in school she would not be the independent lady she is today, or be where she is, with the good job she has held for so many years.

The next Monday our Butchie started his second grade here in Arlington. I wrote Sis letters and sent her little packages about three times a week, I knew she could not read them but would be getting mail anyway. With two of them in school and missing our little girl so very much I did a good job of spoiling Denny Jim. But he turned out O.K.

After our three weeks were over we took the boys and went to Salem and rented a cabin and spent the week end with Sis. On Sunday afternoon we had to take her back to the school. When we turned in the drive way she started to cry. No one will ever know how close we came to just making a U turn and going home. We left a crying girl again. They told us she was talking sign language real well and could now understand she was at school and could go home once in a while. She could also say Mother and Father. That was really a thrill for us. We knew she would learn fast. In two weeks she was to come to The Dalles on the bus. We would pick her up there. We were at the bus depot when the bus came in and no Sis. They called the Bus depot in Portland where she was to be changed onto the other bus. They said she went to the bath room and the bus left without her. They had her there in the ticket booth and would put her on another bus. We had a three hour wait but she was on the next bus. Had her home for the week end. When we took her back she gave us all a kiss and said good by and could not wait to get to her friends and started to play. Their little fingers just flying. We knew then we had made the right decision on Sis's school. My cousin Gladys Roose that was deaf was in public school till she was about 12 years old. Then went to Montana State Deaf school and was put in with small children so she could start from the beginning and she did learn sign language and was a very good worker. As her education was really started so late she did not get the good out of it Sis did. Gladys was offered a job at the Deaf School in the sewing room but she did not take it and returned home to her folks.

I decided I wanted to go to Barber school for some reason. Don't ask me why as I don't know. Anyway we moved to Portland and parked the trailer out by the Columbia River on the road to Vancouver. Jim was on a job at Goldendale Washington He and Rosie were living in a cabin there and would come home on week ends. Opel Peterson in Vancouver was taking care of the boys for me so Butchie was in his second school for the second grade. She had Denny Jim all day. The car was still bent up on the passenger side from my wreck in Mitchel. I was going to school one morning and Butchie was in the back seat and Denny Jim in the front with me. We pulled up on the road from the trailer court and he grabbed the door handle and it came open. He fell out but hung onto the door handle till I got stopped so he was not hurt. Sis now came home to Portland every other week end. On Halloween that year we had a box of apples to give to trick or treaters. In no time flat they were all gone. Jim went to the store to get something to give the kids. He came home and said that people were letting kids out up front by the car load. This was forty some odd years ago and people to this day bring kids by the car load to trick and treat in trailer courts on Halloween. Guess it is good picking in a small area and a lot of houses together. (Got off my track.) About then there was a knock on the door and it was a grown man at the door with a pillow case half full. Jim said I think you are a little old for this and would not give him any. We turned out our light and sat in the dark.

The boys needed hair cuts so I set up shop on the patio one Sunday morning I had Denny Jim on a stool and everything laid out when I discovered I had forgotten a comb. I went into get one and when I came out Jim was sitting there with a silly grin on his face. I asked him what he had done? He said it looked easy, I looked at the back of Denny Jims head and his Dad had taken the clippers and ran up the back clear to the crown with the close clippers. All I could do was clip his head.

We stayed here till after Christmas and We decided we might as well move to Vancouver. Butchie was already in school there and we left Sis in school in Oregon. Jim came home from Goldendale one Friday night and he had the car tied together with ropes in the front end. He had an old man pull on the road in front of him and it was either hit a bridge or the pickup. There was no tailgates on the pickup so it rammed it right into the front of the car. The man said he had been pulling on that road for 30 years and there had never been any one coming before.

Jim had come home on Friday night and by the time I got out of school Saturday night he had something to show me. We went to this car dealers and inside with a light shining on it was a Navy Blue 1953 Olds 98. It had a continental kit and a metal sun visor snap on nylon seat covers a real beauty. Well we bought

it. It got about 6 miles to the gallon. The only reason they could tell us was that it had a Buick Dynaf low in it as the hydromatic plant had burned down in '53 and they didn't work very well in an Oldsmobile. So we had a pretty car that had its fan belt hanging out panting every time it seen a service station.

The man that owned and operated the Barber school had a Old hotel in Tacoma he was trying to sell it. We went and looked at it and should have known better but we gave him our Mobile home as a down payment on it and moved to Tacoma. Third school for Butchie this year. Sis is still in Salem. I transferred to the Molar Barber School in Tacoma. Jim had Denny Jim had the Hotel to take care of. We knew before we were there very long it was a big mistake, but didn't know how to get out of it. I got a note from Butchies teacher one day saying she wanted to talk to me. I went to school the next day and was met by a very cold teacher. She asked me if I could wait to talk to her at recess. After the children had gone out to play she laid it on me heavy about what a terrible troublemaker we were raising. She had never ran into such a child in all her years of teaching and she was surprised that he had brought the note home as apparently he had not brought any of the others home. About then the children came back in and Butchie came over and asked me for a kleenex. That teacher got the funniest look on her face and she came over and asked if that was my Tom. I told her yes and she said she must have gave the note to the wrong Tom to take home. Then she started to apologize and she followed me clear out of the school and then wrote a note of apology She assumed I was the mother of the other Tom in class but the other Tom was African American. I think this teacher had a problem.

In early spring I graduated from Barber school our Instructor took us all out for breakfast on our last day. I was the only woman in my class. We all ordered and everyone got their breakfast but me. They had forgotten mine. By the time it came everyone else was done and they all sat there watching me eat like they only got coffee.

Butchie decided about the time school was out he was not Butchie any more only Butch so we had to remember that, it took most of the summer. Sis came home for the summer. A woman that had worked for the former owners said she would stay in our apartment while we took our trip to Oklahoma. So we packed up and were off for two weeks. We went to Denver and visited Jims

Brother Clyde and his wife Doris. They had just moved to Denver from Amarillo. Along with a partner they were in the process of building the first convenience store in Colorado, it was out on Colfax avenue towards Golden. This was in the summer of 1954. We had a lovely time at their house. They took us to see so many things in and around Denver. Also to see two of Jims cousins that lived there Jack Kennedy and Howard and
Iva Kennedy.

This Kennedy family were from Oklahoma also their Mother was Jims Aunt Carrie. One of Mrs. DeLongs 5 sisters. The Kennedys family's Grandmother was part Indian they lived at Dale Oklahoma when the railroad was being built through their land they were promised X-amount of money for the right away. The railroad was all in except the rails and they had not received their money. He went to town to see what he could do. She took it into her own hands. Moving a small storage shed up on the rail bed . She tied a rope around the building and hooked their mule to it and drug it up there. Stuck 4 posts in the loose gravel and strung one wire around it, then put her rocking chair in front and sat down with a shotgun across her lap. When the workers arrived there she was. She held off 25 men most of the day. The foreman had gone into Shawnee to see what they should do. He returned with the check late in the day. When they came back the next morning all was clear for them to proceed and she had her money.

While going on the trip to Oklahoma we had three children and 2 Davey Crocket 1 Polly Crocket hats tails and all flopping around in the car. Clyde and Doris had 4 Pekenise dogs in a fence in the back yard during the day. We were eating dinner one evening Clyde got up and went to the sink for a glass of water he looked out the window and said the dogs are all out. After catching all of them and everyone sat down to finish eating. Clyde said O.K. who let them out? Denny Jim said I did they were in Jail. So the remainder of our visit the gate was wired shut real tight.

We left Denver and headed on to Oklahoma. Jim told me no one in Oklahoma wore shoes. We stopped up in the pan handle of Oklahoma for gas there were children playing out beside the station and they were bare footed The two men that waited on us had on bib overalls but also shoes. When we left the station I mentioned this to Jim and he said well they own a business so they can afford shoes. By the time we came to a town he about had me convinced to the fact. Got a real big kick out of it when I seen everyone wearing shoes. We went through Woodard. Doris and Clyde had owned their first store here, They were in a tornado there in 1947. One of the worst ones in Oklahoma history.

Shortly after that they moved to Amarillo. I started driving at Kingfisher. Jim and the children were all asleep all at once it got Dark and started to thunder and lightening and rain. The wind was blowing so hard I could hardly keep the car in the road and when the lightening flashed I could not see anything. I woke Jim and told him we had to stop. He said not in this. Have you had the radio on? I said no well he started to drive and turned on the radio and sure enough the storm warnings were on from Kingfisher to Oklahoma City.

We got to Oklahoma City after Dark and I seen my first oil well Jim pointed out the state capitol building and I asked him why they had a Power line running across the lawn. He started to laugh and told me it was an oil derrick. This one still had a tower over it. We arrived in Shawnee about 10 o'clock it was so hot. Mrs. De long sat out a lunch for us and a pitcher all frosty from the refrigerator of ice tea. I learned that evening that when they made ice tea they put the sugar in the tea while it was still hot. I don't drink sugar in my ice tea. In later years when we were all there they made one with and one without as Clyde and I did not like it sweet. After some visiting it was bed time and Jim's Mother brought out sheets and pillow cases to make the bed. I put them on and waited for the blankets. I finally asked Jim if he knew where she kept them. He said it is not going to cool down all night and we won't even need the sheet. Boy was this Montana girl learning a lot on this trip.

While here Mrs. DeLong made a blackberry cobbler it was so good. Sis just loved it then we all had to go pick blackberries so Grandma could make more cobblers for this special little girl.

Jim comes from a family of nine. He lost his father when he was 16 years old. While on this trip I met four of them and their families. Clyde and Doris in Denver they never had any children. Harold who never married. Margaret and Ottis Walker and their three boys. Max, Darold and Robert. Eugene and Debra they had two children Richard and Vickie.

While in Shawnee there were Tornado storm warnings one evening. Grandma DeLong the children and myself went to the storm cellar. Sis didn't like it down there she kept looking around for Spiders. Jim would open the door every so often and ask if we were blown away yet?? Our time was much to short and we had to head back to Tacoma. When we went through the area I had driven through the storm, we seen where it had done a lot of damage. We were either ahead or behind it.

Stopped in Denver over night on our way back and straight on home.

When we arrived home we found there had been a fire in the Hotel not a bad one but a fire. The Insurance company fixed it. The hotel didn't have to many permanent residence. The ones we did have were old men and that was their home. We had one man there that said he had been a logger down by Troy. I told him about my book Tobacco Plains Country he wanted to read it. I loaned it to him and never got it back. We had another old fellow that kept telling Jim the devil had gotten in his radio. Jim would check the tubes and replace the broken ones

Something else I learned when we went to Oklahoma. It was June and rather chilly on the west coast. I didn't know how hot and humid it could be in Oklahoma. I took long pants and jackets for the children. I ended up buying shorts and bathing suits for them while we were there.

Rose the woman that worked for us part time was from Poland, she was a World War II war bride. She had two children and then her husband had left her. She worked part time jobs there in town and maybe got A.D.C. I don't know. One day she told me she was pregnant and was going to adopt the baby out as she could not take care of another one. I asked her who she was going to adopt it to? She didn't know so I asked her if I could write some one I had heard was trying to get a baby. She agreed so I wrote Helen and Ike Norton they were living on Woodby Island north of Seattle. In two days they came down to meet her they all had a long talk and before they left it was all settled. They would pay all the expenses and get the baby. She went into labor at seven months and lost 1 baby. She was having twins. Then she came and stayed with us for six weeks and went into Labor again. I called an ambulance as I had been instructed to do. Thought they would never get there. I didn't want to deliver the baby there in my kitchen. They finally got there after a half hour. She was ready to deliver. There was one young man and a middle age man on the ambulance. The older guy told the young one to get in back with her. He said no I am going to drive you get in back with her . She delivered a very little baby boy 15 minutes after arriving at the hospital. He was fine except so little. I called Nortons and they were there the next morning. The baby was in the hospital for a couple of months. They named him Jimmie. He has grown to be a pride and joy to his parents. We never seen Rose again.

Marge and Jim St.Peter lived in Seattle. Marge and their two children Peggy Ann and Mike had gone to Montana to visit her family. Jim was going back the first of August to get them. Butch rode back with him to spend a month with Grandma and Grandpa Shenefelt and Grandma and Grandpa Price. When they were on the way Jim got sleepy and nearly drove in front of a train. Butch yelled at him and he got stopped. He always said Butch at 8 years old saved his life. I went back to get Butch over Labor Day, when he walked up to me I didn't recognize him. He had gained about 20 lbs. that one month. Now he says he ate to much. Besides Grandma having the cookie jar full all the time. Some days he ate lunch and Dinner with both sets of Grandparents.

By the First of August we knew we could not hold on to the hotel any longer. The utility bills were getting away from us and we had no cash flow to live on. When we bought the Hotel we were told that the soldiers from Fort Lewis stayed there when they were on leave. Maybe they once did but no more.

Jim put his name on the union books and got called out to a job at Bonneville. The kids and I stayed at the Hotel. The old man with the radio trouble got sick and had to go to the Hospital. He died we went through his room and he had no evidence that he had any relatives to notify.

I went to talk to an Attorney at Legal Aide. He advised us that we didn't owe enough to take out bankruptcy. He said to give everyone a written notice we were closing and they would have to be out the first of the month. Then call the bank and tell them we could not finish paying the loan. Send each one of the utility companies a check for $5.00 if they cashed that check we would not have to send more than that every month. But don't miss a month. We sent this every month for nearly seven years, before we got them all paid off. Dennises nose out of joint. Some one else had his Aunt Dolly and Uncle Rosie.

Butch was now in the third grade. One evening I asked him to take the trash out. It interrupted a T.V. program. He took it and ran out, to the garbage cans I thought. The next day a man came over and ask if I would come and clean up my trash that was under his trailer. I asked him how my trash got under his trailer. He said I don't know but there is mail in it addressed to you. When I seen it I knew how it got there. Butch and I had a little talk that night. He went and apologized to the man and lost his T.V. privileges for a few days. It never happened again.

We lived in the children section which was below the wash house. One elderly lady spent her days in the wash house visiting with who ever was washing. One weekend when Sis was home this lady went and complained to the land lord about the noise Sis made when she was outside playing and the landlord came on Monday and told me I would have to keep her quiet. I told him if that old gal would stay home she would not even hear her. I was glad she could make a noise and I would not bother them any more as soon as I could find a place to move to. He said that was not necessary. I went to Portland and found a place to park. Hired a trailer hauler. He would be there the next morning. When we awoke the next morning it was raining like you can't believe. The trailer was leaking like a sieve. When the trailer mover came he came to the door and said he would move the trailer as soon as the T.V. antenna was taken down the trailer was disconnected and un blocked. I took the boys over to Dolly and went to work while he sat in his truck. Got the sewer, lights and water disconnected and the trailer un blocked By now I was covered with mud and crying my head off, while trying to disconnect the oil barrel. The man got out of his truck with a wrench that fit. He disconnected the barrel and put it and the stand on the truck and we finally got moved. When we got all parked I paid him and he did reset the oil barrel for me. So the kids and I got the trailer partially blocked every thing hooked up pans under all the leaks inside. We tackled the T.V. antenna it fell down and broke. Got Butch in school the next day three schools in a little over a month.

When Jim came home Friday night no family no trailer only an empty spot. He went to the office and they didn't know where I went. He went to Dollys and she told him and they brought him over.

We went for a ride one week end out to Aunt Blythe and Veins farm north of Vancouver. Caught Aunt Blythe down in the barn helping the sheep it was lambing season. This was when her children Wayne and Loris were small. She must have told Gladys Roose Green my cousin who is deaf where i was . One day she and her Mother-in-law came to see me. Gladys sat with me on the divan. She wrote to me on paper and scrambled each one up when it was full. She told me that was her car but Mrs. Green would not let her drive it. Fred her husband had a tumor on his brain and had surgery that was not successful. He was in a mental Hospital they had two children. Seems her mother-in-law had a rooming house and Gladys and the children were living with her and she was working Gladys so hard. I sure felt sorry for her. She finally got out of there and raised two fine children and educated them also.

This trailer park had a speaker in the office if someone had a phone call or they needed them for some reason they would call you on the loud speaker. One evening they left it on and the manager and his wife were having a battle royal you could hear it all over the court even with your doors and windows closed. Jim got some of the leaks in the roof fixed but never did get them all. Sometime in the first part of November we went on a job to Tillamook Oregon. When we found out we were going there we went and found a new trailer they would take ours as a down payment on. Or maybe it was the new hide a bed We were foolish enough to leave in it. Anyway we would have delivery on it in Tillamook in two weeks. We were moving late in the day and in a hurry. Going down the other side of the Mountain a car passed us and honked and pointed to the trailer. Jim said look out and see if the door is open. It wasn't so we kept going. When we got to our destination we found out what they were pointing at. We had lost the cover to our heating pipe. One more place for the rain to come in that trailer. Butches school was right across the road from the trailer court. His 4th school in the 3rd grade. After we were here only a couple of weeks our new trailer was delivered. It was a Spence craft put out by Liberty a 1955 40 ft. two bedroom and a bath. I thought dry once more. The day after they had set up our new trailer we had a leak in the bedroom. It took them about a month before they got it stopped.

We arrived in Tillamook towards the end of November and it rained every day we were there except Christmas day.

We hadn't been here long when Jim got a letter to appear in court in Tacoma. We didn't have any idea what for. He went without an attorney. It seemed the elderly man with the bad radio in the hotel had taken a liking to him. While in the hospital he had made out a will and had the Doctor and a nurse witness it and went into a coma before he signed it. So it was null and void and everything went to the state. Jim took a day off from work to find out this man had left him $30,000.00 in cash in a safety deposit box. But he didn't get it. We had no idea the man had any money. Sure to bad he was living the way he was when he didn't have to. We lived next door to Joanne and Bill Tibbs this is the first time we had met them. They had a boy and two little girls all preschool age. A real nice family.

One night Bill and Jim decided to go hunting out along the road. It was dark and not hunting season. We never dreamed they would get anything. Well here they come with a small dear. They took it to an old shed in the back of the court and gutted it and skinned it onto a canvas. Rolled them all up to take out and get rid of. They needed somewhere to cool the dear. They put it in my new bathtub. Telling me to wash it off. They did not mean the way I did. It was in the tub so I ran cold water in the tub and gave it a bath. Then they tell me it had to set for a couple of days to cool before it could be cut up. The next day Butch discovered blood in the old shed. He told the land lord some one must have killed one of his chickens in there. We were taking showers in the laundry room.

Finally they cut it in half and took half of it to Tibbs trailer where Bill cut it up and got it wrapped and in the freezer. I had been sure every car that drove into the court was the game warden. At about 11:P.M. at night I decided that had to be cut up so I had it on the kitchen table. Jim and the kids were asleep. Knock Knock on the front door I nearly died. I threw a tea towel over it and asked who was at the door. It was Betty Lockridge, Jims bosses wife. She said I heard you needed some help with what you have under that towel. She said I cut up many illegal deer when we were at Thompson Falls. So she helped me and after a couple of hours we had it in the freezer. Wrapped up all the bones and fat and got it out in the garbage.

I decided I would need some extra money for Christmas so went to work at the Hotel Cafe the graveyard shift. I would sleep when Dennis took his nap and doze on the divan while he played in the front room and get about three hours sound sleep after dinner. I worked till Sis came home and Butch got out of school for Christmas it helped some.

I was making my Christmas candy and never had any trouble with Divinity but here it would not get hard. I mentioned it to the landlady one day. She said to much rain and salt air here you can't make it except on a clear day. She said that was why they had such great luck with the salt water taffy at Sea side.

The only Vacuum cleaner I had was a round pot you put water into and had to wash it all out every time you used it. We had carpet in our new trailer. We were visiting a couple that lived down at Tillamook bay. They were saying they had bought an electrolux vacuum cleaner and had not used it except to do the car two times. They still owed two $10.00 payment on it and was going to tell them to come and get it. I asked them if we paid it off if we could have it. They agreed and that was a good vacuum we used it for over 20 years.

There was a grocery store in this town that kept a new broom sitting by the register. While ringing up your groceries the cashier would take a hold of the broom handle and ring it up then lean it back against the register. After so many times of saying that is not my broom we all just stopped going there.

We went down to Tillamook bay to catch crabs. The men would go out in a boat and put scraps of meat on a net when the crabs crawled on the net they would pull it up. We would have a fire going on the beach with a five gallon can of water boiling over it. The crabs were cooked there then we would take them home and take them out of the shells and put them in milk cartons and freeze them. One night we started home from crabbing and Jim stopped the car took Sis out of the back seat and swatted her bottom and put her back in the car. I said what was that for. He said Sis knows I asked her and she showed me where she had pushed the cigarette lighter in and stuck it on the seat cover and burned a hole.

We were at Tibbs one night the boys were asleep and we went next door for a few minutes. Sis was home and not asleep so she went with us. Joanne had just gotten some tall slim beer glasses and served us some beer in them. Hers and mine were sitting on the table and she wanted to show me something in the bedroom, when we came out our beer glasses were empty. We asked the men why they drank our beer. They said they hadn't even drank their own. Here sat Sis on a chair swinging her feet with a silly look on her face. She was about 5 this year, she was a little drunk she had downed both glasses of beer in about five minutes.

Just before Christmas I had cleaned the house from top to bottom put a Christmas table cloth on the table with a bowl of nuts on it. I came in from the wash house with the laundry and Jim and the Kids had gotten nut shells all over the table cloth. I lost my temper and said if you want to live like pigs we all will. I flipped the nut shells all over the front room floor. Knock Knock I went to the door and there stood some perfect strangers with some Christmas gifts for us. They were going by and Dolly and Rosie had sent them to us. I had to ask them in I was so embarrassed.

All at once Butch and I were covered with bites they looked like mosquito bites but there were no misquotes. Finally some one told me they were sand fleas they were in the grass as well as the sand and they came into the house. Crawled into the beds and would bite you while you slept. Jim and Dennis were not bitten. Also I was told to sprinkle bath powder in the beds, fleas breath through their pours and the powder fills them up and they die. I had those beds so full of powder it just flew when you turned down the covers and we were still getting eaten alive. I went to the drug store and asked them what you could do for sand fleas. The druggist handed me a box of flea powder. He said they come in the door over the door stoop. Just sprinkle this on the door stoop and it will kill them. It did in no time what a relief for Butch and I anyway.

There was a vent in the ceiling of the wash house or we all thought it was. One of the dryers had a bad meter on it and if you watched it and grabbed it and held it in place you could get two drying out of one quarter. One day Joanne and I were washing and we would yell at each other to grab the dryer. Finally the land lord came out and wanted to know if something was wrong with a dryer? We told him no. He pointed to the ceiling and said I kept hearing you say to grab a dryer. Joanne said we didn't want anyone else to get one till we were done with them. I said how did you hear us? He said I have a speaker in my kitchen I can hear everything said in the wash house when I turn it on. We decided he deserved to hear everything that was said about him.

Before we all moved we let him have it. I don't know if he had the speaker on or not he never told us.

When the job was done we moved to Portland. That way Jim would be closer to the Union hall. There was no jobs in sight. Our new Trailer had a six volt brake system and our car had a 12 volt battery. Someone told us we could split the battery some way with a nail. Well it didn't work. We went up over the Tillamook burn and across Portland hitting down town at five o'clock in the evening. We had no sign of a brake on that 40 foot trailer. We made it once more. We got turned around and had to back from the front of the court all the way to the back. By now it was dark and we parked between two trees. I stood by one with a flash light and Butch by the other and he backed in between the two lights worked great. Jim went down and signed up for unemployment. We got $27.00 a week. Tibbs were parked right beside us. Jim and Bill dug cesspools by hand that winter they got $40.00 for each hole that was $20.00 a piece and they dug about one and a half a week. Not much money but it put food on the table. We also had trailer payments and parking to pay. The car was paid for. Jim had me take it in for a tune up and I said the wrong thing I said over haul. I went to get it prepared to pay about $35.00. The bill was $300.00 we didn't have it so I had to go borrow it. Then I had car payments also. Till that was paid off. I went to work at a Cafe as a cook. I had never cooked before but it was a small cafe with one waitress. People kept talking about the rats running around on the parking lot, I hadn't seen any. One night I went out to the storage room to get pickles. I knew where the pickle barrel was so didn't bother to turn the lights on. I reached my hand in for a handful of pickles and grabbed something soft and hairy. I let loose in a hurry and turned the lights on. I went inside and told the owner there was a big rat had drowned. He said I can't afford to throw away all those pickles. To this day I can't eat those sliced dills they put on sandwiches. He also didn't want anyone to get the meat for the day. He said that it had to be properly rotated. Fine with me. I told him one day I needed steaks for my shift, He handed me a package. I opened it up and they were slimy and green and stunk. I told him they were rotten and took the package to him. After looking at them he threw the package at me. By then I had had it. I threw them back at him took my apron off and went home.

Myrtle and Wayne came out to visit us while we were here. Sharon and Terry were of school age but still small. We at the time had a Parakeet bird which I was always scared of. It would get out of its cage and perch on the top of the drapes and chew on them and poop all over the house. Jim would clip its wings (he ruined my barber shears doing this). The thanksgiving we were in Tillamook the bird went behind the cook stove and didn't come out till evening I thought maybe he got cooked along with the turkey. No luck he wasn't even singed. He would swoop over my head with his beak clicking, I would leave the door open hoping he would fly away but he never did. We gave him to Sharon and Terry they put his cage on the floor of the back seat and he moved to Montana. Now the bird was where I wanted to be. Myrtle said he became real tame and would set on their head. They also had a cat. The bird flew to Sharons head and overshot and lit on the floor and the cat had him. End of bird. His name was Oscar Rosie as we didn't know if it was a boy or a girl.

Joanne was working for Blue Bell potato chip. I went

and put in an application and got right on. Grave yard shift. While Jim was out digging cesspools Butch was in school, Sis was also at school . I would get my house work done and Dennis would set on the floor in the front room and play real quiet and I would nap most of the day off and on. Then get a couple of hours of sound sleep in the evening before I had to go to work again. I started out spotting potatoes. You do exactly that. You cut rotten spots out of potatoes. Then I was put on the cooker. And then the bagger. One night I was on the little 5¢ bags. Yes they did at one time have a bag of chips for that price. My bags stuck together one night and that machine was spitting chips at me , they were all over the floor and my lap by the time I got them loose. Shortly after that I went on the conveyer belt where you glued the top of the cartons together. I hadn't been on that phase of the job long when Jim got called on a short job to Izee Oregon. It was only for a couple of months so the kids and I stayed put.

When he went to Izee he took our car Bill went also but they had a very old car. Anyway I had to stop working at Blue Bell as there was no one at home at night with the boys.

There was an add in the Sunday paper for a 1955 Cadillac for sale for $300.00. Bill called on it and the man said there was nothing wrong with it, he had to sell it and give his wife half the money in a divorce settlement. He wasn't going to give her any more than he had to. Joanne and Bill went and looked at it and bought it.

I really needed to work to catch up on things after his long lay off. Coming home from the store one day about a block from the house I seen a Cook wanted sign in the window of a little drive in cafe. Dales Cafe, I went in and applied for the job. I got it and went to work the next day. A lady in the court took care of the boys for me. When I went to work here came two waitresses and 3 car hops I wondered what I had gotten myself into. I was so busy that night, at that time you had no training period. You were told what to do and you did it. I was about 28 years old at this time.

My first night there the boss told me to make chicken rice soup for the next day. There was a big pot of chicken broth. I put onions celery a few carrots and rice. To much rice, by the time we got it thinned down we had it for three days. When I finished it was as thick as oat meal. Dale came in and never said a word he just thinned it down.

That first night I had about 40 hamburgers cooking and the buns all fixed for them when a car hop came in and set a burger sack up in the service window. She said this man said that would be real good if it had some meat in it. I looked at it and a big bite was out of it and sure enough the meat was still on the grill.

After I had been there a couple of months I got my pay check and it was wrong. I told Dale and he said no it isn't wrong you got a 5¢ raise. The first raise I had ever been given.

They had pin ball machines in the cafe at that time they were for entertainment only. Dale told me if it was a steady customer that we seen in there all the time we did pay them off. The cook had the pay off money in the cooler. One day the waitress brought this man back we both recognized him as a steady around there. I paid him off and got a ticket for it. He was a steady Policeman that came in there. I had to go to court. Dale paid me wages to go and paid the $50.00 fine. They sure teased me about that.

The gals were getting their cars broke into out back after so many calls and broken windows, the Police said don't lock your cars if you have something of value lock it in the trunk and leave the cars unlocked. It worked no more broken windows.

This new trailer we bought was really a lemon it had Jalous windows. Little slots of glass that fastened against each other The wind really whistled in them. Had very little insulation. Nails about every other one instead of screws around the roof and spike nails through the springs instead of cotter keys. But so cold. My sewing machine molded sitting in the closet as did the shoes. We went down to the trailer sales and told them. They said they had storm windows sitting there that would fit it but they were $10.00 a piece. Jim picked up eleven windows and put them in the car and said thanks. If something isn't done about that trailer I will paint lemons all over it and park it on that vacant lot across the street. Within a week there was a man from the factory there. He replaced the nails with screws and cotter keys. The only excuse we got for the insulation was it must have been made on the night shift and they carelessly put camp trailer insulation in it. We never did get a bill for the storm windows.

He went from Izee to Madras we would be there some time so I quit my job and we moved one Monday Morning real early. Joanne and Bill went to California on a job and we have never heard of them again. We left Portland real early in the A.M. so as to get there before work started. I have a husband that at times expects a car to run on fumes. About two miles out of town we ran out of fumes. Long hill into Madras, we were coasting down the hill and met the trucks going out to the job. We made it to the station at the bottom of the hill. After getting gas we went through town to the trailer court he had us backed in to the spot and one wheel was in a hole. Betty Lauckman brought out a lunch to him and said unhook and go out on the job. He did and here we sat all day in a real lopsided trailer and nothing hooked up. Betty said we could come stay with her but we used the courts bathroom and I did a little straightening up. When Jim came home from work he got it all straightened up and blocked. Butch finished school in Madras that year

I went to work at the Cactus in as a cook. It was not a clean kitchen I wasn't there very long. The meat they served was two well aged for me. Bad Job I quit.

We had met a couple that had a little dry land farm here at Madras. We were invited out there for dinner one Sunday. They all decided to do some target practicing. Some one told me that this rifle didn't kick so I props it on the back of a pickup bed sighted it in and shot. I nearly had to pick myself up from the ground. That was the last time I ever shot a rifle. While there Dennis had to go to the bathroom. I told him it was in the little house out back, he came in the house and went up to Elsie and told her her bathroom stunk and there was no flusher on the toilet. That brought a roar from every one. The children rode a donkey most of the day. We all went home tired but had a wonderful day. A year before this someone told us if we sent $2.00 to the Sheriff at Pascodia Mississippi he would send us a trailer license. No questions asked. We nearly all had Mississippi license.

Job finished we all were moving to The Dalles and were stopped by a patrolman. He asked for our registration for our trailers. They were all registered in Oregon or Washington and had Mississippi License. We got a ticket and had to get Oregon plates.

We were not in The Dalles long this time and moved on to Tumwater out of Olympia. We were parked at Black Lake. Had a beautiful place to park for the summer.

We were parked beside Bozo Kelly and his wife they had about 4 or 5 of those little hairless Mexican dogs, when we would come home or go in or out of our door, those darn dogs were in the window next door barking their heads off. Very nerve wracking.

When we first moved here Butch was in school for a short while. When I went to town if we came upon the school bus going home Dennis didn't want me to pass it. We would follow it all around the lake so he could wave at the kids in the back window.

That summer we did a lot of swimming in the lake and had another good summer. Some one told us there was good clam digging at Aberdeen. You needed a tent, our Landlord told us he had one we could borrow. We went equipped with tent, camp stove, sleeping bags, food, shovels, lanterns, buckets. We were going for just one day and night so I didn't take any extra clothes. No one told me how wet and dirty you get digging clams. There was low tide at four in the morning so Jim and the kids get up to go dig clams. They left the tent with lantern, buckets and shovels. The beach looked like a little city with all the lanterns all over it. There was a lot of shouting and laughing drifting back to the tent. About six o'clock here they all come. Happy but so wet and dirty. There were a lot of clams. To solve the situation, they took their cloths off and climbed into bed. They all went to sleep, I shook as much sand as I could from their cloths and hung them up to dry. We had taken a wash tub with us to put the clams in. Someone told me to put them in the tub with some water and corn meal, they would eat the corn meal and discharge the sand. I carried water from the ocean and got this done while they were sleeping. The cloths got partially dry before they woke up. We had breakfast dug in one more low tide then proceeded to break camp to go home. In taking down the tent we tore it on one end right where it had been patched before.

We got home unloaded, cleaned up, and I left the clams in the tub till the next day. When Jim came home from work the next day I had them all cleaned and in the freezer. He had to take the torn tent back to the landlord. We decided we would try to buy the tent. He took it back and asked if they would sell it. The man said sure $20.00, so he gave him the money and the guy said where did it tear on you. Jim said how did you know I tore it? The land lord said did you see the patch on the end? That's where it happened to me when I borrowed it. So we told him right beside that patch. He said you can take it into Olympia to the shoe shop they will only charge a couple of dollars to patch it. So now we had a tent we never used again.

Walt Lauchman was foreman of this job they lived on the other side of the lake. I went to visit Betty one day. She had a little girl Dennises age. Betty had to show me the plug in Walt had fixed the night before. She plugged in the toaster that morning and the plug in had melted and run right down the wall.

We went into Olympia that day to go to the bank. Betty, Debbie, myself, Butch, Sis and Dennis. At the bank they gave each of the children a sucker. Next door was a real nice dress shop. Betty wanted to show me a dress she had found . Butch and Sis were right with me and all at once I missed the other two. We spotted Debbie and Dennis laying on the floor under a rack of dresses on their backs running their suckers back and forth on the hems. We got our children and got out of their i a hurry.

We always had to be home so Jim could watch the $64,000.00 question T.V. program. I didn't care for it, I said no one could be that smart. In later years I was proven right.

It was getting towards the end of summer so this meant school clothes. I made Sis a real pretty coat from an old one of mine it was gray and I got blue velvet for the collar and covered buttons, It turned out real pretty. We were in Penneys in Olympia. Had gotten Butch one new outfit to start, the rest of his came a little later. Sis had to have nearly everything she had grown out of things and worn them out. She still needed two weeks clothing. I noticed Dennis looking at these little Boy's cowboy shirts. Finally he came to me and said "can I have a new shirt that no one else has ever worn?" He got it a black and white plaid cowboy shirt that he picked out all by himself. He wore it till it was in rags and much to small for him.

No job in sight at the end of this one and with school about to start we went back to Portland where I could work and Sis could go to school in Oregon Got Sis back in school, Butch back in Powel Hurst school where he had gone before. Tried to get Dennis in Kindergarten at the church across the street and he would not go. A week later he decided he would go and then I didn't have the money Later someone asked him why he wasn't in Kindergarten and he said because Mom don't have any money. So now I knew it was Job time. I went back to Dales Cafe and got right on as Cook. He had hired another Cook the day before me. Come Christmas time Dale always gave everyone a Christmas card with a bonus in it. I would not have opened mine had I known he had given me $10.00 and the other new cook only five. But I did open it and she did see how much was in mine. Then the trouble started. I took the soup stock out one morning to make soup for the day and the box with the rolls of money had some how tipped over into the soup stock. Now this box was a cigar box with a lid. It really must have jumped. I left it for the boss when he came in. Made potato soup instead. The next event that sticks in my mind. I turned on the grinder to grind bread crumbs and sparks and flames shot out of the front of it right at me. It had been filled up with book matches. When Dale came in I told him if she wanted my job that bad she could have it. I was gone. His reply was "no you little Indian just settle down. She won't be in any more except to pick up her check" He went to the phone and fired her.

The next cook he hired wanted only the afternoon shift which suited me fine. After a month or so Dale came in one day and asked me if I was selling T-bone steaks on the day shift? I told him I had not sold a one. He told me they were really going and he couldn't find on the tickets where any had been sold. He parked out on the back lot a few nights and seen where the steaks were going. The new cook was wrapping them in kitchen towels and putting them in the trash during her shift. When she went home she got them out and put them in her car. There went another cook.

For Christmas this year, Doris and Clyde sent the kids a Pekingese dog. He was red and white registered and all. This was Tinker Boi. He arrived by air freight Jim went and picked him up. They brought him to the back door of the Cafe for me to see. He was a little ball of fur. The first night he cried all night. The lady next door told me to put an alarm clock in the box with him, it worked from then on he was fine. A very easy dog to house break. The only thing is the first two weeks he was the kids dog then for nearly fifteen years he was mine. I had to feed him bath him brush him and clean up after him. He would ride on the back of the front seat behind me every where we went.

At Christmas this year I called Mother and Dad they had a phone now. Mother asked me how I liked my Poinsettia she had sent for Christmas? I told her I had not gotten one. She put a tracer on it and found out it had been delivered to the wrong address. They had no more so they brought me a Jerusalem Cherry. It was a real pretty plant. During the months following Christmas it died down. I was taking it to the trash and the dog got out so I threw it under the edge of the trailer, and caught the dog and forgot the plant where it lay the rest of the winter. Come spring and it was time do a little cleaning around the trailer I dug out the plant and it was turning green. I brought home a five gallon can from the cafe and planted it. It sat on the tongue of the trailer and looked real pretty. Green waxy leaves and first little green balls then they turned red.

Some where along the way we found a two wheeler for Dennis it had real little tires about like a scooter and was belt driven so it had no brakes. He learned to ride it and trying to keep up with Butch on his big one his legs would go so fast it was comical to see him. The boys always put their bikes in the yard by the back of the trailer when we went somewhere. We came home from the store one day and Dennises bike was in front of the trailer smashed. Someone had left it in the road and it had gotten run over. Smashed flat could not be fixed. During the last few months in Portland Jim was working at Kent on a short job. He came home on week ends. I could walk to work and the store. He was home so we had the car to take Sis back and fourth to school. This winter we had gotten rid of the gas eating Oldsmobile and bought a rambler station wagon. It was bright yellow and nearly new. We got about 19 miles to the gallon a lot better than the three the Oldsmobile was getting. This funny little car had the starter on the gear shift. You had to pull up on the gear shift to start the car. It was real nice but shimmied all over the road above 58 miles an hour.

When school was out we moved to Cottage Grove Oregon. Had to have a trailer hauler move us the rambler was to small. When I left Dales Cafe this time he said you weren't a cook when you came here the first time but you are now. If you ever get back in town and need a job you have one. Never seen him again.

At cottage grove we were parked in a trailer court right by the free way. Most of the crew were there and It was in front of a motel where Jim had lived before I met him when he was on another job there.

One morning I heard cars honking and brakes squealing behind the house I looked out and there was Tinker Boi sitting in the middle of the free way. The cars were zipping by him. They all stopped for me to go to him and get off the road. He had gotten out some way and not tied up.

This summer we did a lot of swimming in the town swimming pool. The kids and I had never swam in one so we really did enjoy it. Sis developed boils on her leg during the summer they were so painful we never did find out what caused them. They left as fast as they had come. Our neighbors had a dog. When we moved in the lady told me not to let the children come on her side of the trailer as the dog was tied there and he would bite them. So I told them and they were real good about it. Sis always loved animals and was not afraid of any of them. I looked out the kitchen window one morning as I was doing dishes and Sis was on the porch next door lying by the dog with her arm around his neck and her head on his head. I couldn't call her and did not want to upset the dog. I watched her as she murmured to the dog real gentle and finally got up and walked away. The lady who owned the dog had been inside watching also. She came over and wanted to know if I had seen what had happen? She said if you didn't have the boys I would give my dog to your daughter. I told her we had a dog and maybe we were just lucky that time. But it happened time and again.

By now I was getting real homesick again. The car needed new tires. We got four new tubeless tires. I loaded the car with three children and a dog and headed for Montana and my mountains and home. We drove to Spokane the first night. When I went out to leave the motel in the morning I noticed the tires looked a little low so put air in them and went on. Butch took movie pictures out the car windows. We have pictures of the Kootani river but mostly bridge railing bouncing by but not bad for a little guy. When going up the river between Libby and Rexford it was so very pretty. One place the trees were hanging over the road and it was so cool. Dennis pipes up out of the back seat and said we are driving into a cave. He tried to sound so spooky. They ruined that drive when they put the dam in a few years later.

I parked my car in Myrtle and Waynes drive way that evening and the next morning I had four flat tires. When Wayne came in from work that evening he took one off and took it to a station, they had put worn out inner tubes in the tires when they put them on. So had to get all four of them fixed right. Mom was cooking for the forest service but I did get to visit with her some. Also went and seen Esther. I had my Montana fix once more so could go home. I started home thinking boy was I going to raise cane at that place where I had bought the tires when I got home. We made it to Umatilla Oregon that first night. I had trouble finding a Motel that would let me take the dog in the room. I was afraid if I left him in the car he would whine or bark all night. The third motel I went to the lady at the desk said sure you can take that little thing in the room and I will put you right next to us as you are alone with the children. She gave me a little dish to have water for the dog. He was house broken and never let a peep out of him all night.

On arriving home the next day I found all the trailers were gone only ours was sitting there. When I went in I found a note on the table saying when I got home to call a trailer mover and have the trailer moved to Ivancovitches trailer court in Redmond Oregon. As I have mentioned before I don't know how I always managed to have the money to move on but seemed to. Jim had unblocked the trailer and had it nearly ready to go. I called a trailer hauler and moved the next morning so never did get back to the tire salesman.

When we arrived at the trailer park there were all the trailers from Cottage Grove and Jim had stayed with Claude Michales family till I got there. When they were parking the trailer I took the dog out of the car and fastened his chain around a tree in our yard. The Manager came and told me we could have the dog if he didn't bark. I could not put his chain around the tree as he would rear on it and kill the tree. I unhooked him and snapped it on the top of the garbage can. That is where he was tied up all the time we lived there, he never even pulled the top of the can off. He was always tied up and if something was fastened on to his harness he thought he was tied up. At picnics I would put my purse on a blanket and hook his leash onto it and he wouldn't move it. As for his barking he never did bark much but for a couple of days every time he started to do so we would smack him with a newspaper. All the rest of his life he only barked when some one knocked on the door real late at night.

I had to have the oil barrel filled up so called an oil company and when it was delivered I was real surprised to have Leo Peltier from Montana deliver it.

While we were at Redmond we went to Bend Oregon and visited with Uncle Corade and Aunt Signa also Uncle Celose and Aunt Ora.

When Jim put up the T.V. antenna he put the cable over the telephone wire and we picked up cable T.V. real good. This is something we never have hooked up to even yet. But we used it there.

That fall we all went up to a lake in the Three sisters mountains I don't remember what the lake was it was real cold but we all went swimming and had a great time. It was nearly on the top of the pass that is between Bend and Lebanone.

The children were out playing one evening and riding their bikes. All at once Dennis jumps from his bike and comes running to the house screaming and beating the side of his head. He was yelling it's buzzing it's biting. He said something was in his ear I looked and could see nothing. I poured proxide in his ear and didn't wash anything out. We loaded him in the car and took him to the hospital emergency. The Doctor knew right away what it was he said this is real common in the fall of the year. He put him on a table and took a pair of tweezers and took a moth out of his ear. He dropped it on the floor and had Dennis step on it. Well that moth cost us $12.00. The next evening the neighbor man came over with a pint jar about half full of moths . He said I hear you are paying $12.00 a piece for these. Are you needing some more? I could have hit him over the head with them he thought he was funny.

Butch would give Sis a ride on the cross bar of his bike. While doing this one day she stuck her foot in the front wheel and wrecked them. Neither of them were hurt but it was a good thing Sis had some little majorette boots on or she would have been hurt as it cut the heel from the boots.

Time to start thinking about school again. So we got Sis all ready and had two boys for school this year. My baby was starting and he informed me his name was not Denny Jim it was Dennis James DeLong. The day I took them to school to register them, Butch was registered real easy but when they asked Dennis his name he was so excited he couldn't remember it. We got them all registered and the trailer court was right straight down the road from the school. As they got out at different times I asked Dennis if he wanted me to meet him the first day. He said don't you dare. I can come home by myself. I had been drilling him all week on his name and where he lived. I grant you Ivancovitches trailer court was a mouth full for a five year old, he would be six the end of September one day later and he would have had to stay out for another year. When they left for school I asked him one more time his name and where he lived. He thought for a minute and said Dennis James DeLong and I live in Son of a Bitch trailer court. I told him to just say he lived in the trailer court straight down the road from the school.

Things were going great in school and We were not to far to zip over the hill to get Sis for a week end. I decided I was going to bowl. I never had but one of the gals on the crew talked me into it and I joined a league and had a good time. The Children came home from school one day and the neighbor boy came over and he said to Butch "boy you sure fixed that big bully today didn't you" I asked what was going on and found out Butch had had a fight and the other boy had gone to the Dr. for stitches. Butch had a note that I had to take him to school to the Principles office the next morning. I had bowling that evening and one of the women on the other team was talking about this big bully had cut her sons lip in a fight at school and there would be hell to pay in the principles office the next morning. I didn't say anything just went on bowling. The next morning we went to school. Butch had told me this kid picked on everyone and he got tired of it so when he had the chance he hit him. When we walked into the Principles office here sat the woman and a good size boy with stitches in his lip. She looked at us and then asked her son if that was the boy who hit him? The boy said yes, She looked at Butch again and said to her son we are getting out of here. When he stood up he was a whole head taller than Butch. We stayed and talked to the Principle and that was the end of that episode.

This woman I bowled with smoked and she said her husband didn't know it she kept her cigarettes hid in a wool sox in the trunk of her car. If he smelled it on her she would say it must be on her cloths from the rest of us that smoked. Guess she got away with it.

We all decided to do some hunting while here. Got hunting license and come Saturday we would pack lunch and all take off for' the woods with all the kids. We would find a likely spot and start a bon fire, put a five gallon cream can of water on it, dump in a pound of coffee. That done some one would stay at camp with all the kids and the rest would designate drivers and shooters. They would tell us where to sit or stand to shoot the deer when they ran them up or down the hill. One day Edna Grant and I were posted as shooters. I didn't know how to shoot a gun. I had that one time target practicing. Anyway we were sitting there and a buck came out in the clearing. Edna said shoot it!! I put the gun up and pulled the trigger nothing happened. I told Edna the darn thing wont shoot. She shot and missed she was laughing so hard at me. Seems I had pulled the peep sight down instead of taking the safety off . We women didn't get any deer that day. When we got back to camp the coffee was done and it was lunch time. There were two deer hanging in a tree at camp some of the men had gotten. While we were eating a pickup drove up and stopped he said do you think you will get anything with all the noise those kids are making. No one said anything but just pointed towards the ones in the tree. The same pickup came by later in the day and there were four deer hanging in the tree they just shook their heads and kept going they didn't have anything.

One Saturday Butch was sick so I stayed home with our children. A man in the court came by and said he had shot a deer and did I want it? It had his tag on it and he hung it in the tree by our trailer. When the hunters came home I was proud I had one and had not even gone hunting. Jim and Everett Grant took one look at it and told me it had been gut shot and not washed out. They got the hose and hosed it down and we did save some of it.

When the job was over there we went to The Dalles we were not there working to long before the job was over. Claude Michales stayed with us for a little while he slept on the divan. Sis was home one weekend and the women that lived behind us had sweet peas growing on the fence. Sis picked some, the woman was scolding her for it and Dennis said go ahead and bawl her out she can't hear you anyway He took his sister by the hand and they walked away.

The boys were in school here and Dennis says all he can remember about it was a long hall in the school house. They also remember the cliffs I let them play on. They thought they were so big and high. Butch went back by there as a grown man and drove up to see the cliffs. They were actually only little rock ledges. Coming home from school one day Butch went into the Super Market and he took a 5 cent package of black licorice. He got caught, I could hear him coming across the field. He said the store manager said if he wasn't back in a half hour with his mother or dad he would call the police. He was really scared. We went right over. He was scolded by the owner. His punishment was to sweep the parking lot after school for a week. And after supper at home he had to go to bed and not play. I think he learned his lesson and maybe the other kids benefited from it also. I won t say my kids didn't steal anything after that but if they did I didn't hear about it.

Just before school was out this year some of the children in Virginias school that were from welfare family's received new canvas shoes. Virginia had a perfectly good pair but she wanted new ones also. She sat in the swing and went back and forth dragging her toes till she wore her shoes through. The house mother told us what had happen so she had new shoes also after her next trip home.

There was a company party while we were in The Dalles we got a baby sitter and went. This was the only time I ever ate caviar. Didn't like it and never tried it again.

Soon the job was over. Most of the crew stayed right there. We couldn't move if we wanted to the car wouldn't pull the trailer. We started to look around for a car that was heavy enough to do the job. We drove into Portland and found a 1952 Cadillac. It had good care and was a good car. Also gave us 19 miles to the gallon same as the Rambler. It pulled the trailer fine.

While we were here that winter some of the men wanted to learn to play golf. They paid Jims green fees so he would teach them. We went to Hood River to a nice little golf coarse that wasn't busy. Once again most of the time we women went along and took the kids if it was on a weekend. We took a picnic lunch and ate at the tables in the yard and the kids played while dad golfed. We also spent time sifting sand along the Columbia River. Jim made a sifter out of heavy screen with handles on each side. We found Indian beads and arrowheads. All I seem to have left is one large arrow head. It was a good family outing and we all had a lot of fun.

There was a family lived here that were so dirty you can't believe it. They weren't kids, but had two little boys. One still in diapers. She kept her dirty diapers in the bath tub and didn't even rinse them out. They went into the wringer washer that way, when she started washing any one else in there finished in a hurry and got out. She did clean the washer and tubs when she got done. They invited us over one night to play cards. On our arrival the table was covered with cereal boxes and dirty dishes. She was washing dishes picking one spoon at a time from the mess on the table. He asked us to sit down, where? The divan was covered with cloths she had brought in from the line earlier in the day. He picked them up and threw them in on the bed. She finished the dishes and picked the boxes from the table. He made coffee. We were ready to play cards. I set our cups on the table. Jim tried to pick his up and it was stuck so he slid it off the edge. Then they decided the table needed washed before we could play cards. She brought a nice dish of home made candy over one day and when the family learned where it came from no one ate it. They moved to California and we never seen them again.

There was a dog running loose in the court that tipped garbage cans over all the time. We each had a can in the front of our trailer. The fellow beside us decided he had enough. He hooked an electric fence wire around the can and to a battery some way. When this big dog came up he started to heist on the can and he got an electric shock. He was crying all the way down the road and never came on our side of the court any more. Spring is here and work is opening up. We get a call to move to Lebanon Oregon. Work once more. While we were in The Dalles I had found a Doctor that would give you rainbow pills to lose weight. I had really lost a lot, felt good. The Cadillac pulled the 40 ft trailer real well we had gotten an equalizer hitch. The trailer court was out of town and in some trees it was real nice. Lots of people on this job we knew. The boys were put in school here in Lebanon. School was about out by now. One day I decided I would go pick strawberries. Big backbreaking mistake. When I came home Dennis was sitting on the steps crying. I asked him why he wasn't at school? He told me he had been pushed from the swing and hurt his arm. Butch had gone to the Principle and told him his little brother was hurt and threw such a fit they brought him home. But they only let him out and didn't check to see if anyone was home. I put him in the car and we went to town to find a Doctor. He had a broken Collar Bone so spent the next six weeks in an ace bandage wrap. I didn't pick anymore strawberries.

One evening Cliff Phillips who was Jims foreman came over and asked if he was O.K. bruised stiff or sore. Jim said no he was all right. I asked why he should be? Cliff said didn't he tell you what happened? Well no he hadn't. He had an accident at work that day. A truck with a triple Drum reel on the back had gone over a bank and tipped over while Jim was working on the back of it. The brakes had give out. He felt it going and somehow got in the front end and turned the wheel keeping it from rolling all the way to the bottom. He said all the boss said was, now would be a good time to grease it, as it set with all the wheels up in the air. The next day they hooked a cat onto it to turn it right side up. We took the movie camera out and took pictures of them pulling it up. The kids liked to run the film backwards. To see it tip over time and again.

Our Jerusalem Cherry plant was by now a bush and getting to large for the five gallon can it was in. Such a pretty thing. I asked the landlord if I could plant it in the trailer court. He said he would be honored to have it. Could he pick the spot? He planted it out front between the store and the monkey cage. Yes they had a monkey in a big cage out front. There was a sign on the cage to not put your fingers inside the wire or you might get bitten. Our children fed him cookies and potato chips and were lucky they left with all their fingers in tact.

As the weather grew warmer we found a wonderful spot in the river for swimming and picnics. We all spent a lot of time there. On the Fourth of July we all went into Albany to the Timber Carnival. It was so hot and terribly crowded. We had put down a blanket for our family and people came and crowded in on us till there was no place left for our picnic basket. We decided the river was a better spot for us. So we made everyone move and we folded up our blanket took our family and headed for the river. Had a wonderful time clear through the roasted marshmallows and fireworks.

One day about six trailers and flat bed trucks with dark complected people came into the trailer park. The women were dressed in bright long skirts. Lots of children. As soon as the trailers were parked, one beside us, The men started to unload all these tools and machetes. Then proceeded to build lawn furniture. I went and asked the landlord how long they would be there. He said three or four weeks they are Gypsies they come every year. They won't bother anything where they live. They had never caused him any trouble. The women had their own washing machines, wringer type. They ran cold water from the hose into them and put out the whitest wash I have ever seen. We all wished we knew what kind of soap they used.

They would roll rugs out in front of their trailers in the evening and play their string instruments. Some would dance and sing. Really great to watch them. When they were all done the rugs were rolled up by the trailer till the next evening. The flat bed trucks were loaded with tables and benches and lawn chairs when they came back in the evening most of the time they were empty.

While they were there we had company from Montana. Esther and Clyde had bought a new Station Wagon. They put the twin mattress from Dicks bed in the back. Dick was at boys state so Esther and Clyde were going to travel and sleep in the station wagon. They headed to Oregon. After one night of crawling in and out and no place to get dressed that was enough for them. They did sleep in it while they were at our place. I remember Esther was a little leery of the Gypsies. They spent a couple of days with us.

This was my first experience with blackberries. There was a bush out at the back of the court as big as a house. While I was doing my housework in the morning the children would take sand pails and pick blackberries. Three sand pails full made a batch of jam. We ate a lot of them with sugar and cream or just berries they are so sweet and good.

It was getting towards the end of summer and end of job. School would be coming soon. We were sent on a job at Quincy Washington. We take off on a Saturday morning bright and early. About 10:30 just outside of Arlington Oregon our overload pops out from under the car and broke our brake line. We no sooner got stopped alongside the highway till a patrolman was pulling in behind us. He wanted to know what was wrong? We told him and he said you know you have to have that trailer off the road by three o'clock? We went into Arlington and they said they could fix the brake line but not till after noon before they could get the part. So we called The Dalles and found a trailer hauler who could take it on to Quincy for us. We told him we would be right behind him. He arrived there just about the same time we did. Took a few minutes to find a trailer park but made it fine.

When school started We put the boys in school in Quincy and as we were in Washington at the time school started we had to transfer Sis to Vancouver to school. Once school got going I went to work as a waitress at the Turf Cafe. I worked 4 to 12 as Jim was home with the boys. While working here I had my first time of seeing more than one African American at once. The Turf was a bus stop and a bus full of Air Force men stopped. All in Air Force blues and all African Americans. I took all the orders, when I started to take them out they all looked alike. They laughed at me and when I went out with plates I would say what I had and they would tell me who ordered it. That was a first for me.

Every Friday night one of the prominent business men from town would bring his wife in for dinner. They always sat in the Dining room, it got to be a joke to all waitresses. Whoever waited on them knew they would end up with no tip. He always left a dollar bill on the table and then went out to pay the check, his wife left the table after him and always picked up the tip on her way out. One new years evening the waitress that was in the dining room accepted drinks when offered. We were not to drink on the job. Anyway finally the Cook asked the boss why they were only getting orders for hamburgers out of the dining room? When the boss went to investigate it seemed no matter what was ordered the tipsy waitress ordered hamburgers. Everyone was getting a kick out of it but the boss. So he told the waitress to take off and celebrate New Years. I was put in the dining room for the rest of the shift. I also had my first experience with Spanish speaking men. Maybe one out of ten that came in to eat could speak English. They were seasonal workers up there working in the potato crops. They always sat at the counter and took some time to get their order as the one would translate for all of them.

When we first arrived in Quincy I could not cash a check at the grocery stores. I asked why and they said we were on their list for hot checks. I finally went to the credit bureau and found out the James A Delong from Everett had moved there with six or eight kids. Got this straightened out that we were James E DeLong. They gave me a card to carry. Didn't have and more trouble with cashing checks but one day the Sheriff came into the Cafe and told the boss he wanted to put a garnishment on my wages for a tractor we bought and never paid for. The boss told him he would but that they would have a law suit against them as they had the wrong people. The Sheriff did some checking and came back and apologized to me.

We had put Sis in school in Vancouver, friends of ours in Portland took her out of school one Friday and put her on the plane for us to Moses Lake we picked her up there. She was home for Saturday and early Sunday morning we had to take her back to Vancouver. We stopped somewhere along the way for dinner. Dennis always had liked liver and this day that is what he wanted. When it was served to him it was a real thick piece and real strong. That cured him on liver. Either his dad or I traded our dinner with him and he would not eat liver any more. That was such a long drive to take her back we made arrangements with Chuck and Hazel to pick her up and take her back to school from the air port for us after that.

Butch wasn't feeling to well one day, the boys had twin beds, there was a night stand between the beds. We had an aquarium on it filled with guppies. It seemed every week when I cleaned it there were a lot more. Butch was lying on the bed and he would tap the side of the tank and the fish would all swim to the spot. He hit it a little hard and it broke the fish and water whooshed out on the bed. We picked up the bed spread and put it in the bath tub. Put the plug in and water then shook out the fish. I don't think we lost to many. What to do with all the guppies? We put them in fruit jars and the boys took them to school they must have had enough for each room

Christmas was on us and I was so homesick for Montana and my family, we took of on the train for a week. We had a wonderful time. I have a picture of Mother , Esther, Myrtle and myself sitting under Myrtles Christmas tree. This is the last time I saw my Mother alive. This was Christmas of 1957 I think.

On our way back on the train, when we got on in Eureka they told us standing room only. We stood and sat on luggage, finally were told to go to the dinner we could sit in there. This went on all the way to Spokane. We finally got seats then. Didn't have to much farther to go. When we got from the train in Quincy Butch had gotten a bow and arrow for Christmas and he had carried it. You couldn't put it in a suitcase. He hit the conductor in the head with it getting off. The conductor said that's all right sonny. Not half as bad as some of the things that has happen to me on this run.

Now it is time to send Sis back to school. I called Hazel and told her what day and flight she would be

on. We took her to Moses Lake and it was storming like you can't believe. We waited a long time and finally they said there was a break and the plane would take off. So she left, we had no sooner gotten home till the land lady came to get us for a phone call. It was a stewardess calling from Yakima and she said they were grounded and she would keep Sis with her and call the number in Portland when they did get there. I called Hazel and told her our little girl was in Yakima but with the stewardess so would be all right and she would get a call when they got in. About a half hour later she called me back and said they had Sis . The airport had called her and said they had a child there by herself who gave them the phone number she had and what were they to do with her. She told them she would be right there. She was told Sis was not kept in Yakima at all the plane had came right on in. That was Sis's last plane ride till she went to College.

Our little Butch had quite a year in Quincy. He had tooth aches for years on his front teeth. When he was three years old his front teeth had rotted. Finally a Dentist pulled the four front ones. His permanent teeth started to rot when he was about seven years old. They would not hold filling. We took him to dentists all over, they told us they could not be saved, finally a Dentist at Quincy was truthful and said they can be saved but I don't know how to do it. There is a Dentist in Wenatchee that was my instructor at dental school, take him in to him. We did and they had to pull the four front ones by now. They took the enamel from the rest of his teeth and covered them with plastic. We were told that would probably hold and last him through his school years. He was fit with a partial for the four front ones. That Dentist did a wonderful job. Butch is now 48 years old and has taken care of his teeth but still has them. The Dentist said he believed he had to much acid in his system and it had eaten the enamel from his teeth. It took us a few years to get the bill paid it was $1500.00 at that time with both of us working we were making about $4000.00 a year. But it was worth it our son had no more tooth aches and looked so nice when he got his new front teeth.

Sleigh riding time OH BOY. They went over by the school and weren't gone long when a boy came running and yelling Butch cut his leg off and is bleeding all over the football field. It was on a Saturday and Jim was home he took of running to the field and there laid Butch. He had hit a rock and run the sled board into his upper leg. There was a cattle feed lot close by and the kids decided that was Butches blood they were smelling. Jim carried him home and we found a Doctor. He cleaned it all up and put something like eighty stitches in it. It didn't heal in the center so the Doctor said he would need skin grafting. We had no insurance but knew it had to be done so we went into Moses Lake Hospital and it was done there. It was so very hard to see my little one put to sleep for surgery he had already been through so much that year. They took a patch of skin from his left leg and sewed it on his right leg. It all went well and he went home the next day. He spent about six weeks on crutches over all of that. When he was about fourteen we finally got that all paid for. After he was back on his feet again they were outside playing in the snow one night and a policeman came to our door with Butch, seemed the kids were throwing snowballs at cars and Butch picked a Police car to hit. We were told to have him at the Police station the next evening after school. When the kids were dried up bathed and ready for bed they were sitting on the divan and Dennis looked at Butch and said "you are my big brother and I sure do like you but with all the money you have cost Mom and Dad this year now you just have to go to jail." Jim took him down the next evening and they went in and talked to the Police Chief. He gave Butch some marbles to play with out in the hall then called the man in that had told us to bring him down. He told him he thought a scolding was all that had been necessary in this case and never bring a small child in like that again. Then he told Jim to go get his son and take him home. Butch took the marbles back into him and he told him to keep them.

We had a real cold windy winter there in Quincy. Some of the people were stacking bales of hay around their trailers it looked terrible. I told Jim if he put any around ours I would move out. This was before people skirted their trailers. One day the wind blew so hard it blew our trailer up enough so that the blocks all fell out from under one side. The rest of the winter I just knew we were going to blow over but no one did.

We were all buying our milk by the gallon from a farmer a little way south of town. One person would go out and get milk for everyone. It was a cold slick day and my turn to go for milk. The kids had gone to school so I gathered up 9 gallon jugs and took to the road to go get milk. I had 5 full gallons on the seat and 4 on the floor. I hit a slick spot and by the time I got straightened out in the road I had 9 gallons on the floor. I went on home and the milk was running out under the back doors. I had 5 still intact. Delivered them got more jars and went back for 4 more gallons. I took the floor mats out of the car and put them on the floor of the wash house to scrub with a broom and hot soapy water. Then hosed them of. This went on most of the winter. The milk soured in the floor mats and stunk like you can't believe. Finally when spring came and I could hang them out for a week I finally got rid of the smell.

Some one at work was telling about a trailer moving rig the Bank had for sale it was a 1947 Chevrolet truck someone had bobbed to haul trailers. It had been tied up in an estate for a couple of years and been setting behind the bank. We didn't want to run into another broken brake line on the Cadillac so decided we would find out about this truck. Went to the bank and they showed it to us. The paint had been sandblasted from it while it was sitting behind the bank from the sand and wind. We put a battery in it and it started right up sounded real good. Not to many miles and only $400.00 so we bought it. It still had some prefabricated tires on it with the red dot on them. We took it home and decided it had to be painted. We lived by the silicon plant there in town. When the plant was running it put out a fine powder at times. The town people complained about it so much that the plant paid their payroll in $2.00 bills so the local people would realize how much they helped the economy. Our trailer was blue and white so we got paint the same color as our blue trim and some brushes and one day decided it was time to do it. We had just started and the powder started falling but it seemed to go right into the paint and made a good smooth job. That paint was still on it when we sold it and it never even chipped. I decided to drive it to work one night for some reason. I could shift it and make it go. Never thinking about where reverse was. I drove it and parked it up against the building. Went in and worked my shift and goes out at midnight to go home. The truck started fine but where was reverse? I tried everything. Finally went back into the bar and had to ask a man to come back it out for me. I never drove it again.

By now spring was here. One day I was out getting in the clothes when some of the gals asked if I wanted to go bowling? Sure let me take the clothes in first. I took them in and laid them on the divan (which I never did) got ready and went bowling. We had been there a while and I noticed this couple had came in and were watching us. They looked familiar It finally dawned on me it was Doris and Clyde, Jims brother and sister-in-law from Denver. The last Address they had from us was The Dalles. They were sent to Lebanon then on to Quincy. Finally tracked us down. Seemed they were about to split partnership with their partners in Denver and each take a store, so they decided on a vacation before they really got tied down. I was so ashamed when we went in the trailer and there were clothes all over the divan. They spent three days with us we sure did enjoy them. This was the first time any of Jims family other than that one time his Mother came, had ever came to see us. But my family didn't come either. I guess everyone was working and raising a family.

Job over moving time again now we would try our new trailer towing truck. We decided to go into the Seattle area closer to the union hall. We moved to Kent. The boys were put in school there to finish out the year. I didn't go to work as we kept thinking he would get called out on a job some where. I learned here if you ran out of propane in the middle of a meal you could pour hot water over the tank and get a little more gas out of the tank. Our T.V. always sat on the top of the refrigerator. Now you realize how heavy T.V.'s were in the 1950's. When we moved we always sat it on the floor. When we moved from Quincy, I was following Jim up Stevens Pass. I asked Butch if he and his Dad had taken the T.V. down? He said no. When he got to the top he stopped to check the trailer and it was still sitting there. During our stay in Kent we were living on unemployment and so broke. Our Television went out, we didn't have the money to call a repair man. We were without it till Jim got called on another Job and got his first pay check all it was was a 50¢ fuse. Plus a $5.00 service call. There was a terrible odor up by the wash house for nearly a week they could not find where it was coming from. Finally traced it to a small trailer parked up there. It was locked and the manager could not get in. He said an elderly man lived there. No one had seen him for some time. They called the police who broke the door in and found the man dead. They said he may have been dead for two weeks or so. The heater was turned up pretty high. They finally pulled the trailer way off in a field and took the man out of it. It was still sitting there when we moved.

When we moved into this park the manager said we would have to unhook as he parked the trailers with a hoist on his cat. That way he got them lined up the way he wanted them. So we did and he could not lift the front of our trailer. He said I don't know what you have in there but I guess you will have to park

it. Jim hooked back up and put it right in where he wanted it. The man just stood there. He finally said what have you got in there. I told him just what we had to have. I opened the front door and here in our front room was an Oil barrel, sleds, wagons, bikes, and a front step and a variety of other things. He just shook his head and walked off.

The job Jim got called on finally was at Redmond Washington not to far so he drove till he got that first check we had in a long time. Then we moved. We were in a trailer court with some other construction people. The first time we were back with Shorty and Joanne Taylor since the Mad Turks in Kennewick. George and Meril McBride lived at Snohomish they had bought a place in the country there. We visited them quite often. The trailer court was nice it was flat and by a creek. There was a small store out on the road to get things you forgot in town. We had our fill of oatmeal, beans and macaroni and cheese when we were at Kent. We were parked by a double deck trailer. They had a swamp cooler on the top. We had put up our awning. One nice day on a week end I decided I would bar B Q hamburgers. I wanted to keep the mess down so lined the Bar B Q with foil. It was fine till the grease dripped in on the coals and the foil, it burned and smoked. The smoke went out from under our awning and was pulled into their swamp cooler and down into their trailer. They came running out thinking they were on fire. These same people I cut their T.V. cable in half mowing our grass one day. It lay on top of the ground and ran over one corner of our yard. Snip no more T.V. I had to go confess to them. Jim spliced it when he got home. They finally moved. We didn't know them.

One day Joanne decided we should take all of our kids we each had three and go camping. I don' know where we went. All I can remember is we made lean to's from tree branches and slept on the ground. All I could think of was my little girl wandering of from camp and not being able to call her. So I kept real close to her and was glad to get home. The kids had a good time. All the time the children were growing up their Dad didn't do any golfing. But while here he did go up to Arlington a couple of times. One of the other gals and I decided we would play golf also. We got someone to watch the kids and we played nine holes while the men played eighteen. We didn't keep score as we didn't know how. The men told us to let everyone play through. The courses were not to crowded then. We didn't notice any one behind us and after I swung at a ball about three or four times some one said Lady if you would keep your eye on the ball you might hit it. I was very embarrassed and didn't play golf again for many years.

We got an awful lot of wind at Redmond and it came up one day when the men were at work. Our awning blew up on top of the trailer and the poles were flying around it is a wonder they didn't puncture the roof but they didn't. So that night the men got it down and anchored it a little better.

On the fourth of July the land lord tried to get people to stay off the highways so he said he would furnish the meat if all the women would bring other things for a pot luck picnic down by the creek. The day before the fourth he went down and dug a big hole about three feet deep and four feet long. He had the kids help put a bunch of river rocks in the bottom. Then he put a lot of wood in it. Nearly filled it with wood. Early the next morning he went down and started a fire. When it burned down to nothing but coals he put his meat in. He had wrapped the roasts in foil and then tied them up in wet burlap bags real tight, He then put rhubarb leaves and lettuce leaves in on top of the hot rocks, the meat and more leaves. Then he scooped the dirt back into the hole. This was about 10:00 o'clock. The earth worms really came up out of the ground over the hot rocks. One woman would not eat the meat because of this. About four o'clock he dug it up and unwrapped the meat and put it on platters, it was so good. I have always been going to try it but never have. That evening after playing a lot of games and the kids playing in the creek. There was fireworks a great fourth of July.

Our carpet in the trailer was getting in pretty bad shape. I thought there would be tile under it so proceeded to tear it out one day. Big surprise nothing but plywood. When Jim came home here I was no flooring. We decided that we would get tile squares and lay them ourselves. We found some gray ones that went pretty good with what was already in there and the man sold us some black glue to stick them down with. He didn't tell us to spread it real thin. We used plenty. After a while it started to work up between the tiles. I worked and worked on it but never did get it all off. Our Divan was getting dirty and worn so I thought I can recover that. Bought fabric and took all the old cover off and used it for a pattern. When I got the new cover on it was like a hammock where the back and seat fit, I knew I had done something wrong. I went and got Joanne to look at it. She asked me what I did with the piece of canvas that was sewn down the middle of the old one. I looked and it was still there. We took it all apart again and I sewed this in place and put it back on. Then she pulled it down between the two sections real tight and told me to put a tack between her two fingers. You guessed it I hit her finger.

We finally got it finished and it looked real nice. I had a clean front room with black oozing up between the tiles once in a while. I always was making new curtains for our trailers.

We decided it was time to save our income tax return and go to Oklahoma this year. So with saving a little more it was about time for a two week vacation. The Cadillac was now 12 years old we thought we should get a newer car. We bought a 1955 oldsmobile. We went to Denver first to see Doris and Clyde. They had just moved into a new house on fourth avenue in Lakewood. Clyde decided he would go to Oklahoma with us so we took his new station wagon on down. We had a nice trip it was awful hot. This time Jim's brother George and his wife Maggie and daughter Margie Louise from Louisville Kentucky were there. We had a great family reunion. They were all there but Dale and Lou Ella. This is the first time I ever ate home made Pimento Cheese. They ground up American cheese and pimentos and mixed mayonnaise with it, made real good sandwiches.

When we were going back to Denver Clyde told us when they split partner ship they could see a divorce in the making with the other couple so they didn't want the business in the middle of that. The four of them sat down in the middle of the front room floor and flipped a coin to see who got what. Doris and Clyde got the new store on 80'th and Federal in Westminister and Gambles got the one on Colfax. Doris and Clyde got to keep the old name of DEE GEE kwick stop. He asked us why we didn't move to Denver and we could both work for them? They would train us and it would be year around work. Our past year in Construction had not been good with long stretches between jobs and a lot of days they didn't work because of rain. We talked it over and before we left Denver we told them we would be there as soon as we could get things situated so we could move. When we left Denver we had a couple of passengers as far as Portland. Mrs. Davies and Irene. Doris's mother and her niece. Irene had a wedding veil in a box that we shuffled around in the car. There were four adults and three children. A little crowded but O.K.

We stopped in Salt Lake and seen the Mormon church grounds they were real pretty. Later in the day we stopped at a store and got picnic things and some Dry Ice for Mrs. Davies medicine bag that had to be kept cold. When she went to take the medicine it was frozen solid. So we had to go back to regular ice. Some where north of Salt Lake we stopped at a small town and got a Motel big enough for all of us. Had breakfast the next morning and took off. Along about noon we decided to find a nice park and have our picnic. We seen a nice grassy spot with trees in Boise Idaho. No tables but we spread our things out and sat on the ground and were eating, a man in a pickup drove up and said "We don't mind you folks eating here but please don't leave a mess. You know you are eating in the cemetery". We didn't know. After we finished and packed every thing and everyone in the car we drove on over the hill and then could see we were indeed in the cemetery.

We made it into Portland late in the afternoon and dropped them at the bus depot. They were going to a town on the coast of southern Oregon. We continued on home. The car had started to act up when we were in Oregon.

We took the car to a garage and found out it needed an awful lot of work done on it. Jim told George McBride he could have it if he wanted to take over the payments. We were wishing we had our old Cadillac back now. George took the car and we bought a 1955 Cheverolet.

It was time for school to start. Sis went back to Vancouver. Butch was in Jr. High this year he was in the seventh grade and Dennis in the third. He came home from school the first day with a note from his teacher wanting proof of his age. He said the teacher had told all the kids that were eight years old to stand on one side of the room and those that were nine to stand on the other. He sat in his seat. She asked him why? He told her he was only seven. She thought he was in the wrong grade. I went to school the next day and got it straightened out, He would be eight the end of the month.

We sold our trailer towing truck with no problem. Got what we had paid for it. We didn't think it would pull our trailer to Denver. The people we sold it to pulled their trailer to Texas, back to Washington and to Arkansas and we lost track of them so don't know where else it went.

We tried to sell our trailer but no luck. We ended up trading it in on a new 50 ft. 10 wide Nashua and having the new one delivered in Denver. Doris and Clyde got us a place to park it out on North Federal.

We stayed in our old trailer and they were to pick it up on October 31. We rented a U-Haul trailer, they put a hitch on the chev. for us. We were really loaded. Jim quit his Job we took the three children out of school and headed for Denver. I was driving in Wyoming and the wind was whipping that U-Haul all over the road. I turned it over to Jim in a hurry. We made the trip fine no problems at all. I do wish we would have gone by way of Montana. We didn't. And I was never to see my dear Mother alive again.

We arrived in Denver and our trailer arrived three days later. We got all moved in and the boys in school. Doris and I took Sis to Colorado Springs to school. They ran a lot of tests on her and wanted to know if she had had some private tutoring? She was ahead of her age group in their school. I told them no she had started in Oregon at age four. They said that told them why she was so advanced. They didn't start them till six. They put her in her level with older children but in the dormitory with her age group. We had to change the laundry marking on all of her clothes. Doris and I were sitting there sewing and she was wandering around and she came into the room squealing and laughing. she had run into a little red headed girl she had gone to school with in Oregon. When we left her that day she was perfectly happy.

After all was settled we went to work in the store in Westminister. It was at 80th and Federal. I worked the A.M. shift from 7-3. Jim worked P.M. 3-11. He made $75.00 per week. I did the same thing he did but made $1.00 per hour or $40.00 a week. One day I get a C.O.D. in the mail from a photographer in Redmond Washington. I got it out and unbeknown to me Butch and Dennis had gone to the store by the trailer court in Redmond one day and had their pictures taken. They were in play cloths, but they were some of the best pictures they ever had taken. The Post Office forwarded them, to us.

We went to work in the stores in Denver October 19th 1959 and worked there till September 30th 1968.

We had not been in Denver long when Clyde started to build another store it would be at third and Sheridan in Lakewood. When it was finished, we stocked it and had the grand opening. Then people started to bring things back. They tasted like Kerosene. It was traced to a cement sealer that was put on the floor. One night Doris and I scrubbed the whole store with scrub brushes and a strong soap. It was some better but was still there. Finally they tiled the floor and that got rid of it. Everything except can goods had to be replaced. Grandma DeLong had sent a box of home made noodles. We decided we would have to add more noodles to make enough for all of us. We ruined them all with noodles from that store. Some of the companies picked up their products and replaced them that helped a lot. So it was not a total loss.

There was a family living in this trailer court that had a son Dennis played with they were in the same grade in school. The father worked for Beacons as a driver of a moving truck. I was talking to the mother in the wash house one day. She told me she had some sheets and pillow cases to wash that her husband had brought home. She said they had not bought any linen since he went to work for this Co. When he packed households they didn't miss a sheet or towel here or there. I decided I would never have any moving company pack and move me, even if I could afford it. I realize this was probably one in a thousand and I am sure he finally got caught.

Dennis had a boil on his arm and I was cleaning it up and putting a bandage on it one morning before he left for school. I told him the core would probably be ready to come out that evening. He wanted to know if it would hurt? I told him it could some. He got a funny look in his eyes and passed out in my arms. Scared me half to death, I yelled for his Dad who was in bed asleep. He came running into the front room and by then Dennis had came to and seemed all right He went on to school and the boil finally took its coarse and he was over that ordeal.

Butch and Dennis were outside playing one day and wrestling as usual. Dennis was on top of Butch when he rolled over knocking him off. Another broken collar Bone. Same one as before. The Dr. set it and told him one more time and they would have to put a pin in it. That was the last broken collar bone. He had a Dentist appointment in the same building as the Dr. was in. When we came out of the Dentist Dr. English seen him and told me to bring him in a room he wanted to adjust the ace bandage on his shoulder. He was standing in front of the Dr. getting his bandage rewrapped when he asked me if he had to have any dental work done. I told him one filled and maybe one pulled. He slumped over and into the Dr.'s arms passed out again. The Dr. asked me if this had happened before. I told him once. He told me to bring him in the next day for an exam. They couldn't find anything wrong with him, so decided it was caused from fright of being hurt.

I did some leather tooling for Christmas Presents again this year. I was making purses for my Mother and Mother-in-law. I would start right after dinner and work for a couple of hours on them every night. One evening there was a knock on the door. I went to the door and there stood my neighbor lady. I asked her in, she looked around and then wanted to know what I was building? I told her nothing. She said every evening she heard this tap-tap-tapping in our house and had told her husband she was going to find out what was going on. I told her and showed her what I was doing. Also said if it bothered them I would try to do it at another time. She said no it really didn't bother them they were just curious. Then she had me make a purse for her.

This Thanksgiving we had at Dorises. We worked every holiday and every weekend for ten years in the stores. Dorises Mother started the dinner. The Men would eat then come to work and we would eat when we got home. Christmas went the same way. We spent it at Doris and Clydes. Jims cousins Howard and Iva and Jack Kennedy were there also. Dorises brother Gene Davies had moved to Denver from California and was working in the store also.

Come spring everyone in the Trailer court that had children were given a notice that the first of the next month we would have to move out. They were going adult only. We found a place to park the trailer in Edgewater. Butch went to Belmont Jr. High. This is where he started to take music and he chose a stand up Base Viol. He didn't like to play it with the bow he preferred to pick it. Dennis went to Edgewater elementary school. The trailer court was on a hill and down below was a drive-in theater. We could watch the movies without any sound from our yard.

Butch had a paper route here for the Denver Post which was an evening paper. He had an old green bike that he had taken the fenders from for some reason it was really a bad looking bike. He used it to deliver papers. He had apartment houses. People would move out and not let him know, someone else would move in and when he would go to collect they would say we didn't order the paper and would not pay for it. So this venture didn't last to long.

Clyde had built two more stores, one on 80th and Wadsworth and one out towards Golden on Ralston Road. As we gave curb service in these stores he needed more help. There were a couple of men from Denver working for him. He hired Harvey and Lavonne Johnson from Coose Bay Oregon to come and work she was Dorises Niece. Barb and Raymond Gibson from Oklahoma this was another of Dorises Nieces. And Virgil Delong from Tulsa Oklahoma. His wife Maggie went to work at Coors in the office and worked there till she retired.

Virgil finally quit and went to work at Coors porcelain plant. They bought a house in Golden their two children graduated from High school in Golden. They are still living in the same house now both retired from Coors.

Clyde and Raymond got into it over something and they moved to Pueblo where he went to work in the steel mill They had a third child here and eventually moved back to Oklahoma and got a divorce.

Harvy and Lavonne had two little boys they lived down the street from us. One evening she wanted to borrow our walking sprinkler. I showed her how to set it on the hose. When the men came home from work about midnight. Here was the sprinkler in the middle of the road at the end of the hose jumping up and down. She had put it on wrong so it jumped off instead of hitting the shut off.

We had decided to stay in Denver we had year around work and a steady job we both liked. We looked into using Jim's G.I. bill for a house. We were eligible we found a lot down a little and across the street from Doris and Clyde in Lakewood it was at 6965 W. 4th ave. We were where Quay came to a dead end on fourth ave. Found a contractor and got started. We put our trailer up for sale, didn't have to much equity in it and ended up only getting a house full of furniture for it. After we sold it and before we got moved out of it one of Denver's famous hail storms hit and one side of the trailer looked like someone had taken a hammer to it.

We found a three bedroom house for rent just off of Alameda not far from where we were building. The people at the store decided to surprise us with a house warming there. They arrived with lots of food and we had a real good time.

The house was on Lamar a customer at work asked me where we had moved to? I told her we had rented a house on Larmer and would live there till our house was built. She said not Larmer? She finally ask where the street was and when I told her she laughed and said Larmer is the skid row down town that is why I was questioning you.

Our house was a three bedroom brick with hardwood floors a big two car Garage. Taraza tile window sills. Full basement really a beautiful home. The kids were out playing one day when we got another of those hail storms. They took refuge in the dug out at the ball park. I didn't know where they were and went out looking for them, One hail stone cut my arm and I really got beat with them. After the storm stopped here they came and they were all fine. That evening the contractor came over to tell us we would need a new roof on the house even though that one had only been on less than a week the hail had ruined it. His insurance paid for it. He came to the store one day and told me I would have to pick out the color for my bathroom fixtures or he would put red and black in. I had been trying to make up my mind. I picked blue and was never sorry it was a real light blue. While the contractor was at the store a little girl came in and told me she had two tickets left on the station wagon they were selling raffle tickets on and would I buy them. I told her to sell him one and I would buy the other one. He won the new station wagon.

Butch went to Alameda Jr. High this year he still took music. He would come home carrying that big Base so he could practice on it. Dennis went to North Alameda Grade School. He came home and told me he had a man teacher. I asked him how old his teacher was? He said pretty old. He must have been all of 25 years old. Dennis decided he wanted to take music also and he chose a snare drum. We bought one of them for him.

Sis was home one weekend that fall and the kids and the three across the street talked us into letting them sleep in a tent across the street. They were all settled down when we went to bed. About one o'clock in the morning Sis came in and told me her brothers were gone. I went to the tent and sure enough the three boys were gone. I woke up the mother of the other boy and we looked and looked and were about to call the police and here they came. They said they were over a couple of blocks in an empty field robbing magpie nests. I really don't know where they were. That was the end of the sleeping in tents.

I was working in the store on Ralston road one day when an irate women came in and told me she didn't appreciate me selling her son a playboy magazine. I told her we didn't sell them to children. She said he was on his way home from school and told her he had bought it at this store. I finally asked her where he went to school, and wanted to tell her maybe he stole it. But I didn't. She said he was coming home after football practice and he went to Regis College. So I told her if he was old enough to be in college we probably had sold it to him as he was a young man not a child.

I was driving down fourth avenue not far from our house one day, I felt a bump and knew I had run over something. I had not seen anything. When I put my left leg out of the car a black dog came out from under the car and bit me on the calf of my leg. I got back in the car and backed up and then seen the little dog I had run over. I honked the horn till a man came out of the house I told him what had happened. He said they probably ran out from the hedge to bark at the car. The black dog had bitten two times before that and to go get a tetanus shot and he would destroy the dog. When I got to the Doctors office they had to cut my pant leg as my leg had swollen so much. I don't think I have ever had anything hurt like that did. Three canine teeth had gone in and the fourth one had been broken and only left a real good bruise.

We had bought a 1961 V.W. bug as we needed two cars to go to work as we were working different shifts at different stores

We had this one customer that was always asking if we were in our new house yet. I was finally able to tell her yes. She asked what my decor was and I told her early Salvation Army. She never asked me another thing about my house.

Mother was to come see us with Esther and Clyde so I hadn't told her about our house as I wanted to surprise her. We moved in July first 1961. I had hurried and gotten drapes and curtains up at all the windows. We were invited to Johnnie Fraleys for a Bar B Q on a Friday night. Doris called and told me Esther was trying to get a hold of me. I called her and she said Mother was in the Hospital nothing to worry about but wanted me to know and they would not be coming She said she would keep me posted but no need to come. It was an asthma attach.

I hadn't been to work very long the next morning when Clyde called and told me I had better come if I could they had performed a tracheotomy during the night and she was breathing easier but Esther was with her at the Hospital. I called Doris and she said go by all means and we could take their Station wagon. Jim and Butch packed for all of us. Doris came out and relieved me and we were on our way. We drove straight through. We were in Billings at one A.M. getting gas I wanted to call and Jim said I have been driving all day and you must take over now. If anything has happened you won't feel like driving and there is nothing you can do. This is about the time Mother passed away. She was only 64 years old. She had asthma for so many years and all her labored breathing her heart just gave out. When we were outside of Garrison early the next morning the car started acting funny. So I woke Jim and he took over. When we reached Missoula we went to a ford Garage and they said the fuel pump was going out but they didn't have one. They called the garage at Ronan and he had one and could put it on if we got there. We made it and went and had breakfast while they put it on. When we got to Whitefish we found out we were to late. Went on to Eureka and found that we had quite an assortment of clothes packed in that foot locker.

We stayed for the funeral. Esther, Myrtle and I went to the house and went through some things. We knew Dad would still be living there but Mother wanted her clothes removed from the house. I took her treadle sewing machine home with me. And a Dish I wanted. We each took a couple of things. Also threw away two shoe boxes of those pictures you put in a machine many years ago and they looked three-D . The machine was gone, we could not find it anywhere. We threw the pictures in the trash. When I got back to Denver I was one day in a second hand store and found a lot of the machines for $2.50 but the pictures were from $5.00 on up.

I had found a Dr. in Denver that gave you those rainbow pills to lose weight for $10.00 a month I had been going to him for about a year and had lost a lot of weight. I went for my appointment and his office was closed. There was a sign on the door that said U.S. Government. Closed by the F.D.A. A week or so later there was an article in the paper about a women that had died and they thought it was caused by these pills. The Dr. ended up getting a prison sentence from it. No more rainbow pills for me.

Mother and Dad had adopted Lee a year or so before Mothers death. He was Bobbies son from his first very short marriage. When Mother died Myrtle and Wayne took him and they raised him. He is now married and has two children after working 13 years in California they live in Helena. Lee worked as a machinist all this time till his wrists gave out he is now going to college. His wife is a registered L.P.N. and works for the state in Helena.

Chrystal also joined the family during this period of time. Her mother was married to our brother Harold, they were living in Whitefish and had a baby boy. Her mother died and Harold could not raise two children. He couldn't even take care of himself. Esther and Clyde adopted Chrystal she was I believe 8 years old. She is now married has two girls and lives in Whitefish. She works for a law firm and is a Paralegal.

The baby boy was adopted by a Minister and his wife in Libby. I think he was raised in the Billings area. His name was Murry.

I one day drove the bug to work and parked it facing this high chain link fence that was by the store. I needed some change from the bank. Dorises brother came by and I asked him if he would take my car and go for it. He said sure. I asked him if he new how to get it in reverse? He said he had never gotten into a car yet he could not drive. Finally I looked up from the register and there he stood in the door with a silly grin on his face. He said every gear he put it in it went forward and was up against the fence. I went out and backed it up for him and showed him how to shift it so he could go to the bank for me.

Jim was driving the same car one day when the roads were slick. He arrived at the store with the left front fender all bent in. I asked him what had happen? He said he had stopped at a stop sign, by the stop sign. In other words he had slid into the stop sign.

Butch entered Alameda High School as a Freshman. He played Football his only year. I had bought a 1947 Ford woody station wagon. I hauled a lot of kids to football games as the parents had to see they got there. One day I was stopped at a stop light a women was making a left turn and she clipped me. She got out and looked at the car. I asked her if she hurt my car? She burst out laughing and said I can't tell. It had chunks of wood that had fell off all over it. She really didn't hurt me at all. I was driving down the road one day and the head liner fell down so I stopped and took the box cutter I had in my purse and cut it the rest of the way out. We got a lot of service from that old car. Till Butch got his drivers license.

Dennis is still in North Alameda elementary. They needed a Den Mother when Dennis joined the Cub Scouts. No one had time, most of the Mothers didn't work. Well you guessed it I ended up with 14 Cub Scouts waiting on my front steps once a week when I got home from work. I had them till long after Dennis was no longer a Scout. Finally I went to a meeting and told them if they wanted their sons to be in the Cub Scouts one of them would have to take over as I was no longer available. After a month of no meetings one of them finally took over. I was taking them down in the basement to work on some wooden candle holders we were making for Christmas presents for their Mothers. I was ahead of them and both feet went out from under me and down I went full length of the flight of stairs on my rear and my back. Knocked the breath out of me and bruised me up a little and really scared 14 little boys. But we continued on with our project. In the spring Jim helped Dennis make his pine wood derby car. They drilled holes and melted solder then would go to the store and weigh it so it was just right. Sanded, painted and spent a lot of time on it and Dennis took first place. The next year I had a little boy who had no father so Jim took on two pine wood derby cars. When race time came the other little boy was so happy his car came in first and Dennises came in second.

Dennis decided he wanted a paper route. He chose the Rocky Mountain News which was a morning paper. They would be stacked on our front porch at 4 A.M. Then would have to be rolled up and rubber bands put on them. Saturday evening the Sunday funnies would arrive and Sunday morning the funnies had to be put in the papers. If they missed someone and the newspaper was called that cost the delivery boy a quarter and he only made something like fifty five cents a month on each customer. After a couple of months I talked him into giving that up.

When we had first moved into our new home, one evening it was getting dark and I called the kids in and no Dennis. No one knew where he was. We looked and called and drove the neighborhood. He was no where to be found. I was frantic and about to call the police when here he comes walking down the sidewalk. He had been playing in a kids back yard with a high board fence so we could not see him and he did not hear us calling. The boys were out riding Bikes one day and they locked wheels. Dennis was thrown from his bike and broke his arm. So Butch always said he broke Dennis's arm.

Butch had been having a lot of sore throats this year. Finally the Dr. said his tonsils had to come out. He said we might as well take both of the boys at the same time. Dumb me I let them take Dennises out also and he had never had any trouble with them. I took them both to

St. Anthonys hospital. Dennis was 12 years old and Butch was 17 so Dennis was put in the Pediatrics ward on the third floor north end and Butch in a room on the fourth floor south end. Now this hospital covers a city block. They had their tonsils removed a half hour apart. I made a trail from one end of that hospital to the other that day. I was feeding Dennis crushed ice and ice cream, then made a run to Butches room and he was sitting up in bed eating. I asked him where he got that tray of food? He said I was hungry and they brought me a menu so I ordered it. I took them home the next morning and they were not down long at all. While I was wondering around in the Hospital I went into a wing that was nothing but children with dog bites. Some of them were just covered with little black stitches. Remembering the pain I had with that bite I had my heart went out to them.

We had planted lawns in the front and back had the back yard fenced because of the dog. We had a good size tree in our front yard.

A lady wanted to breed her Pekingese dog with our male. She could not pay the stud fee so we got our pick of the litter. There was only one male so that is how we got Ming. Then later we got Hey Boi the same way. I had always swore there would be no dogs at our house. Years before this when we were living in Portland I had decided the kids needed a dog and had gone to the pound and gotten a big black pup. The next day I took Butch to school and Dennis to the baby sitter and I went to Barber School. When we came home the house was trashed. Everything he could get to he had tore up, knocked over planters and messed all over. We took him back to the pound and got a cute little curly haired black cocker pup. He cried for two days and nights. And with not being home we really had a mess and I knew we would never get him house broken so he was returned also. Then Tinker Boi was a Christmas gift to the kids and we had him for 15 years.

Now these dogs we had in Denver, by now we had three. When they heard the electric can opener running they were all at the back door thinking I was opening dog food. They were good dogs, no problem with barking or anything and they did sleep in the garage most of the time. After Dennis had his tonsils out he was in bed and I went into his bed room and Tinker Boi was in bed with him with his head on the pillow and all covered up. I asked Dennis what he thought he was doing and he said Tinker thinks he's a people. I told him I knew that but he didn't sleep in the bed.

At Christmas time Myrtle sent us a beautiful home made fruit cake. It must have been a good two pounds. It was on a cutting board all wrapped with clear paper and tied with a big bow. It was so pretty I put it under the Christmas tree. I came home from work one day and this little fuzzy pup was laying in the middle of the floor on his back with all four legs sticking up in the air, moaning like the dickens. About then the kids came in from school. I told them something was wrong with Ming. I sat him on his feet and he waddled around a little. Then we discovered that there was only a few crumbs of the fruit cake left on the board. I took him to the Vet, he told us that he would be miserable for a day or so but it wouldn't hurt him. I hope he enjoyed my fruit cake that I never got a bite of. We had him for a long time and finally gave him to a customer in Westminister. Hey Boi was a party color like Tinker Boi. I finally gave him to a woman that worked with me. She told me one day he scratched all the time. She said she knew he was clean as she bathed him every day and even put powder on him. I told her I thought she was drying out his skin. Dogs don't need a bath every day once a month maybe and then brush them good and forget the powder. He got over his scratching. This left us with one dog. Which was plenty.

Butch finished the walls in his bedroom in the basement. We never did get the bathroom finished down there. One morning Butch came up stairs and wanted to know if he could borrow some of Dad's shorts as he didn't have any in his drawer. I asked him where they all were? I had washed the day before that. He didn't know, we went down to his room and I took the broom and swept lots of dirty cloths out from under his bed. Easier to kick them there than walk into the next room to the clothes hamper. Any teenager will tell you that. Our front room was so large it would take a lot more furniture than we had. I decided to build a room divider to separate it into a Dining room on one end. Butch helped me we built it in the basement counter sunk the screws and really did a good job. It was a set of shelves. Sanded and varnished and all done Time to take it up stairs. It was about two inches to tall to go up the stairs. It ended up in Butches bedroom. May still be there. Butch was taking shop and metal shop in school and he built me a real nice one with planter boxes in the top and lattice work nearly to the ceiling. It had shelves under the
planter boxes.

We would all go to the Mountains early in the morning when we had a chance. We would build a fire and have hash browns, scrambled eggs and coffee. It was a pleasant get away from the city. Also picked choke cherries and wild plums.

I decided the kids should experience some camping. I borrowed an umbrella tent. Loaded the three kids and food in the Woody with all the blankets pillows pans and etc. to camp. We were going to this little stream that Doris and the kids and I had found the summer before. The rest were coming up for breakfast the next morning. Well we went up through Morrison and on up into the Mountains. Then with a left hand turn on to the creek. When we got there the creek had been rerouted some where else. But we had to stay so the rest could find us. We proceeded to wrestle the tent and finally got it up. Had our dinner , roasted marshmallows and finally went to bed. Later on cars started parking out front. We were in Morrisons lovers lane. When we came over the Mountain we ended up back down by Morrison. During the night some one hit the center pole and our tent collapsed on us. When the others arrived the next morning. I had no water for coffee. We moved on till we found a stream. I was called death valley Helen for a while after that.

Sis had friends in Denver and this summer we had a slumber party for her for her birthday. They didn't do much sleeping but seem to have a good time.

Clyde and Doris had taken one of Margarets boys to stay with them so he could finish college at Boulder. He worked in one of the stores and was three years older than Butch. He had his drivers license. He and Butch would use Clydes Station wagon once in a while. They ran it off the road into a field once but got it home O.K. Another time they were doing something for Clyde. Doris got a phone call at the store from Butch, he told her Robert was bleeding but they were O.K. The station wagon was crunched. Seems they had been hit by a truck. The station wagon was totaled out. After Robert started college up in Boulder that fall and had started going with Judy who lived in Evergreen he wanted to buy a car. Clyde said no. He bought and old one anyway. When he would come down to Denver from Boulder he would park it around the Corner from their house but we could see it from ours. Then he would say he caught a ride down with someone. He would leave it sit there till he left in the evening of the next day. He finally got caught and there was a big fight but he kept the car. Clyde would not let him talk to Judy on the phone only so long then he would come across the street and stay on our phone for another hour or so. A year later they got a phone call from Robert saying he and Judy had run away to Idaho and gotten Married. When she called her folks her father had to be taken to the hospital he was so shocked. They all converged on me as they thought I had known about it, but I didn't. Robert and Judy stayed in Boulder he finished college and got a degree in Business. They had two children Derik and Carrie They have since divorced but have maintained a good relationship and are in business together.

During the time Robert was living with Doris and Clyde he and Butch went to the Red Rock amphitheater to see Peter, Paul and Mary. They came home disappointed, The music that they could hear was good. The crowd was unruly. Robert got hit in the head by a beer bottle some one threw.

By now Clyde had four stores and was having trouble staying on top of it all, I helped Doris with the book work. In the ten years we worked at the stores there were fourteen hold ups. Never when Jim or I were on a shift. I always said if anyone pointed a gun at me they would not have to tell me to lay on the floor I would already be there.

This summer Doris had some relatives stop to see them one afternoon they had three small children. Clyde had just bought a new platform rocker with wooden arms. When the company had left Doris was straightening up the house and she noticed some one had carved an A in the arm of the chair. She called me and asked if I knew what she could do to hide it. We tried all kinds of furniture oils and Walnut sticks it dimmed it some but it was still there. She told the kids if Clyde asked them who had done it not to know anything about it. The next day I was at work and Clyde called me and said he had my three kids lined up in his front yard and one of them had carved on the arm of his new chair and would not admit it. I told him I didn't think so , he had better call Doris. Later Butch called me and said he didn't even apologize, he just said O.K. go on home.

He hired Dennis to rake leaves that fall and Dennis was doing a good job till Clyde got bossy and was trying to tell him how to do it. He put the bag of leaves in the trash can the rake in the garage and came home. End of leaf raking and Clyde done the rest himself.

It was now 1963. I had always said I would have all my kids out of High School the year I turned forty and I could do what I wanted to. By the end of August I didn't feel to well after school started in September Dennis was in the seventh grade Sis in the eighth grade and Butch a senior in High school I knew what was wrong with me but made a Doctor appointment to confirm it. I was 34 soon to be 35 and Jim was 39. I went to the Doctor and told him I thought I was Pregnant. He said well I don't know make an appointment for a month from now and we will see it could be something else. When I went in in October I said now I am three months along. He examined me and said well come into my office and we will talk. He told me yes I was pregnant and how did I feel about it? I told him great. He looked at me like I was nuts. Twelve years between the last two. He said lots of women my age had trouble accepting another child. When I told the rest of the family they were all thrilled. I had a great pregnancy and worked the full time. I had customers give me play pens carriers and all kinds of things I never had for the other babies.

In March Butch had gotten his drivers license, He had not had them to long when he hit a pickup broad side with the V.W. bug. No one was hurt he had a car full of young people with him. When we came home from work the car was not in the drive way and he came walking out of the house. He handed his Dad the car keys his drivers license and ticket. Jim asked him if anyone was hurt and he said no just the car. He had had it towed to the Volkswagon garage and they wanted us to call them. Jim handed him back the ticket and said" that is yours I will keep the others". He had been looking for work but had not been able to find any. His Dad told him you had better find a job, that ticket is your responsibility. If you don't have the money for the fine I hope you enjoy your stay in jail. He went out looking for a job after dinner and found one washing dishes at the L and M steak house about three blocks from home. The V.W. was repaired and Butch paid the $50.00 deductible. By now he and Jim had gone to court and he was fined $75.00 with $40.00 suspended. He let out a sigh of relief as he had $50.00 in his pocket. Of coarse he didn't know it but Dad would have paid the rest if he had been short. He called one night from work and asked if we could bring him a pair of pants as he had ripped the seam in the ones he had on. He had to have black pants. Jim took him another pair and went in the front door with them over his arm. The owner seen them and thought it was someone with a hidden gun to hold them up. When Jim asked for Butch he was relieved. While here Butch took the woody to work one night and called me to tell me the clutch had gone out of the car. We never had it fixed we should have but had it towed to the junk yard. I then bought an old Chevrolet car. It had a lot wrong with it I drove it for a short while and then put an add in the paper to sell it for $150.00. I ended up taking a 30.06 rifle and an old Ford car for it. The car was in good shape after I got all the trash and cigarette butts out of it. It was really a stinky mess.

Butch would take my car to some hills up by Red Rocks and try to think a V.W. was a Jeep he would climb all over the hills with it. He had made Channel 7 news with his wreck in the bug so I was hoping nothing else would happen.

I had spent my day off cleaning that big house we had. I had even waxed and polished all those hard wood floors. When I came home from work the next day I walked in the front door and could hear the boys laughing again. The Kitchen floor was soaked. Dennis was at the kitchen sink with the spray from the sink and Butch was on the patio with the hose. They were having a water fight through the kitchen window. When I seen it out the door I went, I got in the car and left. When I came back about 45 minutes later it was all cleaned up and they were sitting like angels again watching T.V. Dennis told Butch he thought they had lost me for sure that time.

There was a family lived across from us that had a son Butches age his name was Bob. He went to a private school some where in Denver. He had a little sister about ten years younger than he was. When they had to be gone some evenings they would hire Butch to baby sit with the phone. He would get calls from Australia and all over the world. He had a wonderful job, but also liked to gamble. He ended up losing their home and nearly everything they had. They then moved elsewhere. We don't know what ever became of them.

Doris had given me her old Ford car so I got rid of the older one I had. They had gotten a new 1964 Thunder Bird it was bright yellow and a real beauty. She hadn't been out of the Hospital to long after a hysterectomy the car was three days old I was pregnant.

We came to a red light and made a right hand turn. A lady in a little rambler came through the light and made a left hand turn she hit us in the side just in front of the drivers door and knocked us of the road into a parked wrecker. Really fixed up both front fenders on the new car. Then she kept going. Finally some one got her stopped and she came back. I was not hurt I only hit my head on the sun visor. Doris hit her stomach on the steering wheel and was a little banged up but not bad. They got rid of the Thunderbird before long and got a Lincoln.

Butch was 17 years old now and he found a Harley Davidson Motorcycle he wanted so bad. I wouldn't let him buy it. I could see him splattered all over the highway. So he found an old Ford car and bought it. It cost him nothing but money all the time he had it. Finally he needed a new battery and didn't have the money so we got one for him. Then the rear end went out of it. He sold it to a junk yard for about $10.00 and left the new battery in it.

On Butches 18th birthday I bought him a six pack of Coors Beer. In Colorado you can drink 3.2 beer at 18. He thanked me then said "but I wanted to buy it myself".

Butch always came in and sat on the edge of our bed when he came home and told us where he had been and what he had done. One night I was up reading when he came home and he said good night and headed for his bedroom. I soon went to bed and not long after I heard him in the bathroom, being very sick. He was lit to the gills and really was a sick kid. So he didn't keep it from Mom and Dad after all.

Dennis was in Alameda Jr. High. I was very pregnant by now with Kevin. I had a day off and not long after Dennis left for school I got a call from the Principle that I was to come and get him. He had broke a boys nose and they had to take him to the Hospital. I went to school and had no sooner gotten home with him till the phone rang and it was the boys Mother calling to tell me what a horrible child I was raising. She had no sooner hung up till the Father called and told me we owed a $250.00 Hospital and Dr. bill. I didn't have that kind of money and didn't know what to do, so I called the stores Attorney He said don't worry if it just happen this morning he doesn't have a bill yet. He said call him and be real nice. Just tell him to come to my office before noon with the bills and they will be taken care of. Well the man never showed up and we heard no more from them. Dennis went back to school the next day. The fight was over horse play before school started. One kid got behind Dennis and the other one pushed him backwards over him. He came up swinging and he connected with the nose. I was also called to school for a conference with his teacher. She told me he seemed very juvenile for a seventh grader. I asked her if she knew how old he was? She said no she had not looked and when she did and found out he was a year to two years younger than a lot of his class mates she decided he was doing great.

The baby was due May 10th which was Mothers day. I had been called to court on May third. It was over advertising at the store with Meadow Gold Dairy. It was something I knew nothing about. They really wanted Doris. I had a Dr. appointment and I asked him how I could get out of going to court. I had real high blood pressure and was still working and had to try to take it easy. He said you will only have to go tell the judge you don't know anything about it they have the wrong person or be flat on your back in the hospital.

I went to work on May 2nd and was putting up grocery's about 1 o'clock I went into labor. I finished stocking the shelves till three when my shift ended. I then went home took a bath and fed the boys. I told them I thought by morning there would be a new baby in the house. Dennis finally went to bed and Butch and I sat and played cards till about 10:30 I then called Doris and told her I had to go to the Hospital and called Jim and told him where I would be when he got off work at eleven. Doris came flying up our drive way and ran into the house, grabbed my suitcase and ran to the car. Butch and I stood there and laughed at her. When we got to St. Anthoneys hospital we had to go to the back door to get in there was a big long hall way and she and my suitcase were at the other end and I was only half way down the hall. She had never had any children and could not remember ever seeing a new born. Jim got there about 11:30 and at two o'clock May 3rd our beautiful perfect baby boy was born. This was Richard Kevin. And I did not have to go to court. The women in the room with me just had her sixth girl and between us we had ten children. When we told Sis she had a new brother. She said and I am still an only girl. But when she seen him she loved him as we all did. Esther called me and got through to me in the hospital late in the evening. Jim had let them know in Montana. I don't know how the call got by the Nuns late in the evening. They would not let any of the kids come see the baby. I went home on the third day. Butch was tired of cooking and Dennis tired of eating what he cooked. I came in the house and they looked at the baby and said what's for dinner. The boys and I had painted a used crib and it looked real nice. It was in our room and the dog loved that baby and slept under the crib. The next day I got caught up on the laundry. I was going to take a few months off from work. I took May and June. Then I got a call that they had no one to work the fourth of July. I told them I didn't have a baby sitter. They said bring him with you. We put him in a Banana crate just around the corner from the register and he was there for two days till I found a baby sitter who had him till we left Denver.

The stores had been put up for sale. Clyde had a heart attach and the Dr. said keep those stores and die or sell them and live. After they expanded to four stores they had more than they could keep a tight rein on and things weren't going as good as they had when there were only two. He couldn't put his finger on it but were not making the money they did with just two. They found a buyer in Roberts Dairy from Omaha Nebraska. They bought all four. The company officers came to Denver and asked us all to stay on with them. Then they took Jim and I to Dinner and asked if we would consider Jim taking the job as supervisor over the four stores and me keep on as a store manager and do the book work for the four stores and send it in every day to Omaha. It meant a good raise for both of us. This was in 1964. The first thing Jim had to do was get rid of Dorises brother Gene. He was taking money out of the cash register and going to the bar next to the store in Westminister and spending his time there. While leaving a young school boy in the store by himself. Jim was not to popular with the family for a little while but it was his job and had to be done.

We decided the V.W. had to go and Jim had his sites set on a new car that had just came out. A Mustang. We were going to look at them one night so I warmed a baby bottle for Kevin in the tea kettle. Just before we left I took a tea towel to take the bottle out. In doing so I must have touched the burner with it. I them laid the towel on the top of the cupboard between the built in oven and the stove top. Of we went to buy a new car. We were gone some time and came home with a new 1965 1/2 white Mustang. When I open the front door I could smell burned varnish. The towel had burned the top of the cupboard and up the wall by the built in oven and then burned out. We were lucky the whole house could have burned so very easy. I was known for leaving tea kettles on till they burned dry and the spout would melt off. Or a coffee pot on till it would go dry and the glass ones break. This scared me enough that I was always very careful after that. Our insurance repaired it.

Butch had been cooking at the Pizza Hut a few blocks from home the summer before his Junior year and during his Senior year. Dennis decided he wanted a new bike one of the small ones with the banana seat so he said he was going to get a job as he was only 12 years old I never did dream he would find one . I told him to go ahead. He was not gone to long and he came home all excited and said I have to eat supper and have a white shirt and go to work at Louigis at four O'clock. That was where Butch worked they had hired Dennis to wash dishes for 50Cp an hour. He finally saved enough to get his bike. He didn't have it long when it was stolen. He found it in the ditch and one wheel was broken. We got it fixed and he rode it for a while. He parked it in the garage one night and the next morning it was gone and we never did find it. The police said new bikes and race bikes were being stolen and they thought they were leaving the area.

Butch graduated in 1965. Right after graduation he went to Montana to work for Tommy Price during the summer. He bought a little motorcycle while he was in Montana.

When Clyde sold the stores he gave Jim and I each a $1,000.00 bonus for what we had done for them. We bought a 12 ft. camp trailer with $800.00 of it and decided we would take a family trip to Montana. Jim and myself, Dennis, Virginia and Kevin and our luggage filled the Mustang to the hilt. We loaded up and left for Montana. We went to the Tetons and Yellowstone Park. We had never been to either place. We had a room in the Tetons that was so full of beds a double, two twin and a home made crib that the kids had to walk over our bed to get to theirs. The next morning we went to Yellowstone park. We stopped at a cafe that was by Old Faithful for breakfast. They brought a highchair for the baby. It was an old wooden one and there was enough food dried around the sides of the tray to feed a baby pig a good meal. So I held Kevin while we ate. We had reservations at a motel in the village. A double bed two twin beds and a crib. When we checked in there was a double bed two twin beds and a net play pen with no bedding. We ended up putting swimming towels in the play pen for the baby and a jacket for a blanket. The room was so full of mosquitoes there were no screens and the windows were open. We found a drug store and bought some bug spray, went back and closed it all up and sprayed then decided we would go eat. We found a nice looking cafe and went in. The hostess said I can seat you but there will be no one to wait on you for an hour. Our help is going to eat now. It was straight up 6 o'clock. Jim said so are we and we got up and left, went back to the drug store and had hamburgers and milk shakes. That day we had seen Old Faithful and a lot of other geysers. The paint pots, The river, lake and the waterfalls. The next morning we got up and took off north. At one point there was a black bear in the road we stopped and he came over and put his paws on the car and his nose on the window. He looked us all over then we slowly took off and he walked away. We went to the hotel at the north entrance and had breakfast it was a lovely old Hotel. Clean and good food and good service. We looked over the area there and then took off for Montana.

On arriving at Eureka we went to Myrtle and Waynes. It was not long till here came a motorcycle roaring up in their driveway. It was our Butch. By now he had about enough of living in an apartment by himself in Montana. He was ready to return to Colorado. We told him we had no way of getting his motorcycle home. He said no problem he sold it. We were in the Mustang and he had a lot of stuff with him. He and Jim took two or three suitcases to Kalispell and shipped them home on the bus. We had a nice visit in Eureka and went to Whitefish to see Esther and Clyde. Then we headed home five adults and a baby in a four seated car. The kids kept shifting around in the back so no one would have to ride on the hump all the time. We had a great trip home.

We went through Glacier Park none of us had ever been there. Even though I was raised so close every time I had a chance to go I was working so never got there. We stayed that night in a Motel in Great Falls there was a pool in the Motel the kids made good use of it. The next day we went to Custers Battle Field and spent some time there. That night we stopped in Casper Wyoming. Our last night out we wanted to take the family to a real nice Cafe. Our Motel again had a swimming pool and Sis and Butch wanted to swim so they said bring us a hamburger and a milk shake. Jim, Dennis, Kevin and I went to eat, we went to a nice Italian Restaurant. It had red table cloths and linen napkins and a violin player. They brought a high chair with a metal tray for Kevin. He proceeded to pound on the tray and embarrass Dennis. I took everything out of his hands and held his hands and he thought we were playing so he was squirming and squealing. We were all glad when his food came, he then forgot the play and ate. We stopped at a drive in and got the hamburgers and milk shakes for the other two and the next morning we headed home to Denver. A great vacation.

Butches friends were all glad to see him. Patty Straight, A girl he had taken to his freshman Prom. I had to drive them they were neither one old enough to drive. And three of his buddies. They all spent a lot of time at our house.

Kevins first Christmas he would not leave the Christmas tree alone he was crawling. I came home from work one day and the boys had put the Christmas tree in the play pen so he could not get to it. There it stayed. Dogs nor baby could get to it.

In February of 1966 Butch came to the store one day and said he had something to tell me. I had tried to get him to go to college and he would not go. Vietnam was in full swing by now. He told me he and his three buddies had just gone down town Denver and joined the Marines. It was a real jolt I can tell you. He went and took his physical and did not pass because of his weight. They told him if he lost I think 30 lbs. he could leave with the other guys in about six weeks. He started taking Epsom salts didn't get far from the bathroom. Watched his food intake and lost enough to leave when they did. We took them to the Air Port to go to basic training in San Diego. I cried for two days. He was put in the Fat Farm in basic training. Come time for his graduation from boot camp one of the other boys Mother and I went to San Diego to see them. I drove myself to the airport and left the car there. I left after work and the next two days I had taken off. We arrived in San Diego and got a Motel. The next Morning we called a Taxi and went to the base. Way to early. We wandered around got run out of the obstacle coarse and shown where there was a coffee shop. We found out where the graduation would be and were some of the first ones in the building. I had seen my first palm trees on the base here.

At about 11 A.M. the Marines started coming in by platoons. Three of the four of them were in the same platoon. Ron had gotten himself in a little trouble and got set back a week or so. They were rushing them through a ten week course in eight weeks. When the boys platoon came in I could not find my son. When it was all over we went outside and our boys found us. The reason I had not been able to recognize Butch was because he was the same size as the others. He looked great really lost a lot of weight. They could take us to the mess hall for lunch but didn't want to. They wanted to go to the snack bar which had been off limits to them all this eight weeks. The weather was beautiful and there were tables outside. The third boy who's Mother didn't go told his Commanding Officer we were his Aunts so he could join us. We had a great afternoon. Was hard to leave them. We took a lot of pictures. The boys would be going to Camp Pendelton in a day or so. When we got back to the Airport in Denver said good-by and I went to the parking lot where I had left our new Mustang I started to look for my car keys and could not find them. I never locked a car and so went to look in it and there they were hanging in the ignition, had been there for two days.

I always deposited the money bags at the banks every day. Then I would pick up the other bags I was missing one bag for about two weeks. When I went to the bank about it and told them I needed the deposit slip that should be in it for $1500.00 they said they had no record of the deposit but would look for the bag. I kept going back every day as I knew I had dropped the bag. Finally the banker had the guard go with us and we went to a room down in the basement and there on the shelf was said bag with a note taped to it that said hold. No one knew anything about it and it still had the money in it.

There was no safes in the stores so every night after the stores were closed they would bring the money bags to our house. One night we heard a car honk and got up and no one was there. Went back to bed and honk honk again so we got up and stayed up. Then a car came around the corner and we recognized it and there was a car right behind it. We turned on the porch light and when he came around again he came into the drive way and the other car went on. One frightened young man brought in the money bag. He said he had been followed for fifteen miles from #2 store. That night I hid the money all over the house instead of just putting it on the dining room table. I had $500.00 opening money from each of the four stores plus the daily receipts.

Not long after this we received a phone call at o'clock one evening that #1 store had been held up and 10 minutes later #4 was held up. Two nights later #1 was hit again but the guy was greedy he stopped to clean out all the Salem cigarettes. A customer had seen what was going on in the store and called the Police. They caught him. It was a former employee. I told them I thought it was time to put in safes as all these cooks knew where the money was dropped at night and I was scared.

Before the safes were installed I was going down Wadsworth one morning and had all the money bags on the floor of the V.W. when a policeman made a U turn and turned his lights on. I stopped I didn't think I had done anything but was a little nervous about the money in the car. He only wanted to check my registration as they were looking for a black V.W. like I had that had been stolen. So I continued on to each store and put in the money and went on to work myself. The morning after Kevin was born Jim had been up all night so he gave Butch the keys to the four stores and sent him with the money.

Finally the safes were installed they were in the cement floor in the walk in under the beer section. On week ends I didn't open the bottom of the safes till Monday morning. The employees could get in the top of the safe but not the bottom where the deposit envelopes were dropped. I was the only one that had the keys for this. Once in a while there would be a quart of beer broken it would run into the safe. They could sop it out of the top but what run down into the bottom stayed there till I opened it. Sometimes the money envelopes were floating. I would have to peel the bills apart. Felt like I should have a cloths line to hang them out to dry.

Our house payments had gone up quit a little because the taxes were going up. We didn't think we could be able to keep it so we put it up for sale. It had been on the market for nearly six months and they had brought no one to see it. I called the Realtor and told them to take it off the market. They wanted to know why? I told them there may not be any buyers but there were darn well lookers and we had seen no one in five and one half months. They said we have two weeks left on the contract let us see what we can do. The next day they brought a man out. He looked at it and then left. In a little while he was back and wanted to look at the basement again to be sure there were no water marks in it. Then he went to look at the insulation in the attic. Later he came back with the Realtor and they said he would take it if he could move in in a week. I told him he could.

The next day after work I went looking for a Mobile home. I found a three bedroom Magnolia. Jim went the next day to look at it and we bought it. They said when we were ready they would pull it over in front of the house then to the park of our choice. I had trouble finding a park as we had a Teen age boy Dennis. They didn't want any teen-agers. We had wanted to stay in the same school area and Dennis was now a cook at the Pizza Parlor and he wanted to keep his Job. We finally found a lot at a park in Morrison. It was full of weeds and Dennis would have to go to Bear Creek High school. Also would have to quit his job. Jim and I would have farther to drive to work. But that is where we moved to. Dennis rode the bus to school. We now had a marine in Vietnam. He was at Cho Lai. Before he went over he sent Kevin a T shirt that said "My Brother is a U.S. Marine," it was real cute. We had not been here to long and Jim had the yard looking beautiful. He had terraced the bank behind the house, hauled rocks in from the trips to the mountains and made beautiful rock gardens. Our kids spent a lot of time at the other end of the court in the swimming pool. One day there was a knock at the door and Jim was laying on the divan, when I answered the door a lady that lived down by the pool stood there. She said "would you trade spots with me ? Your children like the pool and I am right across from it. And you have the prettiest spot in the whole trailer court." Jim pipes up and said " Hell no all it takes to have a nice yard is a lot of work and a little elbow grease". She turned and walked away.

Sis came home on the bus from school one week end and she needed a prom dress to take back on Sunday. She and I went to the Villa Italia shopping center and after hours of looking we finally found a really pretty blue frilly one to fit her. She was not to easy to fit as she wore a size 3 or 4.

I let Kevin out to play in the yard one day he was nearly three by now. He always stayed in the yard. I looked out to check on him and he was gone. The search was on I could not find him anywhere. I finally started going door to door. By now I was frantic. At one trailer a lady told me there was a Sunday school class going on in a trailer. I went there and he was sitting on the floor with a lot of other kids. She said he came in when they all did so she thought I knew he was there. He went home with me and didn't attend any more.

Jim came home one day and was real upset. We sold Money orders at the stores and they were sold in unison by number. He had just found out that a teacher that was working nights moonlighting at the stores, had been making out money orders to himself. He was going way down in the pile then when he got his teachers check he would pay for them. They boomeranged on him and there was money orders to the tune of $800.00 that we came to that were missing. Jim called in the Police and then this man confessed he had done it. He would get a loan and repay them if we didn't prosecute. He would lose his teachers job if they found out. He turned to Jim and said I suppose that means I don't have a job. Jim said what do you think. He brought the money and never came back again.

We were having money disappearing out of the bottom of the safe at #2 store and I was the only one that had the keys. Jim worked one day and dropped $500.00 at the end of his shift. That night after the store was closed he took a sleeping bag out and slept behind the counter all night. No one came in. We knew it was someone with a key as the place had not been broken into. When I took the deposits out the next morning the envelope he had dropped was gone. Some one besides me had to have a key. I told the crew we all had to go take a lie detector test. Place and time was set up. One women told me she didn't want to take the test. I asked her why and she said she had eaten some candy bars and drank some pop she hadn't paid for. I told her we were looking for something much more serious than that. I took mine first, then the rest of the crew except one man didn't show up. He never came back to work again and the money stopped walking away. Jim called the other place where he worked. He drove a dairy route. They said he just quit with no notice and why were we looking for him? A few days later they called back and said he had a lot of unpaid accounts on his route and when they went to collect them the customers had paid receipts to the tune of $3000.00. If we heard anything to let them know. Well said man had taken off for Texas and applied for a job giving the stores and the Dairy as reference. When we got the call we just called the police. He was brought back to Denver. He had a master key to the safes. I don't know where he got it. But that mystery was solved. We had a lot of headaches with the stores and could see why when Clyde got the four stores going the profit dropped. Jim was supervisor over all four stores and so he worked all hours. He went to stores at closing time and caught people packing out sacks of groceries that had not been paid for. So we had a real turn over of help. I was managing a store and doing all the book work for all four right down to the quarterly reports. I sent the time cards into Omaha and our checks were cut there and sent out. For ever so long we had people coming to work late. I had one man that was at least five minutes to twenty minutes late every day. I told him after a year he owed the store a whole weeks wages He told me I was nuts. So I said no you owe it to me as I am the one working till you get here. I proved it to him on paper. Shortly there after the company installed time clocks. Then they got to work on time.

I had one man that brought a wooden stool to work and he would set in front of the cash register on it. But he never dusted or faced a shelf and didn't always even empty his trash when he closed up at night. I would hide the said stool in the back room but he always found it. One morning I opened the store it was still dark and when I went behind the counter to put the money sack at the register I stumbled over his stool and one hand went into the trash can he had not emptied. I took the trash out to the incinerator and lit it. I went back into the store and looked at that stool thinking that will fit in the incinerator so I took it out and chucked it in. When he came to work that night he asked me where I had put his stool ? I told him I didn't have time to set down at work and he didn't either if he did his work. He threw his store keys across the counter at me and said You can work it yourself I will never work for another woman as long as I live. I told him that was O.K. he didn't work any way. That was a long day for me. I don't like to work the night shift and in ten years worked a very few.

I had started to sell B-line clothing. It was sold at house parties I did this about three nights a week. Was doing pretty good with it. I had a party one night and it was the biggest ever. It was a little over $800.00 I was on cloud nine when I backed out of the lady's drive-way. I backed into a little low slung car across the road. Put a little dent in the door so I went and told them. Gave them my insurance information and all. He called the Police and I got a ticket for backing out of a drive way. They said you are to back in and drive out. Had to take a half day off work and go to Golden to appear in court. The Judge only fined me $10.00 and said next time just leave your name phone number and Insurance information on the windshield.

When I got back to the store I proceeded to burn boxes. It was dry out behind the store and my fire got away from me and burned a redwood fence by an apart-ment house. I had to call the fire department and the stores insurance put up a new fence. Talk about it not being your day.

Sis got off the bus one Friday night and she had a shoe box she was carrying ever so careful. When we got into the car she showed us what she had. She had a little female kitten some one had given to her. The people that had her had clipped her claws so short they had been bleeding. She had put Vaseline on them. That was all we needed was a cat. Me with two jobs two teen-agers and a three year old. And a dog. Oh well we fi-nally got the cat trained to a box. The dog didn't care to much for her. She would get on something and pounce on him when he went by. Eat her own food then stand guard over his so he couldn't get to it. She was a Siamese. She was into anything we left out. I put cook-ies in a tupperware container on top of the refrigerator. We had not been in bed long when they hit the floor. She had gotten up on a chair then the dishwasher and up on top of the refrigerator. I went round and round with that cat.

On Halloween we dressed Kevin up in his yellow snow suit he looked like a little doll in it with his dark hair he was a pretty baby we were very proud of him. Jim took him trick or treating. It was cold there was snow on the ground. The first couple of trailers his dad took him to and he was given candy he thought that was pretty good the third trailer they went to a kid came to the door with a mask on that was all it took he was ready to go home.

One night shortly before Christmas I got three phone calls wanting to know if I had seen Butch on T.V. He was on the nightly news. I had not seen it. He and an-other marine were standing in Chu Lai looking up at a plane that was flying over playing Christmas carols. When Butch first arrived in Vietnam he wrote newsy letters then finally they were like weather reports and why don't you write. I had written every day. He was not getting any mail. I finally contacted a Ham radio operator that had written us telling us if we had to get a hold of our son he could help. Well he got a message to Butch some how and let him know he had letters some where and we were all fine at home. His mail finally reached him. I sent many packages also.

We had planned to go to Oklahoma for Thanksgiv-ing. Should have known better. We were all packed and waiting for Jim to get home when he called and said some one had called in and quit. That meant he would have to work Thanksgiving. So we called Grandma and stayed home.

Come spring we were going to Oklahoma for vaca-tion. We left the Mustang home for Butch as he was coming on a 30 day leave and wanted to go to Montana. We now had a Station wagon and took that to Okla-homa. We stayed at Betty and Genes farm. They had three boys about Dennis and Sises age. Doris and Clyde were there. The kids rode horses and had all kinds of fun. Gene told them he would take them to Thunderbird lake swimming but first they had to hoe the peanuts. They were game but he had not told them there was about ten acres of them. But they did get to go to the lake. Oklahoma has red soil and the lake has red water. Clyde put on a pair of Genes cut off bib overalls they were stripped. Kevin wore stripped bib overalls and he threw a fit as he thought Uncle Clyde had some of his on because they were short.

When we got home Butch was in Montana but he came home that week end. We had a good month with him but he informed us he had signed up to go to Vietnam for another tour of duty. Another whole year of worry and sleepless nights. This time he went to hill 65 just south of Danang. He received a meritorious mass before his Commanding Officer while here. He evacuated some much needed equipment and had worked through 24 hrs. straight to do so. We got a letter on it and it was on the Radio and in the paper.

He wrote and wanted a Colorado Flag about the size they flew over the schools. I looked high and low and could not find one. I called Betty Ware and asked her where I could get one she had been raised there and I thought If any one would know she would. She didn't but said she had a political sign in her front yard and she would make some phone calls and see what she could do. Later I got a call from the Office of the Lieutenant Governor and they said if I would meet him in the Mall and agree to have my picture taken for the Paper with him handing me the flag they would give me one. Well Butch got his flag. His next request was for a bottle of slow gin for his birthday. I bought a fifth of it, packed it in popcorn and peanuts in the shell and sent it. I always packed things in popcorn and peanuts so they could eat the packing. When I told a man I worked with what I had sent Butch for his birthday. He said "hey its against the law to send liquor through the mail". I didn't know this and it was to late I had already sent it. I could just see the bottle breaking and all that pink gooey stuff running down through a mail sack. He wrote that it had come through fine. I was relieved. I sent an awful lot of can food spam, vienna sausage crackers cookies. I think a lot of the 4th Battalion 11th Marine Division enjoyed them. I worked long and hard on a Christmas wreath made from wrapped candy and tied onto a wire circle with ribbon. Also a small pair of scissors to cut it off. He said it didn't last very long. His Aunt Claudia sent him a Montana Christmas tree. He got it in I believe April. He unwrapped it and it was all brown. He hit it on the table and every needle fell from it.

He wrote just not to long before Christmas that he needed a 45 automatic. He could get amo but not a gun. He was on amtracks and when he propped his rifle against the tracks if it fell over in the sand it had to be cleaned. I bought one and was going to be legal this time and I called the Post Office and asked them how I could send it ? They told me you can't. A gun dealer could send one if they had a letter from his commanding Officer stating that he had to have one. They didn't tell me I couldn't send pieces. I took my trusty screw driver and ended up with lots of pieces. Every can of Christmas candy , cookies and gifts I sent had a piece in them. He got the whole thing and re assembled it. He sold it to some one before he came home.

While Butch was at Camp Pendleton before his first hitch in Vietnam, I was going to work one morning and all at once I had a real funny feeling and started to cry. All I could do was think about my first born going to Viet Nam. I stopped the car on Wadsworth Blvd. and had myself a good cry then went on to work. When I got home after work I told Jim that I felt Butch had gotten his orders that morning. He called that night and he had received his orders to ship out. He flew to Chu Lai.

Doris and Clyde had bought a farm at Salida. They had also gotten a herd of Black Angus cattle. They were not farmers. They were told the cows would calf in the spring. Ya all winter instead.

The theft at the stores was so out of hand Jim came home one day and told me to send letters of resignation to the head office we were quitting We had been there nine years and nine months and after ten years we were to get a month paid vacation. He said "I have 18 employees and the ones that are honest are so darn lazy I don't dare leave them alone and the others are such crooks I don't dare leave them alone (He had caught another Manager knocking down that day.) I sent in the resignations and told them we would stay two months and train someone to take our place. So Dennis went to Salida and started his Junior Year in High School as that is where we were moving to when we left Denver. We worked out our two months and when we got our final pay checks we had gotten paid for our months vacation and had a real nice letter saying if we wanted to go back to work for them we would always have a job.

Doris had taken Kevin for the last few weeks before we moved. Her Mother Mrs. Davies had a trailer parked on the farm and we fixed a place to put ours out there also. It was at Poncha Springs, between Salida and Beuna Vista. Grandma Davies and I decided we needed some Pigs. I bought two little pigs from the man we bought eggs for the store from. On Friday night after work we were going to the farm so we went forty miles north of Denver to get the pigs. I asked the farmer what to bring to put them in ? I thought a gunny sack, he said no just bring a big box. We put a paper towel box in the back of the station wagon and went for the pigs Well we put them in the box in the back. Hadn't gone five miles till they were out of the box and all over the back of the station wagon. I told Jim to stop and put them back in the box. He said pigs were your idea get back there and take care of them. He was laughing so hard he missed the turn on the valley highway, we went through down town Denver at five o'clock, just as every one was going home. He would stop at a light and set there and laugh at me back there trying to keep the pigs in the box. He was pointing back at me and everyone we stopped beside was having a ball over it also. We had to go by #3 store and pick up some bread we were taking to the freezer. I suggested we put the pigs in a 55 gallon barrel and stand it up in the back of the station wagon . It fit fine. Our poor little dog was about to have a heart attack by now. The pigs were coming up out of the barrel and hitting their snouts on the roof of the car. I finally opened a loaf of bread and was putting one slice in the barrel at a time. You know there is twenty slices of bread in a loaf. After two loaves they settled down. We stopped up on south park somewhere for dinner. I went in and washed and washed but could still smell those pigs. We had hot beef sandwiches but I didn't eat much of mine. We arrived at the farm and Clyde and Jim said the pig pen there would hold them fine. We put them in the pen. After a while Grandma Davies went down to take another look at them. She came right back and said I hate to be the bearer of bad news but the pigs are gone. We looked and looked seen them a couple of times across the road but couldn't catch them. It got dark. The next morning the neighbor across the road called and said the pigs had walked up into his corral which was sheep tight and he had shut the gate They went and got them and put them into an old chicken house till the pen was reinforced.

Well we had a chicken house so I decided we needed chickens. I told them how Mom and Dad would buy baby chickens and fatten them up and butcher them for fryers. So they got fifty chickens. They were growing fine but were not big enough to butcher, when all at once in the morning we would find some of them dead. They were real flat as if something had sucked all the liquid out of them. We finally set a trap and caught what it was. A SKUNK. Then they had to shoot it as it wasn't dead. The chickens couldn't use the coop any more It was locked up. We finally butchered the chickens but they weren't big enough. I never used any of them. When we finally moved the trailer it moved fine. I had taken the dog and cat in the station wagon with me. That darn cat was all over scratching and howling all the way. I was glad to get there with her . She disappeared for a few days after we let her out, then finally showed up. She then ended up having kittens out in the garage. When they were big enough to not need to nurse anymore she disappeared again and never came back. The next spring Clyde found her remains in a manger of an old barn we never used. It looked as though she just laid down and died.

I got a job about a mile away in Poncha Springs at a Cafe as a waitress. The people that I worked for were real nice. The tips were good. I later sold the Mustang to their oldest son who was a senior in High School. A year later he wrecked it and was killed in the accident.

While Dennis was staying with Doris and Clyde before we got moved down there he was trying to get his drivers license. Clyde let him drive but only on the farm. When he took him down to take the test he didn't pass the driving part. The patrolman asked Clyde if he was letting that young man drive. He said he drives all over the farm. The patrolman said for God sakes let him drive on the highway, how else is he going to learn to drive ? Next time he passed. Clyde was out digging a fence post hole one day and Kevin was laying on the grass watching him, Clyde asked him what he was thinking ? He said Kevin looked up at him and said this might be your farm but it is my yand (land). He was at three years old always trying to get an argument out of Uncle Clyde.

The Cows had calf's all winter. Doris had baby calf's in the house part of the winter. Their mothers would not accept them so they had to be hand fed. It was a cold winter and they had to feed cattle all winter long.

Jim had gone to work at Vista Market in Buena Vista about thirty miles north of the farm. He was assistant manager. He would bring home the produce scraps for the pigs. They ate it all except Pineapple those only got rolled around.

Dennis started to Ski here at Salida he did his practicing at Monarch Ski area and made the school Ski team. He did a lot of cross country skiing also on the team.

The July before we left Denver Dennis, Sis, Kevin and myself took a trip to Montana for my 20th class reunion and to visit. We had the station wagon and loaded all our luggage and coolers in the car and took off. I decided it was a hundred miles closer to go through Yellowstone Park. It is but takes a day longer because of the bumper to bumper traffic. We had food in the car and Dennis would make peanut butter sandwiches for us going down the road. When we got to Myrtles house in Eureka I took our table knife in to wash it. When we left to go home Lee discovered we had left it and he knew we were going to starve on our way home with no way to make sandwiches.

We went to Esthers cabin at Bitterroot Lake. This is the first time Dennis and Virginia ever tried to water ski Dennis did better than Sis. He and Chrystal spent most of the day the fourth of July on the lake. Someone made a little pool with rocks for Kevin by the shore. Wayne has a cute movie of him throwing a fit to get on the dock till he figured out how to crawl under a barrier on the end, then he was all smiles. The next day I left for home real tired. I went by way of Salmon Idaho. I don't know why!! We were all so tired I stopped there and got a motel real early. The next day we hit a swarm of grasshoppers near Arco Idaho. It was like someone hit the windshield with a custard pie. We could see nothing, I had a box cutter in my purse, after removing the razor blade between the kids and I we scraped the windshield with it. When we got to the next town we had to stop at a car wash and wash the car and the radiator. By then the car was really stinking from the dead bugs. They were driven up under the chrome all over the car.

I had to be to work the next morning. It is something like 800 miles from Salmon Idaho to Morrison Colorado. The kids were not old enough to drive. Late in the afternoon I told Dennis I was going to stop in Wyoming and call his dad that we would be home a day late. He convinced me he would stay awake and talk to me so we could go on home. By the time we got to Cheyenne Wyoming they were all asleep and that highway on into Denver was like a long lit ribbon. We got home at one o'clock in the morning and I got up and went to work the next morning at six. I made up my mind I would never drive that long in one day again and I never have.

One day that winter just before Thanksgiving we had 42 inches of snow one night and day. We were snow bound for a couple of days about a block from the highway. I seen the mailman stop at the box on the highway, I knew it was a letter from Butch. I got lots of cloths and a pair of boots on and wadded in that snow to the mail box to get a phone bill.

Come spring and things started to melt around there. Clyde planted alfalfa and started to irrigate. One day he had Kevin following him around as usual and Clyde jumped across a ditch. Kevin tried it and he fell in. Here they came to the house, Kevin soaked to the gills. He said he fell into the itchen gitchen ditch. One whole side of the calf barn had windows in it with lots of little panes. All at once they started getting broken. Kevin had found out that a rock would go right through the glass.

That spring we had branding and castrating of the calves. Dennis was catching the calves and one got away from him. He had a new rope in his hands and he got mad and gave it a throw. It wrapped around Dorises leg. She said it hurt so bad she didn't know weather to cry or wet her pants. She ended up with a permanent crease in her leg from it. Then the calves had to be given scours tablets. They were catching them one evening and it was getting dark. Dennis made a lunge for one and he hit a barb wire from an electric fence. It caught him right across the face. By the time I got to him he was laying in the manure with his hands over his face and the blood was pouring out between his fingers. Clyde and Jim got him into the pickup and we took of for the hospital. He had cut his mouth inside and out. He had stitches on the outside but not on the inside. I took him home and he had taken his bath and I heard him talking in the bathroom. I went in to see if he was all right He had his shorts on and was standing in front of the mirror hanging onto the sink. He was saying I am not going to pass out I am not going to pass out. I asked him what was wrong and he told me he had just looked inside of his mouth and it was all cut up. A real mess. He healed up from that without any bad scares.

Jim and I went to a Marine parents night in Denver and we won a free phone call to a Marine in Vietnam. There was no phones where Sgt. Thomas E DeLong (Butch) was. The red cross said to call him and tell him to call collect and then we could send in the bill and we would be reimbursed for it. Butch had gone from Chu Lai to Danang by ship he said if he was on there ten hours he was sea sick eleven. Then he went from there to Hill 65. That was his only time on a ship. And he wanted no more. One morning at three O'clock the phone rang and it was a man with a real foreign accent wanting to know if I would accept a phone call from Sgt. DeLong. I did of coarse it was Butch calling from Malaysia He was on R&R. It was real good to hear from him. That call was paid for but not the next ones. But it was worth it. Before he came home from over there I also got a letter that he was in the hospital in Danang with malaria. He said they had an air condition room for them there. It wasn't long till he was back out in the field at hill 65.

While we were in Salida Doris wanted me to learn bridge. I went with her once and I don't think her friends were to pleased with me. I kept getting it mixed up with Pinochle. They asked me back one more time. I don't think so. I felt it was out of courtesy to her. I declined.

One man said every time he went by the farm he seen Clyde a Collie dog and a little kid some where. Always the three of them. They had loaded some cattle in the pickup one day and Clyde was going to have them jump out. Dennis told him to back it up to a dirt pile and they could walk out. Well they got into an argument over it and didn't talk to each other all summer.

Dennis went to work at a Dairy farm after school was out. He got up real early and went to milk he worked till about three in the afternoon and came home and bathed and changed his cloths and went to work as a cook at the pancake house till ten at night. We had bought an old 1947 Chevrolet car. He drove it and called it the old gray ghost. Towards the end of the summer I told him he should stop working one of his jobs as he looked so tired all the time. He said he felt fine and he had told both of them he would work all summer and he didn't want to go back on his word. We had to take him in for his football Physical and he was put in the hospital with severe high blood pressure. He was in there for a week so he stopped both jobs. Finally the Dr. said take him home he is spending his day doing wheele' s in a wheel chair in the hallways and sitting in front of the nursery window watching the babies.

One day out of the blue he said "I am being selfish asking Dad to drive to work all winter. I can go to school in Buena Vista my senior year. Lets move

Virginia had graduated from High School in the spring of 1968. She graduated Salutatorian of her class, and she got a scholarship to Gauludett College in Washington D.C. Patty Draxler was also going back to College and her parents offered Virginia a ride. They went by car and had only room for one suitcase. I sent the rest of her clothing in suitcases on the bus. It took them over a month to get there. We were so proud of her at her High School graduation. She gave her speech in sign language and the interpreter could hardly keep up with her she was very nervous and really went fast. I would give anything to have been able to financially helped her in college but at this time we just couldn't. She was a determined girl and made it through on her own. She worked at the college post office most of the time she was in college.

We moved into a trailer park in Buena Vista got Dennis in school. I had to find a job, had been told to go to the Green Parrot cafe on main street. I went and applied and got a job as a waitress. Now I had waited on tables all over the country and I thought I knew this job start to finish. I had to have a black skirt, white shirt and white shoes. I found a baby sitter for Kevin at a woman's house a half block from the trailer court. Jim or Kevin would pick him up when they got home as I had to go to work at four O'clock. My first night working there she said I will give you two booths tonight and see how you do. I seen the other waitresses taking relish trays and bread sticks to the tables so I did likewise. But I was not getting any orders out of the kitchen. I finally asked the cook why. He told me I had not asked for my sides of spaghetti That was the kitchens signal to start your order. So I got that straightened out in a hurry. When we closed that night Mable said she was having an employee meeting and would like for me to stay for it. I had told Jim I would get off at eleven. She started pacing and telling about the new restaurant we would be moving into within the next month. She walked back and forth. We drank coffee, some of them had drinks from the bar Mable had a lot of drinks. Finally at two in the morning Jim came looking for me. The one and only time he ever did that. I worked for them there at the Green Parrot for about a month and the new Restaurant was about ready to move into. One night the cook was standing at the grill cooking and the roof was leaking so bad he had a towel over his head as it was dripping right from the hood on his head. Mable said enough is enough all of you that want to help show up in the morning after nine o' clock. Tom is going into Denver and we will open the new building tonight. They had all new dishes and silver for the new Restaurant but we had to move pots and pans and supplies. We loaded everyone's cars and made trip's till it was all moved. Then we all showed up at our new jobs that night. The fan was on over the grill but not hooked up. When we started to turn in orders and the gill and fryer got busy we found out why we were not to be there yet. The kitchen filled with smoke they opened the back door to let it out. Everything was going well and the place was full when boom I! the lights went out. The grill was gas. The cook and Mable moved their cars to the back door and turned their lights on into the kitchen, we had candles on the tables. The orders that were in were filled and within a half hour the power company had lights back on. It seems the Restaurant over loaded the transformer they had installed.

The trailer park we moved into was right in town within walking distance of everything. We got Kevin a small Bike after we moved in here, he was trying to learn to ride it and ran into a fence. He came in the house crying and said the fence jumped in front of him and made him wreck.

Dennis wanted to Ski and they had no team at Buena Vista. The Salida coach told him he could travel with them as a one man team from Buena Vista. Which he did and very well at that. He beat out some of the other teams. He was presented with an outstanding Skier of the year trophy at the athletic banquet that year. He received a Ski Scholarship to Fort Lewis College that spring when he Graduated.

Kevin was with the same Baby sitter most of the time we were in Buena Vista except for a very short while I had him with another one till he came home all bruised one day. We went and confronted her with it and she said she had left him with her granddaughter for a short while and she had hit him with a two by four on the bottom because he didn't mind her. He never went back there again. Mrs. Willenburg was not to clean and had chickens running in and out of the house but she took good care of him and was good to him.

Doris and Clyde sold the farm at Salida and bought a home and a small apartment house in Colorado Springs. We didn't see much of them for the next few years. I don't think they kept the Apartment house to long.

While we were here in Buena Vista the first morning of hunting season you would have sworn we were in the middle of a war zone. There were a large herd of Elk at the edge of town out by the drivein Theater. The game department had used Helicopters and charges and all sort of things trying to break them up but to no avail. That morning at day break there were hunters opened fire into the herd, they killed bulls cows and calves. There were 30 hunters in jail by 9 o'clock. It was really a massacre and was written up in one of the hunting magazines.

Dennis had a great senior year of school he Lettered in Football. They played one game on a dirt field at one of the schools. He also received a knee injury. He had told me if he got hurt I was to stay in my seat in the stands. Really hard to but I did while they carried him out. He wanted to go back in and finish the game. Dr. Mcgown (a wonderful man who never missed any games) told him he could if he would have me bring him to the office as soon as the game was over. He did we did and the Dr. had to drain his knee two times in the next week. He was on crutches for the next two weeks. He suited up and sat on the bench those two games.

He didn't play basket ball but was manager. At the Snow Ball he was an attendant for one of the Snow Princess. Then when Prom time came I kept after him to ask someone to the Prom. Finally 3 days before the Prom he asked a girl. We were just under the deadline to get him fitted for a tuxedo. I called and they said if we got to Salida that night before seven they could get it ordered. We also had a corsage to get ordered and the girl didn't have time to get a dress so she put red velvet bows on her sisters wedding dress. They made a very handsome couple and were voted King and Queen of the Prom.

When the Year Book came out at the High School for Dennises Senior Year, he had pictures all through it. Boy with the prettiest smile, Prom King, Football, Skier of the year. He really had a great Senior year.

We went to Arizona to visit some friends on our Vacation Dennis did not want to go as he wanted to try out for the Senior play. We left him home by himself. Jim Kevin and I and Jims golf clubs plus luggage loaded into the V.W. bug and away we went. When we got there I called to see if Dennis was all right He told me he was homesick. When I said but you are home his reply was but none of you are here. He tried out for the play and got the lead male part. When we arrived home the land lord told us he could not believe that a 17 year old had been left for a week by himself and had no party's or any noise over there at all.

Dennis was driving the V.W. one night and had a flat tire, he and his friends could not find the place on the side of the car to put the funny little jack so the other three boys held the car up while he changed the tire.

While Dennis went to play practice Jim and I would both be at work. He would get Kevin from the baby sitter clean him all up and take him to play practice with him. By the time the production was put on Kevin knew everyone's lines and big brother got a lot of attention from the girls because of his cute little brother he had with him all the time.

One girl was killed in the play and everyone thought she did such a good job of acting like she was dead. Sad thing was a day or two after graduation she was by herself in the car and hit a bridge and was killed.

Dennis found work at the Texaco station. He worked for Tony Propernick, after school and on week ends. He was saving money for college. He wanted to go to Fort Lewis College in Durango Colorado.

In 1969 Butch came home on leave from the Marines. He had finished his second hitch in Viet Main and was heading for Virginia to go to school for six weeks then on to some embassy where French was spoken. While he was there he went to Washington D.C. to visit his sister who was attending Gaulladet College there. He could not get over the fact it sits in the very bad part of D.C. So we knew then why the students there were on such strict regulations and the high fence all around the College. She did get an excellent education there however. This is also where she met her husband Bill Randal.

Then Butch was sent from there to Paris France as a guard at the embassy for two years. This job is an honor. He worked with Sergeant Shriver and John Foster Dullis while there.

The Vista Market that Jim was Assistant Manager in was having trouble with people breaking in and etc. so Jims boss asked him if we would move our trailer to a spot behind the store. We would have free rent and they thought if some one was close it might help. We had it there for about eight months. The wind whistled down the railroad tracks that ran beside us. We had a metal storage shed beside the trailer and while Jim was home one day eating lunch, we looked out the window by the table and the shed was dancing around and lifting on one side. We both ran out and grabbed hold of it to keep it from blowing away. However we had boxes blowing all the way down the track. He anchored it down before he went back to work and I picked up things all afternoon to bring back home.

It was not long after this we put the trailer up for sale. A preacher in town bought it. He paid for it with all kinds of checks that had been made out to him or endorsed and given to him there were even some Social Security checks in the lot. We moved to a small two bedroom house we rented from Tony and Mary Propernick. Tony gave Kevin a Bike one day and told him when he learned to ride it it was his. It had been their sons and was a little one with a banana seat and big handlebars he rode it for ever so long.

Dennis had graduated from High School this spring, Sis was home from college and said she didn't want to go back. I told her she had to find a job then. She got a job washing dishes at the cafe I worked at. She also wanted her drivers license. We went down and she took her test and of coarse passed the written one with flying colors. When she and the patrolman came back from the driving part, she stayed in the car and he came on in. I asked him how she had done and he said I wish the people around her that can hear would be such good drivers. She has her license and is waiting for you in the car.

I had this little blue V.W. with a sun roof and she would take some of the waitresses home from work and they would have the roof open and there would be heads sticking out all over.

Towards the end of summer she had decided she would go back to college. I don't think she wanted to wash dishes the rest of her life, and she missed her deaf friends. She was washing dishes for twelve waitresses. On Sunday she worked a split shift. She left at one o'clock one day and when she came back at four there were bus tubs of dirty dishes all over and the sinks were full of dirty pans. We had been very busy and no one could get to them. She came in and took one look and started to cry. She came and wanted a piece of paper and a pencil. She wrote on it Mr. Tom today I quit. Them she went and gave it to Tom Gianellie the boss. This was about two weeks before she flew back to College.

Dennis and I loaded the V.W. trunk and back seat to the top, put Kevin on the load in the back seat, Bike and skies on top and took off for College. We arrived and all of his stuff was unloaded into a tiny room at the dorm he shared with two other boys. I really don't know where they put everything. He washed pots and pans in the cafeteria. He had $ 1500.00 when he went to college for the year. He made it on that. Wish we would have been able to help he and Sis some. But the money just wasn't there.

Butch had left a car, pickup, camper and a big Motorcycle with us when he went to Paris. The car was not paid for and he didn't make the payments so they came and got it. He asked us to sell the pickup and camper for him so we did and sent him the money. We had the motorcycle around forever till he finally came home and sold it.

Kevin started Kindergarten this fall he was now 5 years old. His class had a big black rabbit in class that was trained to use a litter box. The teacher had a lot of animals in the room. One day she sent a note home to me that she wanted to talk with me about him. I went to school and she said he was a very smart child and had an adult vocabulary. She wondered why. I asked her if he was using bad words? She said oh no he just talks like a grown up. The only explanation I could give her was that he had been raised in a home with two adults and two teen age brothers and a sister. She said that was probably it. Also did he have a big imagination? I said no. Well she said a day or so before that he had told them in show and tell he had a brother that was a Sergeant in the Marines. I told her he did have, all she said was how unusual.

The summer before Dennis left for College he had a lot of trouble with Mr. Jones the city police. He had gotten a speeding ticket coming down from Monarch pass. Going up with that V.W. He would have never gotten a speed ticket. In Colorado you get points against your drivers license for each ticket you receive. Next he had a parking ticket for parking where his boss told him to park when he went to work. The police said it was where there was to be a sidewalk even though there had never been one put in. I got a call one afternoon at work from Dennis saying "no one was hurt but you have a crushed bug" . They had been out to a swim pool out of town at one of the mineral pool areas. A friend of his had dove in and caught his leg on some kind of bolt that was sticking up. He had to go to the hospital which was in Salida about 20 to 25 miles away. They put him in the V.W. and Dennis took off with him. Going down this country road to the Highway. There was a Buick Station Wagon coming towards them. She had no turn signal on and when she got right in front of them made a left turn . Neither car was going very fast but when a Bug hits a Buick you can guess who got squashed. The woman got out looked at them and went on down the road to a house. Dennis asked her to call the police and ambulance. She told him to do it himself. After getting his friend out of the car and laid on a sleeping bag by the side of the road he ran back to the pool to get help. He didn't get a ticket for this. The Lady did for illegal left turn, leaving the seen of an accident She was also a R.N. in the hospital in Salida. We had to take Dennis to court to her trial so he could tell them what happened. Our car was repaired in Salida but wore out a set of tires on the front in a three month period. When we got it back there was still blood on the dash and glass all over the floor. In Colorado you must have a brake and light sticker on your windshield which is renewed every year. We had not noticed that this had not been replaced on the new windshield. Jim had to go into Denver and was stopped by a patrolman as the lights on one side of the car front and back were not working. Then also no sticker. So back to the garage it went. One sloppy job all around. Next Dennis was going down the street and seen some of his friends going the other way. He went to a motel and made a turn by going into their circle drive. Here comes the city police. That is against the law to make a turn and not stop and do business in that place of business another ticket and that was three. Enough to take his drivers license for three months. The Senior party was held at a three two night club. In Colorado you can drink three two beer at 18 Dennis was the only one not allowed into the party as he was only 17.

He now started to ride a bike to work. He got picked up for riding a bike at night with no head light.

Mr. Jones the city police came into the Cafe one night and told me if that son of mine so much as spit on the sidewalk he was going to throw him in jail. I asked him what he had done now ? He said he didn't know but he had run from him. When I came home from work Dennis Jim and Kevin was sitting watching T.V. I asked Dennis what had happen? He said he and his friends were at the A&W It was only a block from the house. They had just walked outside when Jones pulled up so they took off running down the alley to our house. He followed them. They went inside and left the lights off. He was all over the yard looking in the bushes and behind trees. They were inside watching him. Finally Tony came out of his house and asked him what he thought he was doing. He said he was looking for Dennis. Tony told him to get back on the street where he belonged and leave the kid alone. He was gone by the time Jim and Kevin got home.

After he told his Dad and I this he said he was going up town. I told him he wasn't and out the door he went. About 30 to 45 minutes later the police car drove in the driveway and the door slammed and I heard Dennis say I'll see you. The car left and he came in the house. I jumped in the middle of him and asked him what he had done now. He said I went to the Police station and Apologized to Jones and he brought me home. End of trouble with the Police. And kids think they are picked on now?

The Vista Market had put in a burglar alarm after we moved from the back of the store. It was hooked up to the owner Managers house our house as Jim was Assistant manager, the Police station and the State Reformatory that was at Bueni. Jim had just walked in the house a little after 7 one evening when the phone rang. I answered it and it was saying Vista Market has been broken into over and over. I handed it to him and he took off in a hurry When they all came pulling up front there was the butcher standing inside in front of the door. Jim had locked him in when he closed the store. He had set the alarm off when he went to the front of the store.

This butcher shop had sawdust on the floor. When we had our trailer parked out back and they put new sawdust on the floor in the shop someone decided that would be good to put over our water pipes to keep them from freezing. Not thinking of all the meat scrapes and blood in it. It was spread out and tucked in real nice one evening and during the night I do believe we had every cat and dog in Bunie under our trailer. So that all had to be removed and he covered them another way. I don't know why we didn't use thermatape. Maybe it was not available as yet.

Tom came in one night and handed me a big roll of keys and said he and Mable and the kids were going on Vacation and would I watch the place for them. I had before when they had gone to Vegas for a week a couple of times. I told him sure. He said here is the recipe for my spaghetti sauce and don't show it to any one and here is the salad dressing. He put the dressing on each salad and would not tell anyone what was in his five containers. I said where are you going? He said in the morning we are flying out of Denver for two months in Europe. I told him he didn't have a bar tender. He said you can do it. Turn the time into the book keeper he will make the pay checks. Here is where you order the liquor and groceries. I am confident you can do the rest. Also make the deposits and do the pay checks for the bar at the Green Parrot. We will pay you a dollar an hour instead of ninety cents you are getting now. Big deal now I would not be making tips as I did waiting tables.

That fall we had all gone in one morning to face 38 bushels of cherry peppers. They were washed and packed in gallon jars then a shot glass of pickling spice was put into each jar an filled with a vinegar and water solution and some salt then the lids put on in a couple of weeks they were all bubbling and working. These are the peppers used on the relish tray. So we had a lot of them ahead when Ginellies left he also served Lupino beans on the relish tray. He got them dry and soaked them in hot salty brine for a couple of days they puffed all up then were rinsed and ready for use. He had a lot of them fixed ahead for me. I knew how to mix up the meat balls and the waitresses stood and rolled them then the cook would bake them and put them in gallon cans and freeze them. One day we were rolling meat balls and this one gal said I think I am going to faint. And she did-before she hit the floor a couple of us caught her and laid her down. Dr. McGowen was called. By the time he got there she was awake. He said she had stood with her knees locked and that would make you pass out. He said you girls move around a little when you are doing these things.

We had doors going from the kitchen to the dining room and the coffee shop. One was for out and one for in. One night I had four dinners on a tray up over my shoulder going to the dining room. I started out and here came a gal in the wrong door. Tray and all flew over my shoulder and dumped. I kept going to the table. When I arrived there the Lady said was that our dinner? I told her it was and it would take about 20 minutes to get it up again. He said what the heck just bring us another drink we can wait. When we went home that night there was lasagna in the gals purses which was on the other side of the kitchen. The next day when I came to work there stood Tom with a saw and some glass. He said come over here you are the shortest one and so I will measure you to put in these windows.

On Sunday we opened at noon the rest of the week we opened at 4 P.M. One Sunday there was a phone call from a church in town and they wanted reservations for 12 people at 2 O'clock and they wanted me to wait on them. We each had seating for 16 people in our station. So that took up most of my station. I put the tables together, took the wine lists from them and was ready when they came. Surprise they sat and drank till 3:30 before they ordered dinner. Here I was with only one table to turn over for an hour and a half. They finally ordered 12 steak and lobster. Had after dinner drinks and left at 5:00 o'clock. When they left the Minister said he would be back to pay the tab. Which was all right No tip was left on the table. At this time you usually got quarters for tips very seldom a dollar bill. Well we got busy and I had all my station full when he came back and he paid his bill and handed me a roll of bills. I went and stuck it in my tip jar in the kitchen and thought it was probably 4 dollars. When we closed that night I unrolled it and there was a 20 and 5 ones. Those that had been teasing me about having my tables tied up all after noon had to eat crow. No one had ever gotten that big a tip there or at that time.

Well now Tom and Mable were gone. The first night I was tending bar and I had 12 waitresses on the floor. All at once I had crying waitresses coming to me in the bar-they said the cook was drunk and was being abusive and they couldn't get any orders out. I went into the kitchen and there was our big deal CHEF sitting on a five gallon bucket with a glass and a bottle of wild turkey whiskey (nearly gone). I told him he could leave and not come back. He stood up and looked down at me. He was over 6 foot tall. He said you can't fire me. I told him to come back in two months and talk to Tom. I paid him off in cash and had him sign a receipt. He left the back up cook took over. I moved the dish washer up to back up cook and called another dish washer. Every thing ran smooth after that. When Tom got home that guy was long gone.

When I would go to the Green Parrot and to the New Cafe to make the bank deposits in the mornings Kevin would come He loved to sit at the bar and have a Roy Rogers drink full of marachino cherries while I counted the money.

They had been gone about a month and I received a collect call from Rome one evening. This is where Tom had been raised till he was 15 years old. They were visiting relatives there now. He asked me how everything was going? I told him I had fired his Chef the first day. He asked why and when I told him he said he would have done the same thing. Asked how the business was and when I told him I had put $14,000 in the bank that month he said good job. We will see you in about a month. A month later they came walking in one evening. They were quite satisfied with the way things had gone.

I was getting a little tired of the evening shift after three years now and so applied for a job in Fords Grocery. Jim worked at Vista Market. There was only the two stores in town and where he worked didn't hire two from one family.

I got the job and so that ended my job for Ginnellies. People would come into the store and want to know where we got our groceries? I would tell them one week at one store and the next week at the other.

Wally had a store at Saratoga, Wyoming it was not doing to well he didn't know what was wrong. He asked Jim if we would go up there to work for a while and I could work in the store up there as he did hire relatives in that one. Well Jim went up as assistant manager. He went up and stayed in a motel and found a 3 bedroom up stair's apartment for us. The next week end we rented a U—Haul truck and moved to Wyoming. Our Apartment was a whole upstairs over an Insurance office in a big house on main street. We had three bedrooms front room dining room and kitchen and an enclosed back porch.

Got Kevin in school, found a baby sitter and we both started work. I think they knew in the store Jim had been sent up there as a spy. They were not a very friendly bunch of co workers when we first got there. The baby sitter left Kevin with her son one day and when Kevin told me what the boy wanted him to do I found another sitter in one big hurry.

They sold UGLY fruit in the store there and one day all the box boys were finding reasons to come by my register and pat me on the back. When I got home and took my smock off I found every time I got a pat on the back there was a little sticker from this fruit that said " I am Ugly " Stuck to back. They really thought they were funny

Saratoga has what is called the Ho Bo pool. It is a very large mineral natural heated pool. We would put our swim suits on in the house and put a robe and coat then go to the pool after dinner. It was so relaxing. When you would get in the car the windows would all fog up from the heat in your body. You could sleep like a log. The way this pool got its name during the depression the bums would get off the train and wash their cloths and take baths in this pool. Since then the city had cemented all around it and put a high chain link fence around it. It was free of charge. Only about three feet deep, maybe 24 by 70 feet in size. When it was real cold the vapors from the pool would freeze on the fence into ice sickles. It was real pretty.

The river ran through town and there were a lot of Ducks that were fed popcorn and bread that stayed there year round. In the real cold weather the river would freeze. These ducks would come flying in and try to land on the river and would just scoot on their bottoms on the ice. Real hilarious to watch.

The wind blows in Saratoga like no where else we had ever lived. In the middle of the night there was a big crash in our bed room and the curtain was standing straight out. The wind had blown out the glass in the window. Here we are up in the middle of the night sweeping up glass and Jim went and found a big box to take apart and nail up in the window. The land lord said oh that is common around here. The next day they replaced it.

Myrtle and Wayne had been to a R.E.A. meeting in Dallas Texas and when they flew back to Montana they came by way of Laramie and Jim went and picked them up they came and spent a few days with us. We all enjoyed the Ho Bo pool while they were there.

Dennis and Sis came home from College for Christmas. We had a nice Christmas Vacation with our children. That was the last Christmas Sis has ever been home. This was 1970.

Butch called from Paris a few times. Then he called and told us he was getting Married to Jillian Spensly from England. So when he came home he would have a wife. This was 1971.

In February Jim Kevin and I went to a small town south of Saratoga that had a real nice Restaurant in a big house. We were going to dinner for our anniversary. On our way there we were surrounded by antelope They were all over the road so we just stopped and waited for them to prance around. They even came and looked in the car window at us. We were probably there 5 to 10 minutes. Then went on our way and had a marvelous meal as I remember.

By now Jim has discovered what was going on at the store. We made a trip to Buena Vista and he told Wally that his manager was taking things out of the store in Wyoming that he was not paying for by the car load. Also turned our resignation in as we were moving to Rexford Montana and opening up a little store that had been closed for a while. Dennis went to work for Tony again in Buena Vista. Sis came home and moved with us to Montana. We again loaded everything in a U-Haul and took off. We had rented a house in Rexford from the same people we had rented the store building from. Got all moved into the house which was pretty clean but painted terrible color's any one could imagine. Kitchen bright Yellow. Bathroom Purple. Front room and Dining rooms Dark Green. One Bedroom Dark Blue and the other one dark pink. The cook stove was very dirty down under the burners. I took it all apart and soaked it in a bathtub of strong ammonia water. Finally scraped all the food and grease off.

Next was a trip to a wholesale house in Kalispell. We ordered all we could afford. We were determined not to go in debt. for any merchandise. We didn't have a variety of brands. But a good selection of necessities.

This was the spring of the year and school was out. Sis was home so we didn't need a baby sitter for Kevin. One day Jim and I were over at the store working and when we went home there sat Kevin with a hat on. It seems Sis thought he needed a hair cut and the clippers were there didn't look to hard. Well I tried to straighten it up some but he was clipped nearly bald and wore his hat for a while.

In July Sis had her 21 St. birthday. Aunt Myrtle gave her 21 red roses she was so thrilled with them. Sharon and John came down and took her out for a legal drink. She and John played pool and she beat him.

Come fall Sis had to return to College Dennis wrote that he was going back to Fort Lewis for another year. Kevin started the second grade. Things were going slow at the store but we were hanging on. We bought a used ice machine from the Vets Club in Libby. Now we had ice to sell. It was getting about time to move to the New Town of Rexford. They were busy moving all kinds of buildings right along now. We had to have somewhere to live up there so we bought an old trailer in Kalispell. We didn't know it had gone through a flood till we had it all set up in New Rexford and found the mud and silt still under the sink in the kitchen and bathroom. The Insulation had been wet and pulled down in the walls and it leaked so bad when it rained the water ran down the wall in the front room. There had been a washer in the front end kitchen. The drain pipes were so full of black greasy looking stuff from detergent build up we thought we would have to replace all the pipes. We finally got them cleaned out. Jim fixed most of the leaks in the roof. One we never got stopped. We moved the thermostat down and then we could keep warm.

When Darrell Roose moved the store building he told me I would have to box everything up and sit it on the floor. By now it was into late fall and was pretty chilly. I packed it all except a few rolls of paper towels I sat around on shelves to see where they went. When they set the building down in the new town the towels were still sitting on the shelves. We were operating within two days in the new town but cold wow. We only had a space heater in there and it was not set down on the foundation yet. We had this for about six weeks. Very miserable.

Finally everything was back to normal and Kevin was in school in the new school. Marilyn Byers was his teacher. Mary Moses was the Principle.

Two things in Buena Vista we never ran into anywhere in the country. The Miners at Leadville only were paid once a month. They would come in and buy a whole months supply of groceries at one time. Sometimes six carts full.

The other thingwas the Vista Market in Buena Vista every so often they would find a bar of Dial soap some where in the store with a bite out of it. The tooth marks were right in it. But they never found where anyone had spit out the soap. And it was a big bite. We never had anything like this in Rexford.

Mrs. (Arnold) Beers house I believe was the biggest house they moved and when it came up to the new town there was a big audience. It moved fine. The next one they said that would fall apart when moved was the Frontier Bar. As it was a large log building. It also moved fine. I helped Eddie Grob wash down the walls after it was set down. Don't think that had ever been done. We found a new color and got an awful lot of cigarette smoke off.

There were not to many people moved to the new town. Lots of them took their money and bought elsewhere. We could see that there were not enough people there to support a store. Kevin started the second grade here. We stuck it out through the winter.

Sis stayed in Washington D.C. and worked for the Postal Department and did not come home for Christmas or the summer. Dennis came home after his third year in college. He and Jim went to work on a construction Job down by St. Regis. He had brought home a German Shepherd Dog (Gashi) She had 13 pups on Mothers Day. We kept one white male. Shorty Ritch took the rest of them and got rid of them. Then she got over protective with the one we kept (Kasanka). She bit Richard Payton and one of the Truman boys. We built a fence but she would dig under it.

I had taken Ceramics in Wyoming and so Myrtle and I started a ceramic shop in the back room of the store. We each had $70.00 We came to Kalispell and bought green ware, tools, brushes, paint a coffee mug mold and a gallon of slip. Then it dawned on us we needed a Kiln. We had no more money so I put it on my credit card. We put all the money we took in on the Kiln and paid it off pretty fast.

Dennis went back to Fort Lewis College at Durango Colorado for his fourth year. I called him the end of September and asked him how things were going? He said everything was fine. When I called him in October he told me he had not gone back to school. He had met a real nice girl from Albuquerque New Mexico. They were going to see her folks then on to California and to Montana. How they ever made it in that old blue panel I will never know but they did.

We had a chance to sell the store inventory to Nina Street and her daughter. We made no profit on the sale but gave us a chance to get out. We found a lot in Eureka owned by Ethel White to park our trailer, we were going to get a hauler. It was a 12 wide by about 64 long. Darrel Hagarud said he would move it with his pickup. We moved on a Sunday Morning with no license and no permit. Scared heck out of me but we made it. When the phone man was hooking up our phone the dog decided to take a nip at him also but didn't get through his pant leg.

We moved the ceramic shop to the stage area in the old grange hall where Myrtles flower and gift shop was.

Dennis and Susan came home. He went to work for Plumb Creek mill. They lived in the little house behind Montana Market. While working at the mill he got cull 2X4's and they carried them by hand up the hill and built a very small house. On Ralph and Darceys land. They later sold it to Mr. Stacey and he moved it to his land.

They lived at the Dance Pavilion on Glen lake for a while. While here they had a friend from Colorado killed in their yard on the 4th of July. They were not home and found him when they came home. They moved shortly after that and lived here and there till they bought the property they now own and have a lovely home on it which Dennis built. He worked many years as a carpenter in the area and has now been with Lincoln Electric for six years and loves it.

We bought a 1960 Chev. car from Ruth Bronson after we moved to Eureka. I started looking for work and went to work at the Eureka Cafe. I cooked for Ray Davis. It was a very clean cafe. They were nice to work for.

Jim went back on Construction and was working in Spokane he got home about once a month.

Kevins teacher told me she thought I should have his eyes tested. She thought he could not see as well as he should. There was a Optometrist from Whitefish came up to Eureka one day a week. I made an appointment for him and sure enough he needed glasses real bad. We ordered them and paid for them. The next week when he came up I was busy in the ceramic shop so sent Kevin up to get his glasses. He came back crying and said the lady told him he could not have them till they were paid for. I got on the phone and was not to gentle with them. She said she was so sorry and to send him back up and they would give him his glasses plus a dollar that they had overcharged us. He has worn glasses every since.

By now Myrtle and I had bought about 200 plus molds and were mixing our own slip in two old Maytag washers.

We were having ceramic classes now and one night just about a month before Christmas a lady came in and wanted to know if Myrtle had sold her pretty tree she had in the foyer in the front of the shop? She said no.

The lady said well a young man was carrying it down the street when I came in. Myrtle went out and looked at the empty corner with the most dumb founded look on her face. She called the Police they had no trouble tracking the tree as it was flocked white and had red satin balls on it which were strung from her shop down the street around the police station and behind the Stockmans bar. There they stopped where a vehicle had been parked beside the bar. At two in the morning they found it in the back of a Pickup parked across the street at the Eureka Cafe. On going inside they found a very drunk young man in a black sweater with white flocking all over him. He said his Mother told him to go find a pretty tree so he came to town and took the prettiest one he could find. Myrtle had to go to the Police station the next morning to claim her tree it was really in a sad shape.

Her Christmas tree had been a joke for a long time she got her moneys worth out of it every year. It was in Red Balls and Bows for Christmas. In February it still had the red Bow on top and red hearts for Valentines day. March and April was the Easter theme with Yellow ribbon on the top and plastic pastel Easter eggs. May was real pretty with Pink cameos and a Pink ribbon on the top. That white flocked tree stayed beautiful all this time. One year we were asking Myrtle when the tree was coming down and she said I guess I will put flags and fire crackers on it for the fourth of July. We told her if she did we would light the fire crackers so needless to say it never went to July. But every one in town enjoyed that tree.

While we were in Rexford in the old town and still in the house. Butch came home from England and France with his wife Jillian They had picked up a new Volkswagon Bug in New York and drove. Butch said every time they seen a little hill after they got in Montana Jill wanted to know if that was the Rockie Mts. and every little puddle had to be Glen lake. When they got to our place He went through the barrels of stuff he had left home and we had hauled over the country all the time he was in the service. Threw most of it away. He did sell the Motorcycle we had been hauling around for him. It was a big one I think a BSA. While they were there Kevin was in his sleeping bag and Butch shook him down in it and tied it shut.

Myrtle and I went to Spokane for a series of classes to get our certification to teach Ceramics. So we were both Duncan Ceramic teachers when we got done. I later sold my share of the shop to Ruth Bronson. Myrtle then sold her the flower shop and bought her share of the Ceramic shop and moved it to the basement of her home and ran it for a long time there.

Come spring Jim bought a trailer in Spokane and he found a place for it at Airway Hts. I sold the one we had in Eureka to Ethel White (it is still in use today). Rented a U-Haul truck and Dennis drove me to Spokane and came back on the train. The Court we moved into was managed by Bobbie (Garrison) and David Maloy from Eureka. We were parked right beside the office. It was a nice trailer a 10 wide and we had no way to move it so after some time we traded it on a new 35 ft 8 wide with a tip out.

Kevin transferred to school here. He liked this school real well. He joined the Cub Scouts got to go to one meeting and we were on the move again. We had bought a used pickup to pull the trailer. This move took us to Othello Washington. Jim was working in town they were rebuilding the city lights. We had purchased a 15 ft. camp trailer for Jim to use on Jobs. We left the 35 ft one in Airway Hts. and lived in the little one that summer. It got up to 1120 there for quite some time. We had no air conditioning so spent a lot of time out in the shade of the trailer. One day I was sitting out there making an afghan The one I was working on was nearly finished and was over my lap and a woman came by and wanted to know what I was covered up for in that weather. I made six of them that summer for Christmas Presents.

Went to Moses Lake to get my Drivers License as I was driving on Montana ones. Took Kevin with me as I had no one to leave him with. Passed the written one at 98%. When I went out to drive the patrolman told me to turn right at the next corner. I went to the intersection and turned. He said take me back you don't follow directions. The next corner was the alley. I flunked. When we got home Kevin ran down the street and yelled at his Dad and said Mama flunked her driving test. The whole crew heard him. I went back the next week and got a different Patrolman. I told him what had happened and he said he must have had a mad on or something. He took me around the block and that was all. I had passed drivers tests 2 times in Montana 3 times in Oregon 1 time in Idaho 2 times in Colorado 1 time in Wyoming and the 3rd time in Washington I flunk it. So one time out of all that isn't to bad I guess. In Othello there is a feed lot for cattle they feed them about 9 at night and stink like you can't believe. This is no sooner over and the Or Ida plant dump their potato scraps. In the dead of summer when you have gone to bed and have the doors and windows open in that heat that is really a smell, to look forward to every night.

When the job was done we moved back to Airway Ht. Kevin started school again. He didn't go very long and we were on the move again. Jim went to work at Clarkston Washington. This was supposed to be a 1 year job. He took the camper down first. Got a place to park the trailer and came back for us. When we took off I was following him and could see smoke coming out from under the pickup. I couldn't get him to stop with honking and flashing lights. I finally passed him and stopped so he did also. We sat there a while for the emergency brake to cool down, he had left it on. When we got to the top of that big switch back hill going down into Clarkston, I made him go ahead of me I didn't want that trailer running over me. The trailer spot had grass and weeds waist high on it. We finally got it all cleaned up and grass planted before it snowed.

Kevin was enrolled in school again. Jim was working and I went to work for Sears Order house for the Christmas season. We traded our 60 Chev and the camper in on a 1972 Volks Wagon Bug. It was a super Beetle. Wish I still had it 50 miles to the gallon on that one. It was Navy blue. Myrtle and Wayne and Dennis and Sue came for Thanksgiving. Dennis and Sue took our V.W. on a trip to see her folks in New Mexico. They also went to Colorado to see Jims oldest Brother. We had a very cold icy winter here. There was one couple lived in a silver streak trailer and she could not get out one day her door froze shut after he went to work. She was in the front window waving at every one they just waved back. When he came home from work he finally got the door open.

When the Christmas season was over I was asked to stay on as a permanent employee for Sears. Christmas eve was a hard day I had to call people and tell them their packages had not came in. They cried, cussed me, and acted as though it was all my fault.

Jim came home and said the end of the month was the end of the job. They had ran out of money. So this meant pulling Kevin out of school again. Me having to leave my job. And another move. We went back to Airway Hts. Once more. Put Kevin back in school there. Jim put his name on the union books and we sat it out once again. I went to work in a Cafe not far from the trailer court. While we were here they were getting ready for the Spokane Expo. One day President Nixon landed in Airforce one at the air base down the road from us. We all went out to the Highway to see his car go by. There was a Helicopter flying over it with guns sticking out of the sides. He went to down town Spokane to open the Expo.

Jim and Kevin and I went to the Expo one Sunday it was wet and miserable but I am glad we went.

Bobbie and Dave had a baby girl while we were there they named her Heidi. One evening they came flying in our front door with her wrapped in a blanket. Dave laid her on the table and unwrapped her. Here was this little thing with no clothes on. They were giving her a bath and discovered a tooth. They wrapped her in this blanket and ran over to show us. She was a sweet baby and really did like Jim.

In April of 1972 we had our first Grand son Jonathan Paul DeLong was born in San Diego, California. He was a very large boy. He and Jillian were both fine. I flew to San Diego in a couple of days. They were home from the hospital I thought I could help and was so thrilled to see my first grandchild. It was the day daylight savings time went in and Butch had not set his clock and was an hour late picking me up. He was working for an air conditioning co. He had got out of the Marines at 29 Palms and they had moved to San Diego. They bought a very nice comfortable three bedroom house. In a very pretty neighborhood. After about 4 or 5 days I decided they did not need my help and I went home.

In May Virginia was graduating from College and getting Married. She Married William (Bill) Randall from Corinth New York. He had Graduated from Gaulledet College the year before her and worked for the Government.

Jim Kevin and I flew from Spokane to Dullis Airport I thought that was in Washington. Sis had to drive out a long way to meet us. She had never seen her Father without a flat top so she got quit a laugh out of that.

We went to Bills apartment and stayed the night there. Bills family arrived that evening, They brought the kids some furniture. We put the mattresses from the two beds on the floor and some slept on the box springs. We made out fine. I had ordered the wedding cake and finger sandwiches. Bought mints and nuts. I had Myrtle order the flowers through her flower shop. The dress had been bought and altered. Sis wore a size 3 when she was married. She was a beautiful bride. Her dress was satin covered with Shantily lace. Jim had rented his tux in Spokane. We took it with us. The wedding was in a stone church on 16th street in Washington D.C. Bills family went home after the wedding. Sis had arranged for Jim, Kevin and I to stay in a room in the Dormitory at the college.

The next morning they had breakfast for the family's of the graduates. Then we were taken on a bus to a big cathedral somewhere in D.C. Our daughter graduated top in her class. We were all so proud. State Representative Brotsman from Colorado presented her diploma. She had entered College from Colorado. When they presented the diplomas they said for the family and husband or wife of the recipient to stand up. We stood up and so did Bill. A young man across the aisle told Bill to set down. He signed back to him and told him they were married yesterday.

After graduation we went to the kids apartment and they left for their Honeymoon in the Pocano Mts.

We called a Taxi to be there at 6 the next morning. Took it to a place in town that the shuttle busses run to Dullis Air Port. It was a beautiful ride early in the Morning there were long boats on the Patomic with oarsmen in them. They seemed to be flying over the water. In May everything was leafed out and blooming real pretty.

We boarded our plane and had breakfast. Landed in Denver, they brought breakfast again between Denver and Boise. We declined We were back in Spokane a little before noon. It was a wonderful trip. We have always been so very proud of our dear sweet daughter.

Well back in Spokane and no work in sight so we decided to move to Redmond Washington so as to be closer to a larger union hall in Seattle. We moved back into the same trailer court we lived in long ago before we moved to Denver. I immediately found a job cooking in a small cafe there in Redmond. We were there till fall and still no work for Jim. While reading the Sunday paper one day I found a help wanted add for a couple to manage a camp ground. We made an appointment for my next day off for an interview. We got the job if we wanted it. They wanted us to go look the place over before we made up our minds. It was an American Campground between Packwood and Randall Washington. It was in a beautiful setting on the Cowlets river. Between Mt. Raineer and Mt. St. Helens. (This was in the fall of 1972. Before the volcano blew). There were 800 private camp sites, 120 public ones, Three swim pools, a big lodge, small grocery store, meeting room and a laundry plus 11 out lying bath rooms to take care of. We were paid $600.00 a month and our apartment and utilities paid. We took the job.

Went back to Redmond and I gave a weeks notice at my job. My boss said the only way I could quit was to send my twin sister in to take my job. I had only been there a couple of months and they gave me a going away party. We hooked up the trailer and were on the move again to the camp ground. Kevin was real thrilled about the swimming pools. Jim had been told he had to sweep the pools every morning when he took the PH. He agreed then said to me how in the hell do you sweep water and what is a PH? I told him if we couldn't find out any other way there were always Libraries. But there was a man that showed him. Every one would comment on how clean and clear our pools were, he kept them beautiful. Last time we were by there they are all filled with dirt and planted in grass. It seems when Mt. St. Helens blew they were all filled with mud balls and dirt. So the companies big wigs decided to cover them rather than clean up the mess.

Kevin entered Packwood school that fall he rode the bus. Also went to Sunday school in Packwood. He liked it there real well and went the whole Year. Jim would mow the lawns with a little tractor mower and he would let Kevin run it some time even though he was only about 9 years old. We went to Montana for Christmas. I joined Weight Watchers while there. When we got home found the closest Weight watchers meeting was in Chehalis, about 60 miles away. We had to go into Chehalis once a week to get stock for the store. We went on Wednesday as that was when I could go to W.W. Jim would set in the car the Hour I was in there then we would go home. I was losing weight real well. But not as well as Jim who was eating the same thing. So I finally talked him into joining with me. At that time it was $5.00 to join and for a couple $3.00 a week We continued this all the time we lived there and had great results.

Jim built a zig zag rail fence along the drive way it was real pretty. There was an open field on the other side of it. One week end there was a ball game going on in this field. Jim and Kevin were playing. Jim bunted the ball and when he took off running some way he pulled the Achilles tendon loose. You could see it all rolled up and the blood under the skin. I took him to the Dr. and he had to stay off it for a while. The Dr. told him this happens real often in baseball players, basketball players, and all athlete plus old men!! It was really beautiful there, the rainfall was somewhere around 100 inches a year so every thing was so green and lots of under growth. There were tree trunks in the back of the campgrounds that were a good 14 feet across, so at one time there had been big trees maybe a forest of them in this area.

I had an old delivery truck with the steering wheel on the right side that I hauled all my cleaning things around in to clean the outlying bathrooms. There was a total of 38 showers 38 urinals and 76 toilets plus the sinks, floors and buildings themselves. They were not all used every day but had to be checked anyway. The 18 months we were there I never ran into a real bad mess.

We had a problem in the wash house with people and the dryers. For some reason people like to stuff a big commercial drier real full. They would put in their dime. (yes a dime) It would run for a short time and stop. They would come and tell me it was broken. I would go out and pull about 6 loads of cloths out and mound them on the sorting table. I would then put in a normal load about a third of the pile. I would also inform them even if the dryer could turn with the heavy load in it they would be all wrinkled up and it would cost them a good 60¢ to get them dry. Then I would have to go behind the dryer and put the belt back on.Also people sure leave dirty washers.

We had a minister from Seattle stayed there for a week. Every night he would show slides in the meeting room he had taken in the holy lands it was real interesting.

People at this time seem to think Cut off's were bathing suits. We could not let them in the pools with them. The strings on them plug up the filters and most of them had been worn for a week. Jim told one man who had on dirty greasy ones that was not a laundry. We had two couples there tenting for a week that were from England. One lady had a very brief bikini. One evening Jim was at the kitchen sink I was in the store helping an elderly man. You could see into our kitchen from where the cash register was, Jim started laughing I asked him what was so funny? He said this young woman with the brown bikini had jumped into the pool and lost the top to her bathing suit and the other three were splashing the water while she was trying to get it back on. The man in the store said I will go wash your dishes for you if you see that kind of stuff out that window.

Jim had cleaned the 2 pools down by the lodge one day and came back up to the house. A young boy came running into the store a little later and said one of the pools don't have hardly any water in it. Jim took off at a run he knew what he had done, he had left the back wash on. If those pools were empty with the high water level there they would come out of the ground but he saved it.

We had a pet deer in the camp grounds when we went there, her name was Rebeca. It seems her mother was killed on the highway and the people at the camp ground raised her. She was a real pet and a real pest at times. She would come up on the steps of the store and reach her head in around the corner and take what ever she could get a hold of candy bars, cough drops what have you. She loved potato chips, marshmallow or people food of all kinds. We had some people tenting in the camp grounds and he had gone to town and bought a pizza. When he came back he put it on the picnic table and they were getting other things out and when they turned around she had the pizza on the bench and she was having a feast. Late one evening we had a camper arrive and the woman got out to come in and register. All at once she was screaming I looked out and she was backed up against the front of the pickup and Rebeca was standing about 3 feet in front of her. So I went out and lead her away. The poor women had never seen a deer close and she was just shaking when she came in. Late that summer a man came up to the office carrying a little baby dear he said he found it lying in the brush when he was out walking. Jim told him to put it back exactly where he found it. It was only a day or so old. They took it back and found another one. Some deer had twins. Jim was hoping the mother would come back after the one had been disturbed. He told the other guy to go on about his business and he went down the road and sat on a log and watched. And it was Rebeca that finally came out of the woods and went to her babies.

Over the next few months she was around as usual with her two babies following her. Come hunting season we put a big red ribbon and bow around her neck. She disappeared. Some one in Randall was bragging about this big doe he shot that had a red ribbon around her neck. Sad but those things happen.

I took Kevin to a Dentist in Packwood he had a tooth ache. The Dentist felt he should have a root canal and sent us to a Dentist in Tacoma. He kept this 9 year old in the Dentist chair for 7 hours. When he got out he was a shaking crying child. We found out last year that root canal we had paid for 23 years ago was never finished.

We had a wind storm go through the area and it blew down 23 large Maple trees only one fell on anything. It fell over one end of a bathroom. At that time we had a crew of Helicopter loggers staying there with their trailers. All Jim had to cut these trees up and get them out of the way was an 18 inch chain saw. The loggers ask him if they could cut it up into fire wood lengths for him with their big chain saws? They had a bet as to who could cut the most. He told them to go for it. After their contest they piled it all up for use in the camp fires. That maple was so hard he would still be there sawing. The Helicopters would haul those whole trees right over the camp ground on big cables.

Crystal was working in Seattle and she had a blue motorcycle. She decided to come spend a week end with us. She arrived on her motorcycle. Blue motorcycle, blue helmet, and blue sunglasses covered with bugs. I think she kinda hated to get back on it and go back to Seattle it was quit a long way. Next time she came she drove down in her V.W.

Esther and Clyde came to visit us for a few days from Montana. We had our 35 ft trailer parked in the camp ground all hooked up. They stayed in it and seemed to enjoy their stay. We had a lot of people want to rent that trailer but I would not rent it out. I did not want smokers or pets in it. Esther enjoyed picking warm fresh blackberries to eat. They were all over the campground. First were the little ones that grew close to the ground. Then came the big ones. The vines grew big as a house all in a tangle. Jim would have to take an ax and cut them back out of the road every so often. They just took over.

Butch and Jillian came through on their way to Montana. They only stayed two days. We wished they could have stayed longer. They had their beautiful little baby boy who was about a year old. They swam in the pool by the house. They were there when Esther and Clyde were. Esther got mad at Butch because he was throwing the baby in the pool. They came to Montana and stayed about a month and stopped by over night on their way back to San Diego.

Myrtle and Wayne came out that fall for a week. By then the third crop of black berries were ready to pick they were a smaller variety on smaller bushes and very sweet. Myrtle started picking berries to bring home with her. She was putting them in one layer in pop cases and beer flats. They were in her flower van. When she had about a double layer of boxes all over the back end. Wayne told her those berries grow all the way to the ocean and you can't pick them all. She went home with a van full anyway.

When I felt I needed some time to myself and to just get away for a while, I would grab a pail and go pick berries. At one time I had 23 gallons in the freezer!!

Over the fourth of July week end we had a lot of Reservations. One young man came in on the 2nd and made reservations for camp sights for tents for 25 people. I asked him if it was a family reunion? He said kinda. He paid the deposit and left. The evening of the 3rd here they came Roaring into the front end. They were on Harley Davidson Motorcycles. Leathers, boots, chains, Long hair, beards and the whole works. I sent Kevin to the neighbors I was scared of them. We had a sign that said no Motorcycles in the camp ground. So we told them they would have to leave them up front. Jim took them back to see the camp sight. When they came back up he said give them back their deposit. They said they wanted something more private. I told them about an closed forest service campground on down the road about 5 miles toward Randall. They thanked us and asked if we would send the rest of them down there as they came by. We had them pulling in as late as 11:30. We found out later they went to the ranger station and got permission to use the camp ground. Left it real clean and spent a lot of money in town the 4 days they were there. They were Dr.s and Lawyers from the east coast on their annual vacation on their bikes.

Dennis and Sue stopped by. They had been picking Apples in Yakima and were headed to California to be farm workers. They had an old V.W. bus. They got to California the buss broke down and they hitch hiked home to Montana. End of migrant work for them.

Over Labor Day Bill and Sis flew out from Washington D.C. to visit us. It was Bills first trip to the northwest. They also picked blackberries. Sis fell in the brambles and Bill laughed at her for a while before he pulled her out. They enjoyed feeding the Deer and walking in the forest. They borrowed the Volks Wagon Bug and drove to Reno Nevada. Some where along the way the horn stuck on them. They could not hear it. When they pulled into a station the attendant came out and let them know and he took some wires apart to make it stop.

Bill wanted to see some Indians. There were some camping in the camp ground. So he took the car and drove back by them. He came back and said "they are just people" Maybe the people back east think the west Indians still wear feathers. They seemed to have a very good time and we sure did enjoy having all of our company that year.

Come fall and Kevin was back in school. He entered the 5th grade this year.

After labor day the business at the camp ground really fell off for the winter. I asked our boss if it was permissible for me to go to work in town for the winter? He said as long as the work was done in the campground he didn't care. I got a job Cooking the morning shift at the Randall Cafe. I worked there all winter and even with cooking I kept losing weight on my W.W. diet. In a year I lost a total of 70 lbs. (took me 7 years to gain it all back) Fought it every since.

While working here we fed those Helicopter loggers and put out 150 lunches. It was a good place to work and I enjoyed it. The roads got real bad and I had to have snow tires on the bug. I worked there till we moved the next spring.

One night I was awakened by a thump. It brought me right out of bed I turned the light on in the bedroom and Jim was not in bed. Then turned the hall light on and could see him on the floor in the bathroom. I rushed in and he had came to by then. I asked him what had happened and he didn't know. Said he got up to go to the bathroom and came to on the floor. I got him on his feet and asked him if he could make it to the bed. He thought he could and was leaning on me when he went down the second time. We both went down.

When I got Kevin on the school bus, we got in the car and I took him into Morton to the Hospital. The Dr. that was on call there asked him what he had been drinking. Jim told him if he had been drinking he would have known why he passed out. They never did find anything wrong with him. I think he had washed all the potassium out of his system. He had lost an awful lot of weight fast. For about six weeks he was so weak he could hardly walk across the floor. I told him I didn't care where we went either back to Colorado or to Montana I was tired of being so far from any relatives when we needed someone because of illness.

We talked it over and decided to move to Montana as soon as the snow was gone from Whites Pass. We gave a notice at the camp grounds. They told us we were such good managers they didn't want to lose us. They sent us to all the other camp grounds except the Dude Ranch. We knew we didn't want that. Horses no way. They thought maybe we would see one that we would like to move to so we would stay. We visited them all but none of them jumped out and grabbed us.

They had the Silver Streak rally at Ilwaco Washington. There were around 400 Rigs. All of the Managers for American Campgrounds went to the one there and cooked a Pancake Breakfast for them. We fed a little over 800 people. They had Cranberry Juice which was donated by Ocean Spray plant near there. Ham and eggs scrambled together, pancakes and coffee. We were set up in the wash house. There was a huge tent set up out back with picnic tables in it. Jim was on coffee detail he swears he made 500 gallons of coffee. We served from 7:AM to 11:AM. I was on pancake detail. There was two 40 inch gas grills side by side. The Pancake crew consisted of one mixing the batter. The Boss pouring it from a pitcher onto the grills. I followed him and turned them all over. Then went back and served them to people and he followed me pouring more. This went on for a solid four hours. I was a smoker at this time, One of the men came and told me he would take over after about two hours so I could go have a cigarette. The first pancake he went to turn over he threw on the floor. It landed on the Bosses shoe. After we all had a good laugh he handed the spatula back to me and said "It looked so easy". So I was on the pancakes the full 4 hours. Even though it was a lot of work it was really appreciated by all the people we fed. We enjoyed the week end on the Ocean. I was wishing for a storm. I really like a storm by the ocean. But it was nice weather all week end.

Come the first of April we moved back into our 35 foot trailer. Hooked it up to the pickup. Jim drove that and I drove the VW Bug and we headed home to Montana. We had a good trip no trouble. We went to Whitefish This was in 1975. Put Kevin in school in Whitefish to finish his 5th grade. We neither one had Jobs. Esther had told her Sister in law Opal Role who lived in Columbia Falls that we were coming to Whitefish and I would be looking for work. That I was a cook or waitress. Opal had a friend Ann Gosney who owned the Pines Cafe in Columbia Falls and needed a cook. I went to apply and got the job. I worked for her for a while then she leased the place out and I went to work at the Veterans Home. Jim had not found any work and I had spotted a 12 wide 65 foot two bedroom two bath trailer house I wanted. Went to Kalispell and made the deal on it then went to the bank in Whitefish and told them I wanted to take out a loan to buy it. We were making out the papers and I was asked where my Husband worked? I told them he was not working. The man said is he retired. I said no unemployed. He looked at me kinda funny and I said I am applying for this loan not my husband. We finished the paper work and he told me he would call and let me know. That afternoon he called and said to come get the check for the trailer sales. We had it delivered to a trailer court down behind the Catholic Church in Columbia Falls. It was not far from the schools and from where I was working. School was out by now. We hadn't been there to long when Jim got a call from Claudia Higson and told to come put in an application for a county job at the new Animal Shelter that was opening up. He had never done that kind of work before but after 11 months anything sounded good. He got the job. The new Shelter was built at the county dump. They had to run a notice in the Daily Interlake . The Kalispell News Paper. Stating that Jim was not related to Joe DeLong who was county Commissioner at that time because of nepotism. It had to be run for so many weeks, I don't remember for how many.

We no longer needed a baby sitter. Kevin was never at home alone very much tho.

After 8 months at the Veterans home I was a very tired employee. My supervisor found I could do the work by myself so she took my helper to the canning room. I worked the morning shift most of the time and that meant breakfast and the big meal at noon. There were 40 in the nursing home and 98 in the dining room plus about 28 employees. At this time they still had a garden there and do you know how much fresh spinach I had to wash and cook for that many people. They got a lot of angel food cakes for dessert as the salt free and diabetic diets could eat them also.

One day that still stands out in my mind. I had a very large roaster full of roasts. Upon removing them from the oven, I hit the lid on the top of the oven and it tipped the roaster up and my forearms were seared to the roaster top. I had to get the meat sliced and on the table. Meals could not be late. By the time I had the dinner out the liquid was dripping from my elbows on both arms. I opened the freezer and laid the burnt arms right on the ice on the shelves. Then put burn medicine and gauze on them, they were very sore around that heat from the grill, stove and oven for a long time.

Another time I was putting the huge mixing bowl on the mixer full of boiled potatoes to mash them. I caught the web of skin between the thumb and four finger on the little prong that the bowl fits over. Ran the prong right through the skin. That smarted for a long time also.

After 8 months I turned in my notice and quit. Every time some one talked to me I would cry and go home after work and sit and cry. Jim told me no job was worth it to find something else. Esther and Myrtle took me to Radium Hot Springs up in Canada for two days when I was done I think they thought I was about to go to pieces. It was lovely up there and we really did enjoy ourselves.

I then went back to work at the Pines Cafe. Ann had leased it out to a couple from Columbia Falls I don't remember their names I only remember she was a Red Head and didn't really know very much about running a restaurant. I worked for them that winter. One morning I went out to start my car and it was bitter cold and it would not start. The neighbor man was getting in his car he worked at the aluminum plant and I asked him if he would give me a ride to work. He did and I jumped in his car and left the keys in my car and the key to the restaurant was on the key ring. He let me out in front of the restaurant and went on to work.

I stood there for a minute going through pockets and all and it dawned on me that my key was in the car at home. I tried all the windows and found one in the dining room that was unlocked. Out back I found a five gallon bucket. When I put it upside down by the window I was up high enough so I thought I could hoist myself in. I threw my purse in and started to try to get myself in. After I was up high enough to get in I could not get my hands on anything, so had to go in head first onto the floor. Once I got in I was thinking If someone had gone by or the City Police had seen me I might have had some explaining to do. And my rear end and legs in white pants sticking out of the window would have been easy to spot. By the time the waitress got there I had the grill hot and the place warmed up and ready to open.

While working here I reached under the steam table one day for a pan and found out I could not lift my arms or my head. Hurt wow!! I finally got moving around finished my shift and went to the Dr. It seems I had twisted and broke an arthritis spur loose on my upper neck. Didn't even know I had them. Five all told at that time. This lead to Physical Therapy after work every night for six months. I had to drive to the Whitefish Hospital. Hot sand packs, A vibrator and tension on my head. After six months I decided that was enough. When it hurts to much to this day I take a pain pill and go on with what I am doing.

I also had an apparatus that fit over the door and under my chin. It had a bag of water hanging on it for tension. I had to sit with this on for five minutes every evening before I went to bed. It is still around somewhere.

The boss lady told me she was going to give up the restaurant. Ann put it up for sale.

I then went to work at Mt. Shadows Cafe. It was being run by some fellow by the name of Bob from

California. I could see the writing on the wall that he would not make it there so I went looking for other work. He did show me how to flip eggs over in an egg pan.

There was a Golf Course being built at Columbia Falls out on Tamarack Lane. It was now in the hands of a Couple from Polson. Their name was Bert and Grace Palauson.

This wonderful couple that ended up with the place to finish, had no idea at all about a Golf Course. They got the Restaurant running before they had the Golf Course finished. I heard they were looking for a cook. Graces Sister in law that lived in Columbia Heights was running the Restaurant and Bar for them. At that time it was in the old farm house and they had built a Dining room on to it.

I got the job. I worked out that season for them. Also kept my job at the other restaurant . Morning shift there and then home to change uniforms and take a bath then to the golf coarse till closing.

One day UPS delivered a couple of boxes and Grace looked in the boxes and wanted to know what all those things were. She was told they were cups for the greens. "She said why so many don't we only need one?" The men working on the course got quite a kick out of that.

They closed the Restaurant that winter.

Dennis and Sue were living on Pinkham. Madeline Utter gave Susan a lovely baby shower. The baby was due in February. They wanted to have the baby be born at our house. I said no I thought they would go to the Hospital. On February 28th I heard that Susan was in labor and they were at some friends house in Coram. As soon as I was off work I took off for Coram. It was snowing and I slid off the road I was driving the VW bug and three men stopped in a pickup and they all got out and pushed me back on the road. I drove around till I seen their Pickup parked in front of these apartments. The second door I knocked on was where they were.

I told them who I was and said I was staying till the baby was born. Dr. Kaufman was there for the delivery. I made coffee and the Dr. said we would have a long wait as her labor had stopped. It finally started again. This was leap year. At two minutes to midnight on February 28th our beautiful granddaughter Yousha River Lilly DeLong came into this world. They handed her to me and told me to clean her up. I took her into the bathroom where there was a very small dim light bulb and nothing to wash her with or to lay her on. I took a diaper and wet that in warm water and tried to clean her off. I wanted to take them home with me but the Dr. said not till morning. I went home. The next morning bright and early they came to our house. I had called Esther that the baby was ok and they were coming to the house. She came over and took her into the bathroom and cleaned her up real well. We put clean clothes on her and tucked her into bed with her mother. The whole family slept most of the day.

Kevin was in the 7th grade this year he wanted to take band. We bought him a saxophone, that lasted about half the year and he lost interest in that. He took shop this year and made a plant stand and two small stools. He did a very good job on them I am still using them twenty some years later.

One night right after we had gone to bed we heard gun shots and a lot of screaming down about three trailers from us. We stayed in the house. Soon there were Police cars all over. Then we found out a man had been shot and killed that lived there. Kevin played with their boys. They moved soon after.

I discovered a lump. When I went to the Dr. He said it would have to be removed. I told him he could do it on my day off. He agreed we set the date and I went into the hospital in Whitefish after work and was scheduled for surgery early ~the next morning. Dr. Johnson who was a wonderful Dr. and I had all the confidence in the world in him. Jim and Myrtle were there the next morning when I went into surgery. The Dr. told me they would do a frozen section and if it was cancer did I want to wake up and decide or did I want him to go ahead and do a mastectomy I told him to do what he had to while I was asleep. All went well and when I woke up I asked Myrtle and Jim what I had left? They told me no cancer. I told them to go home and let me sleep. Then come get me that evening.

I went home that afternoon and to work the next morning. I had a drain in the side of my breast on the right side and I am right handed. When I went home that day after using a spatula all day I was mighty sore. Went into the Dr. the next afternoon after work and he took the drain out and told me I had a benign tumor about the size of a walnut but all was well. He put me on hormones and I have never had any more tumors.

I got a phone call from Grace and Bert they wanted me to run their Cafe and Bar at Meadow Lake. She said her sister in law was just to old. I knew this but didn't want to step in her place and cause hard feelings. So I declined the offer even tho I really wanted it. They hired some young man that said he was a Chef. A month later Grace called me and said we are really in trouble would you come out to the restaurant. I went out to see what was wrong. The place was closed and she said I think all the meat is rotten. First I went into the most stinky walk in ever with spoiled produce all over. I lifted the lid on a electric roaster that was sitting on the floor and it had spoiled chickens in it. The mold followed the lid right up. I told them that everything had to be gotten rid of cleaning out the whole walk in, scouring and disinfecting. She said that is not all I think he let all the meat spoil and then froze it. We thawed some out and sure enough. So we threw everything away. Cleaned and disinfected and aired out every container there.

We sat down and discussed things. They told me they would pay me for every hour I put in and they put $3,000. in a checking account with my name on it. They wanted me to pay for everything from this account. Pay roll and all. I was to deposit all the money that the Bar and Restaurant took in. If I ran out of money and needed more I was to let them know.

I agreed to take the job , but needed to give my boss on my present job a notice. I did that that day gave him a two week notice. Hired some waitresses but needed a cook. I called Myrtle. Wayne was in Essex all week working and she had sold her flower shop to Ruth. I asked her if she would come to work for me during the week. She informed me she had never cooked in a restaurant but let her think it over. She talked it over with Wayne and he told her she had cooked for the family for a good many years he was sure she could do it. So she called and said yes. The next week we opened up and I spent one day showing her where things were and then I left her alone while I finished out my two week notice.

The first day I left her alone was Memorial day weekend. I would go out after work and be there in the evening she was glad to see my arrival every day. After two weeks I would relieve the bar tender and waitress for their days off and Myrtle for her days off. I had a note on the microwave as to how long to cook the lobsters. They were 10 oz. lobsters and I would fillet them and clean them then wrap them in clear wrap and freeze them separately Worked great. I decided to get some slipper lobsters that were about a 6 oz one and serve steak and lobster. One night I was tending bar and the waitress came out and said Myrtle needs you in the kitchen. When I went in there she had this little lobster by the tail and she pounded it against the serving table, sounded like a rock. I said well what did you do to it? She said I cooked it for the amount of time the chart says to. I about died laughing. I told her to just watch the little ones and she could tell when they were done. She left that laying on the table and every one had fun with it that night they would pick it up and give it a whack when they walked by.

One night when I was waiting on tables. I had orders for about 20 rib steaks. Myrtle said on a 30 inch grill you have to be kidding. (At that time they were not rib eyes but the whole steak bone and all) I told her to cook the well done one first and put them on the cool end of the grill then the med. and pile them up on the well then get the med. rare on and then the rare. Serve the first ones off and then the other ones would be ready. Worked great. In September Myrtle had her 50th birthday the girls gave her a birthday party really the only one I think she ever had. That helped her get through the big 50.

On Esthers 50th she said she didn't want anyone to even mention it and we didn't and I think she was sorry then.

Back to Meadow Lake. We would go out early and play 4 holes of golf and then go in and start our days work. At that time #4 was right by the club house. I had one waitress from Kalispell, her husband was bar tender. I can't even remember their names. She came into the kitchen one day and said can you turn the air conditioner on. I am sweating out there. I told her women don't sweat they glisten. She looked at me and said they might but I sweat.

After she left because she was pregnant I hired some more they would work a few days and not show up. One day I had no waitresses. I called three in Columbia Falls that I knew were waitresses and were not working. Each of them told me if they went to work they would lose their County help and child care while they were getting free schooling. They would not work. I desperately needed some one for that night. I called Esther. She said she had not worked as a waitress since high school days many many years ago. She agreed to wear a white pleated skirt and white blouse & help. (my waitresses wore white uniforms and black aprons) I gave her an apron and she went to work. She gave great service as she waited on them as she would like to be waited on. And knew so many of them after all her years as a nurse in Whitefish. They couldn't figure out why she was moonlighting as a waitress. Till she told them only one night as I was desperate.

I had a chart in the waiters station as to what cleaning I wanted done every week. Well Ester kept saying after we closed that she wasn't quite done yet. I finally went out to see what she was doing. And she had done nearly everything on the list . She thought it had to be done every night. We had a very clean dining room and waitress station let me tell you. Then she came into the kitchen and wanted to know what she was to do with this? She reached in both apron pockets and brought out two hands full of dollar bills. I told her that was hers, she said don't I have to share? I told her no and she kept those tips in a little metal box for years. She may still have them. When she waited tables in high school tips were unheard of.

I let the help all have a free drink after work. So they would sit at the bar and stay in the building While I went up to the office and did my daily report and got the deposit made up. I would go by the bank on the way home and drop it in the night deposit. I really appreciated them staying there. Two nights a month I didn't ask them to. Those were the nights I did pay roll. I would lock myself in then go up to the office upstairs. The window looked out on that black parking lot with only my VW parked out there. If I would end up with my payroll off even a penny I would be there for a long time. It had to come out right. This was before computers so it was all done in ledgers. On leaving on one of these nights Just as I unlocked the kitchen door, there was a WHOOSH noise right by the door. I slammed the door shut and it locked and I ran all the way to the car. Locked myself in and sat there but could see nothing. The next day I was telling the maintenance man about it and he really laughed. He said that was the sump pump that pumps the water out of the old cellar under the kitchen. It only works late at night. What were you doing out here by yourself after two in the morning?

The place was broken into while I was there. The glass in the kitchen door was broken out. They went through the kitchen and dining room to the bar and never moved a thing in the dark. They must have known the place pretty well. Straight to the bar and didn't take any bottles from the back bar but broke the lock on the liquor room door and took the two garbage cans we kept under the bar and emptied the liquor room out.

When I went to work and seen that broken window I was leery of going in. But they were long gone and we never found out who done it.

I needed a dish washer and took applications. I hired one young girl and she came to work all dressed up with a big hat on. She was not worth a tootely twat. I ended up sending her home after a couple of hours. Her mother brought her back out and told me to make her work. I told her no I could do it myself better than stand and make some one do it.

There was a young man working on the golf course and he told me his sister was looking for work. I told him to tell her to come in the next day and be prepared to stay and work a shift. She came and I hired her. One of the best workers I have ever seen. Our water taps in the sinks (no dishwasher) were both marked Hot. I noticed her hands were beet red and asked her if she was allergic to the dish soap. She said no it was the hot water. I told her to cool it down. She said both are marked hot so I thought I was to use straight hot water. When I told her to take a break and eat lunch she didn't want to. She kept finding things to do

I finally made her sit down and eat. She told me her brother told her I fired people if they didn't keep working. He thought that was real funny. When she told me I could have scalped him.

When she quite and went to college. I hired Mary she was a great gal also. I got two in a row. Eventually Mary left and she and Tina moved to Arizona. Mary still lives there but Tina came back to Montana. She Married and had a family and is now one of my bosses at work.

Bert and Grace came in one day and wanted my check book. They said according to the bank statement I had an excess of $10,000 in the account and they wanted to buy a greens mower. So they wrote out a check for that amount.

When we finished the season and had closed for the winter, Bert and Grace came to our house to get their books. They were satisfied with everything. They left and about a half hour later here they came back. I couldn't figure out what could have been wrong. They came in and I asked them if something was wrong. They told me they were very satisfied and had a little something for me in appreciation They laid 15 $100. bills on the table. I had not expected anything like that. I bought a fourth of a city block north of the schools in Eureka with it before I blew it on something.

Esther and Clyde had gotten a divorce after 36 years of marriage. They sold their house south of Whitefish and Esther moved into an apartment in town. In fact she moved quite a few times.

Dad had fallen in his apartment in Eureka and they brought him to the Whitefish Hospital. When he was able to leave the Hospital Esther took him to her apartment and was taking care of him and working. She had him for about a month then put him in Colonial Manor Nursing home in Whitefish. He was such a large man and it was just to much with her working and all for her to take care of him. He had cataract surgery on his eyes. He was in the hospital here in Kalispell for a week. He was very frightened and wanted all of us girls with him. He came through it fine. Then he could see again and wanted Louis Lamar books to read. I scoured all the second hand book stores for them. When he would finish a stack of them he would say I think it is time to get some more. He started putting a mark in them so I would not buy the ones back he had already read.

Dad kept wanting to go back to Eureka. So he finally was moved to Mountain View Manor in Eureka. He was there for nearly ten years. He had excellent care while he was there.

Myrtle and I took a trip in January of 1977. We had a new VW rabbit. Jim said he and Kevin would be fine. We left in a terrible snow storm. No snow plow's out between Kalispell and Lob. We made it fine to Missoula. From there to Garrison the road was like a white hammock. Myrtle was watching the markers at the side of the road part way to keep me from running off the road. When we got to Garrison our gear shift was frozen. We ate breakfast and stayed there till it thawed out.

After we got over Monida pass the roads were good and we drove to Salt Lake. Myrtle was driving and I was reading the Map. Bad move!! We were trying to find a Motel 6. Where I had her turn off the free way we ended up down by a soup kitchen in not to good a part of town. It was dark by now. Myrtle said I see the Capitol buildings lit up on the hill. I am heading that way. She did and We finally found the Motel.

The next morning we went through the Mormon square. Even heard the tabernacle choir. Went through the Bee hive house. (Brigum Youngs home).

We then headed for Salida Colorado. We arrived there in the evening. Found a Motel that had a Triple A sign. We rented a room and the place had no heat. We ended up sleeping with robes and finally coats on. There was mold up 6 inches on the shower curtain. Really a miserable night. We were up early the next morning and on our way. I took her to Buena Vista and showed her where we had lived there and where I had worked.

Then on to Denver it was so cold and the wind was blowing like you can't believe. I showed her where we had worked in Denver and the house we had built.

Then we headed south through Colorado Springs, Pueblo and on over Raton Pass to the little town of Raton we had a nice warm motel room and a leisure dinner.

The next morning we took off bright and early and went through Sante Fe and Albuquerque and on to Flagstaff Arizona and stayed there over night. Seeing a lot of sights along the way.

The next day we took of along Route 66 and drove to Kingman had lunch there and headed south to see the London Bridge at Lake Havasue. Spent time along the way getting out to see some cactus and just enjoying ourselves. Between Lake Havasue and Yuma the car started shaking all over you would have sworn it was about to fall to pieces. We kept going. Got into Yuma in the evening and spotted a VW garage but it was closed. We were traveling on a tight budget and thought if it cost to much to get the car fixed we would head back home. The only Motel we could find a room in was something else. Good thing it was dark when we found

it. I think I was driving by then and Myrtle said there is a vacancy sign, I made a U turn in the street and we rented their last room. Went in and locked the door and sat there and laughed There were no drawers in the night stands or chests only the frames sitting there. The beds were clean and we were tired so we went to bed.

The next morning when we started looking around the shower Had mold up about a foot on the walls and there was dirt and sand on all the window ledges. We decided to lock the door and go eat breakfast when we walked outside there was a swimming pool full of junk out front and really a scuzzy place. So decided to load up and go find the garage, then eat and take it from there. Went to unlock the door and found you couldn't lock it. So we had spent the night in this place and the door wasn't even locked. This motel cost us the most of any we stayed at on the whole trip.

We went to the garage and when I drove in a man came out and he said your catalytic converter has gone out. I told him I didn't know what went out but could they fix it. He said give us an hour. We went and ate and when we came back the car was fixed. I asked him what we owed and he said nothing it is still under warranty. So we were two happy travelers that went on our way.

We went through the Territorial Prison at Yuma before we continued on to California. I had been calling home every other night and all was well. We went from Yuma to San Diego. At one place we were in a tower observation point and seen a sign that said you are on the top of the San Leandro Fault. We didn't linger there to long.

Arrived in San Diego and found a nice Motel. We walked all over looking around and seen some brochures in the Motel lobby about tours. We called the company and booked a tour for the next day to Tijuana Mexico and of San Diego. It only cost us $12.00 each. They picked us up the next morning and took us to a departure place and loaded us all on big Buses for Mexico. We had fun shopping and looking it all over. Myrtle was bargaining in a shop and I thought we would miss our Bus but we didn't. Arrived back in San Diego and were put on smaller Buses and taken all over town, They even took us to Blacks Beach (the nude beach) but I guess it was to cold, no bathers that day. Went on a tour of the harbor , that was all so interesting. We then went back to our motel. Up early the next morning and headed north. I was driving on the freeway and Myrtle said our next turn off is coming and I started to make a lane change and Myrtle said STAY WHERE YOU ARE . I looked over on her side and there was a truck wheel as high as our car.

Myrtle was driving and when we got to Hursts castle it was to late for us to go see it. We had planned to see it. While we were driving up Big Sur it got dark so we couldn't see that. We stayed at Carmel for the night. The next morning we had planned to take the 16 mile drive up the coast. Wayne had told Myrtle how pretty it was. He was stationed down there before he shipped out for Korea. We went down and seen the beach at Carmel it was beautiful. Then took off to find 16 mile drive. Ended up in a line of traffic and we finally reached a gate where a man came and wanted our tickets. We said what for? He said this is Pebble Beach and the Bing Crosby golf tournament is on today. We told him we only wanted through to go up 16 mile drive. He said Oh no it is closed the next two days. So we turned around and headed north on the free way.

We drove up north of San Francisco and stopped at the first smaller town we came to. After getting registered in a motel, and settled in we took a bus to town. I am not sure where we were but I think our guardian angel was sitting on our shoulder. We got off at some kind of park and it was getting dark. We were walking around and seen some men drag a girl into a car. We tried to get a cab but they wouldn't stop even when you got right in the street. We finally got back to where we had gotten off the bus and caught another one. We seen where someone had taken out a gas pump in an accident and the police had a bunch of people spread eagled up against an apartment house in another place. When we got back to our Motel we decided where ever we went was no place for two middle—aged women from Montana.

The next morning we went into town in the car. We found a place we could get a tour of San Francisco. The one we really wanted was filled up .That would have taken us out to Ellis Island We took a city tour tho and it was real interesting. We went up on top of the hill and it was a clear day we could see all over the harbor and the city. Down to the bay where all the expensive houses were. Down the street that is so crooked. Across the Bridge to Treasure Island. (A lot of the places that since then were so badly damaged in an earth quake). Then they took us to Fishermans wharf, The driver said you can get off here and take the trolley back or ride back with me. We got off.

Had dinner on fishermans wharf and walked around and looked everything over. When our curiosity was filled we took the trolley. That was an experience for both of us. We got off the trolley and if we had gone the way I thought our car was parked I don't know where we would have ended up. I don't have much sense of direction and can get lost real easy. Myrtle found our parking garage after we took a stroll through part of China town.

Now we headed north again. We had stopped at the Missions and wineries all the way through California.

San Juan Capistrano was real pretty and quite impressive. When we went in there were pigeons flying all over and landing on people. I wanted no part of that. With my fear of birds. Myrtle bought some pop corn and fed them while I went by. We spent some time here It was really interesting. There is a chapel that has a sign outside the door that said no talking inside. It is so beautiful and inspiring you don't even want to talk when you go in. We saw the rooms the Priests had lived in. The missions are all built a days horse back ride apart. I really enjoyed this part of our trip. All the missions and also the wine places and vineyards

While we were traveling the program of Roots was on TV so we had to stop every night and find a room and have our evening meal over by the time it came on.

We stayed in Brookings Oregon after having gone through the Redwoods and on north that day. Had real good Abalone for dinner that night. I called home and Jim told me he had taken Kevin to the Dr. that day he had chicken pox. He was OK and to go ahead and enjoy the rest of our trip. I was a little anxious to get on home then.

Only drove through Oregon as I remember and on north and through Randall and Packwood Washington, over Whites Pass and to Spokane.

When we started our trip our zipper bank bag had $600.00 in it and we had paid everything out of it. It was getting a little thin by this time.

When we arrived home we had $2.00 and some change to divide up. Unbeknown to the other one we each had $100.00 hid in our purse.

Shortly after we returned from our trip I got a Phone call from Tom Price in Eureka saying he had gotten a letter or a call from Butch saying he was flying into Calgary from London and wanted someone to pick him up. Could we do it? We were having terrible storms and I was afraid to drive up there. I called the airport in Calgary when his plane came in and had him paged. I told him I was afraid to drive and Dad had to work. It seemed Tommy had a bad back and could not drive that far. I asked him if he had enough money to take the bus to Elco and I would meet him there. He checked on the ticket and called me back and told me what time to pick him up. He came home from England with an old guitar case and a old suitcase. He had on very worn out cloths. This is all he had left to show for all his years in the Marines and his five or six years of marriage. I left my car in Eureka and rode with Tommy and Norma to Elko to get him. Then I brought him home to Columbia Falls. Finally helped him get an old pickup and he went to Eureka and found a job up there. He had rented a house?? up on Pinkham. Later he borrowed my VW and went to Denver. When he came back he was pulling a U Haul with it and had brought a woman and her two little girls with him. They all lived in the house?? on Pinkham.

Jim was coming home from work one night and on the straight stretch of road between The Blue Moon and Columbia Falls a deer jumped over the fence and lit on the hood of the car. It really fixed it's front fender hood and windshield. This was the VW Rabbit. When the accident was called in the CBers in the valley had a ball with that one a rabbit killed a deer on highway 40.

We sold our trailer and I sold my property I had bought in Eureka and we bought a house in Whitefish. Esther had married Paul Drager and was working in his Insurance Office. Myrtle was working at Essex, cooking in the Isaac Walton Inn. They had rented an Apartment in Whitefish. So now the SISTERS THREE were all living in the same town again.

Dennis and Susan had bought some property up Therroult Creek out of Eureka and were living in a tepee the first summer there but now had built a nice house it had two rooms downstairs and one up. Dennis had dug a well under the house and they had a pump on the kitchen sink. It didn't have Electricity or a bath room but was a nice warm house.

They stopped by the house in Whitefish on my day off and left Yosha with me while Dennis took Susan to Kalispell to take her out for dinner on her Birthday. Yosha had always enjoyed playing with the clothes pins when she was there. She was talking now. When I got out the clothes pins she looked at me and said a Good Grandma has a toy box. So we went to Ben Franklins and we built a small toy box. She wanted books in it even then.

I decided to bake a birthday cake for Susan so they could have cake and coffee before they headed home. Yosha was sitting on the table with one of her little books watching what I was doing. When I got out the mixer she wanted to know what that was? I told her and she said Susan don't have one of those. (She took a streak of calling them Dennis and Susan). When I turned it on she about jumped out of her skin. She said whats that? I told her Electricity run the mixer. She looked real puzzled and looked up at me with her big brown eyes and said. Well Susan don't have any of that either.

She was a doll. We went up and spent Christmas eve with them and Santa came to see her.

In November of 1978 Shianne Willows came to join their Family. Always such a pretty baby and so tranquil and always smiling. She had beautiful dimples. Now they had two beautiful little girls.

In August or September of 1978 the woman that had been living with Butch up on Pinkham left and went back to Denver. Butch had been working in Libby on a job and he met Annette Kajik from Pennsylvania. She was 12 years younger than he was. He brought her to Pinkham. Here she had been raised in the city and moved into a dilapidated house with an outhouse and no bath tub or shower. He had chickens running around and if the door was left open they came in the house. She went out to get the mail one day and when she started back to the house there was a moose between her and the house so she climbed a tree and stayed there till Butch came home from work. They soon moved to Eureka to an apartment in town. He had gone to work at Plumb Creek mill now.

Jim started to have night mares nearly every night now from having to put all the animals to sleep at the animal shelter. There was a maintenance job at the golf coarse opened up and he was hired. This was a job he loved. He hasn't worked at hardly anything else since.

The Golf Coarse was put up for sale and was purchased by a group of Wheat farmers and business men from east of the Mountains. They hired John and Pat as managers and I worked for them for a while. Finally got tired of cleaning up messes from all the young people that were working in the kitchen so I gave my two week notice and went to work in Whitefish at Mr. P's. That was a real nice couple to work for Barbara and Elmer were tops in my books. I finally got tired of cooking and decided I wanted something else. I applied at Haines Drug Store and was hired. I worked there for awhile.

This spring they were having a walk-a-thon to raise money for the nursing home in Eureka it was over 20 miles. Esther got lots of pledges. I don't think they thought she would walk over 5 miles. She walked all the way. Wayne took dad out from the nursing home to see how far she was. He told her you can't get in the car you can make it and she did. I had a bag of Dr. Sholes soap and soak hanging on her door knob when she arrived home. As a joke. she was stiff and sore for a few days but made it all the way.

I had gone to work now at Ben Franklins. I was hired to take care of the candy department. The morning I arrived at work Jack said have you ever sold Fabrics? I told him no, but I sew. He said my fabric lady quit and that is where I am going to put you. They had to show me how to measure and cut fabric and I didn't know one kind from the next but learned fast . I worked there for some time.

I then decided that I had always wanted my own Restaurant so I started to look for a building. I found one in Columbia Falls. It had been a Pizza parlor so it had a grill and vent system, some tables. Refrigeration and a nice sized dining room. I made a trip to Missoula bought dishes and equipment at the wholesale house.

Back home I made red and white tablecloths for all the tables. Did a lot of cleaning. Called the health department for a checkup, passed that with flying colors. Had all the license and all that is necessary so we were on our way. I made all the spaghetti sauce, Lasagna and everything we served. Pan fried the chicken. It was very popular. I had bought a portable three hole steam table. I kept the sauces and spaghetti hot in this.

I had a Christmas party to cater for Melbys store Myrtle was cooking at Essex. This party was on a Wednesday which was a slow day for us. I asked her if she could come down and work for me that night while I went and took care of this party. I told her it would not be busy. I took the steam table with me to keep the food hot. I told Myrtle she could keep things hot on the stove. When I came back after the party the restaurant was closed and Myrtle, Jim, Wayne and the waitress were all sitting down and looked bushed. Well needles to say it had been the busiest night we had there. When I came in the door Myrtle said "Wednesday night is never busy"??

I took in enough to stay ahead of the creditors as I paid for everything that came in. My help all got paid. I am the only one that was not getting a pay check. The rent was a little high. I had not signed a lease as I didn't know how it would go and didn't want held there with one. When it finally started to take off the man that had the building could see it also and he came and wanted to double our rent. No way could we do that. We moved all the equipment into the garage at home and closed up.

Esther, Myrtle and I decided it would be fun, in 1975 before we got two old to do so to take a memory walk out around in the country where we lived as children. We packed our lunch and took off from Myrtles house in Eureka bright and early one morning in the spring it was a beautiful day.

This article appeared in the Tobacco Valley News on June 26th 1975. It was written by Esther Paul, my eldest sister.

A SENTIMENTAL WALK...

Myrtle Richmond of Eureka and Helen DeLong and Esther Paul of Whitefish, the three daughters of Eva and Francis Shenefelt, set out from the Richmond home in Eureka on June 12th on a thirteen mile walk. Their plan was to cover the area in which they had lived as children 45 to 55 years ago.

The first stop was the place now owned by the Netzloffs, where they searched for a large rock on the top of a hill. This rock was special as it was there that mother placed Helen and Myrtle while she worked nearby in the field.

During these times, Esther was left at the house to do the daily cooking and housework.

After leaving the rocky hilltop, they began to look for the "root cellar." In those days, the root cellar was very important as it held the food supply for the family.

"Mother insisted that the cellar be immaculate," The

women said. "Although the floor was dirt, it was smooth and clean at all times.

When they arrived at the "cellar." they found that the years had taken their toll. Only the hole in the hillside remained.

They easily found the rocks used under the former family home, the barn and the other out-buildings. The precious garden spot and the very good spring of water were also discovered. In fact, the spring is still being used by the family in the new home close by.

From the Nezloff ranch the trio walked around the lake and on to the Black Lake school. The miles are longer now they decided. While children , Myrtle and Esther walked these miles for several years. When snow was to deep for a little six year old girl's legs, they rode a horse.

They really preferred to walk, as the horse had to be saddled and unsaddled, fed at noon and the stable cleaned twice each week The daily trip to and from school for the two girls, aged six and eleven, was eight miles.

The next stop was the homestead of their Grandparents John and Sara Shenefelt. Esther was born on this homestead, which is now owned by a cousin Darrel Roose. Their walk then led them down the big sand hill where they had all spent many happy summers playing with cousins and friends. These children were the O'Brians, Rooses, and the Rhodes girls.

Lunch was enjoyed on the grounds of "Aunt Myrtle and Uncle Earl Rhodes" place. Although the log house is no longer there, a peaceful restful scene was provided by the lovely old lilac bushes which were in full bloom.

After the pause for lunch, they went down the hill to the Tobacco River (what a shame that some thoughtless person burned so much of the planking on the lovely old Pigeon Bridge). While looking down from the bridge, they recalled the baptisms as memories they would never forget—The minister waist deep in the flowing river, each one to be baptized dressed in white and the others softly singing old hymns. Times were very difficult during those years, with few having much money. However, most people helped each other and almost all believed and trusted in God.

From the Pigeon Bridge, the sisters walked up the river to the old Pigeon homestead where their mother (Eva Baillargon) had grown to woman-hood and married their father, Francis Shenefelt. The location provided a lovely, romantic setting for a home wedding sixty years ago on June 30th.

Next, they went up the hill to the new highway, stopping on the way to the Hubert McKenzie home. This was the homestead of the sister's uncle Roe Shenefelt After first camping under the still standing old pine tree, Roe and Laura Shenefelt built their first cabin. Later, they constructed the handsome house which Bonnie and Hubert McKenzie are now carefully and lovingly bringing back to its former self.

Back on the highway, the trio spent time in the cemetery where many close family members and friends are buried. Among those buried in the cemetery are their mother and both sets of pioneer grand parents.

Many happy memories came back as thy neared the Art Nutting ranch. This house had been built for Francis and Eva Shenefelt when they were a young married couple.

Later, the young family moved to Fortine for a few years. Myrtle was born at the Fortine ranch, which is now owned by the Keith Burgess family. Later, the family returned to the present Art Nutting ranch, where Helen was born. While living there, Esther attended the Iowa Flats school, traveling by horse and buggy.

After a short pause at Paul's Four Corners, they walked on to the Richmond home where they were greeted by Sharon and John LaBonty with ice cold tea. Never had tea tasted so good!

Esther said. "Thirteen miles in six and a half hours walking time can be a very long walk if you do not do it more frequently than we do, but we enjoyed and loved each mile that we walked.

There is no place like the area around Eureka in the spring of the year to get out in the country and walk.

Myrtle and I took over the restaurant in the Bowling Alley in Whitefish. We built it up till we didn't have enough seating to take care of our noon crowd. The bar was not open at noon time so we seated people in there also. We did all the work ourselves Myrtle cooked and I waited on tables. Toward the end of the bowling season the people that owned the bowling alley decided they wanted a bigger piece of the pie and told us come the first of the month our rent would go up. It was a 400% increase. A good share of the equipment was mine. We told them no way. We were out by the first off the month. They ran it about six weeks and had no business left and they closed it up.

Myrtle, Wayne, Jim, Kevin and I took a trip to Washington D.C. Kevin was 16 years old and didn't want to go. But he went anyway. We went by Train. Kevin contacted ringworm on his face. He swears he got it of the head rest on the train. We had to change trains in Chicago. Our train was late getting in there, they were holding the train for the westbound to arrive. When we got on the train none of us could sit together all night. Bill and Virginia met us with their Van in Wahington D.C. They were living in Upper Marlboro Maryland at this time. They had a very nice tri-level

home. We had a very enjoyable week there they took us to see everything we could think of. One day they took Kevin to some amusement park in Virginia. They had a German Police dog. He was a little frightened at all of us talking. He had been raised in a deaf family and wasn't accustomed to us. We went to Mt. Vernon While there Myrtle and I each bought a start of Ivy that grows there. We brought it home in our suit cases. Mine later died but Myrtle still has hers. It is a very pretty plant.

We took a bus route through the south to come home. I may be the only one who enjoyed it. We went through The blue ridge Mts. of Virginia. Beautiful country, when we arrived in Nashville we had a lay over, or we waited for the next bus. We were within walking distance of the old Grand Old Opera building so we went and were able to go through that. It was very interesting. We were not able to go see anything else. Went through Memphis but didn't stop.

We were on our way through Arkansas and on to Oklahoma. We stopped in Shawnee and stayed at Betty and Eugene's. This was Jims brother. We visited the rest of the DeLongs while there. Eugene took us to an automobile museum and to an Indian museum at the University in Shawnee. Then another day to the Cowboy Museum in Oklahoma City. We were then on our way to Salida Colorado. We stayed with Doris and Clyde. Jims oldest brother. On arrival there my suitcase didn't make it. We had all only taken one suitcase. They found mine at the bus stop on the top of Ratone Pass. It arrived the
next day.

We went to the top of a real pretty observation Mt. there you can see all over the valley. Then they took us to the top of Monarch Pass. Myrtle got into some kind of pollen there and she had an asthma attach so they left and came on home.

Jim and Kevin and I stayed out our visit and then came on home. We came by way of Salt Lake. Myrtle and Waynes route was north through Denver and Wyoming. I really enjoyed the trip. The rest didn't think to much of the bus ride.

When we arrived back in Whitefish every one had to go back to work. Wayne on the railroad. (he was working in Whitefish by now) They had sold their house in Eureka and were renting a house in Whitefish. Jim back to the Golf Course in Columbia Falls and Myrtle and I were working at Ben Franklins.

In November 1978 Our little Shianne was born. Dennis called and told us she had arrived at home during the night. This was Shianne Willows. Another beautiful baby girl. This one looked like the DeLongs where Yosha looks just like her mother. All went well.

The following March Butch and Annette presented us with Nichole. She was so fair and blond (still is) another beautiful baby. She was born in the Whitefish Hospital at high noon. I went up during my lunch hour to see her. Butch and Annette were waiting at our house for the blessed event and he had woke me up at about 4 in the morning and said he was taking her to the hospital. He didn't want me to go as he knew I had to go to work the next morning.

On their way home from the hospital they stopped in at Esther and Pauls insurance office to show them their little Princess.

They soon bought a trailer in Eureka and had it moved to Fortine. They lived in it for many years. Probably about 13 years

When Shianne was about two and a half, Dennis and Susan wanted to go some where. We told them we would be happy to keep the girls while they went. Shianne was a very shy little one. When they left they told the girls good-by and I told them to just go we would all be OK. We had a full window in our front door. I had a sheer curtain in it. Yosha was fine when they left. Shianne went to the door and was really crying. She pulled on the curtain and pulled it down. Mom and Dad started back, I motioned for them to go on. They got in the car and left. She turned around and looked at us and her face was covered with tears and her nose was running. She all at once put on a big grin as much as to say well it didn't work did it. They were as good as gold. I really think better than mom and dad were, as they kept calling about every hour all evening long.

One summer Susan went to Missoula and was certified as a Red Cross life guard. She worked at Chrystal Lakes as a life guard and as a waitress. Dennis was working as a carpenter in the Eureka area and some in the Flathead.

Butch was working full time at Plumb Creek mill at Fortine now. Annette went to work at Chrystal Lakes as a life guard the next year after Susan. Nichole had learned to swim in Fortine Creek and she would Jump in the pool at the Golf Course and everyone was very surprised when she would bob to the top and swim to the edge and climb out only to jump in again. One day she seen the big kids jumping from the Fortine bridge into the creek. She wanted to do it also. Her mother was below and her dad on the bridge with her and they let her jump. What a belly flop. She told me Grandma that hught. I not do that any more.

Kevin by now was being a stinker. He didn't want to go to school and his grades were going down, down. On his 16th birthday (He had his drivers license by now) we let him take the car. About eleven o'clock I get a call from the Whitefish Police station to come get my son. The car would have to be towed as he had laid it on its side over by lion Mt. some place. Where did we want it taken. I told them to bring it to the house. After it was brought home I went down to get him. There had been a whole car full of kids and they had beer. They let the rest of them go home but as he was driving I had to go get him. He was not allowed to drive for a while.

We traded the Rabbit in on a 1980 Ford Fairmont. Jim drove the VW to work and I walked to work. The Ford got 40 miles on it. Sitting in our back yard. Finally found out Kevin had a set of keys made from his dad's keys one evening so he had his own keys. He was driving the ford to city beach every day while we were at work.

We put the VW up for sale and the day before the man from Kalispell was to come look at it. Kevin was driving it with permission and he ran into the back of the city water truck. He said the brakes failed him but there was nothing wrong with the brakes he was not watching where he was going. We knocked $200.00 from the price and the man bought the car anyway. Have been sorry every since that we sold our last beetle.

While I was at work one day a young real-estate man asked me if I would sell my house. I told him no. He said it was the size of houses that were selling at that time. Think it over. I finally told him if he could get me $34,000 above his commission he could sell it . We had paid $17,000 for it four years before He prepared a sign for the front yard and never put it up. The first couple he brought to see it said it was clean and didn't stink and they wanted it.

The following Sunday I was real good to the family and cooked a pork roast with gravy and all the trimmings and ended up in the hospital to have Gaul bladder surgery. To much fat I guess.

The next day the Realtor came to the hospital with flowers and papers for me to sign. We had a month to get out.

Started to look for a used Mobile Home. I looked and looked took Esther with me we really seen some leaky stinky dumps. Finally I seen one at a trailer sales they were using for an office. I talked them into selling it to me. It was a real nice clean, light, roomy one with a lovely big front end kitchen. We had it moved to Columbia Falls into the court we had lived in before. Jim was working at Meadow Lake golf course and I went to work for Peter Putzers Real Estate as a receptionist. Worked there a couple of months and decided that was not for me.

I went back to work for Ben Franklin in Whitefish. While I was working at Ben Franklins Myrtle was working there also. When we would get off work on Friday night Jim and Wayne would pick us up and we would go to the A&W for our dinner. They had put in a McDonalds across the street and one night we decided to go there instead of the A&W. None of us knew what to order. The men were hungry so they ordered a big meal not knowing what it was. Myrtle and I had sandwiches, frys and a drink When our dinner came the men had kids meals. A little sandwich small fries a little coke a cookie and a toy. We laughed over that many times. The next week we went back to the A&W.

Jims job at Meadow lake would be over soon for the winter so we moved the trailer to Greenwood trailer Court in Whitefish. It is still sitting in the same spot there and still being lived in.

While we were there I told Jim and Kevin to be more careful when they backed out of yard as they were going to hit the carport behind us. I went out one morning to go to work and there the car sat with a tail light broken out. When I came home that night I asked them which one of them hit the car port and neither one of them knew. Well $80.00 later Jim owned up to doing it.

Kevin joined the Army reserves and they sent him to Fort Leonard Wood Missouri for basic training for I think 8 weeks. He was still going to school part of the time. Not as much as I thought he was.

We had decided to sell the trailer it had electric heat and was very expensive to live in the winter. We put it up for sale and it sold right away. We then moved into a two bedroom apartment on Lake side.

Jim had been laid off at the Golf Course for the winter. He applied for a job on the Mt. and was hired to do snow removal and some maintenance work. He would leave the house early in the morning and by the time he got up the Mt. he would have a car full of young people that were hitch hiking up to work. I walked to work over to the store. Some mornings I would arrive at work and my hair would be frozen. When I walked across the viaduct I was always leery of walking under where the pigeons roosted. but never got dropped on.

While we were living in this apartment Dennis and Sparrow a young man he was working with from Eureka were working in Kalispell. They stayed with us for a while . They were both very nice house guests. While here one day the sliding glass doors froze closed. When we got home we couldn't get in. Kevin crawled in the Kitchen window and took the hair dryer to thaw out the Ice at the bottom of the door.

In January we decided we would go to Arizona and visit Doris and Clyde. They didn't seem to be doing to well. Kevin drove most of the way down there. In one place he had a Patrolman motion for him to slow down but otherwise did fine. Through Salt Lake, Las Vegas and Phoenix. We were there a week and decided to come back to Montana and consolidate things and move to Arizona. Kevin didn't want to go. He didn't want to leave his friends in Whitefish. Beings he had no job and was not going to school he didn't have much choice.

We had a rummage sale one cold Saturday in the front room. Sold our Furniture and gave some away. Quit our jobs. Jim still has a card all the young people he was working with gave him. Each one signed it and wrote a little note to him.

We rented a Ryder Rental truck, loaded it and took off. Kevin drove the truck and Jim and I rode in the car. We went down from Utah through the Navaho reservation and Flagstaff. The only time in all our trips back and forth we went that way. A double lane road but no freeways.

On arriving in Casa Grande we rented a mobile home from some people that lived in Calgary. It was a turn Key rental. Kevin insisted on washing the silverware and dishes before he would eat from them. We only took our clothes and necessities, and put all the rest in the storage shed. It was a nice 12 wide 65 foot trailer we paid $300.00 a month and that included the utilities (other than the phone). When the rain came, in Arizona it rains like someone is pouring it out of a bucket, and stops the same way. We found out the roof in the kitchen really leaked. We had a constant pail sitting in a couple spots.

We tried to get Kevin to find a job or go back to school he did neither. We spent a lot of time in the Swimming pool.

I got a job at a new TGY store in the fabric department I was hired the day before they opened up. Jim got a job at Francisco Grande golf course working on the irrigation and as a greens keeper.

Through Clydes church we found another trailer to rent. It was in El Rancho trailer park a couple of blocks down the road, not as nice a park but the rent was $65.00 on the trailer and $85.00 Parking plus utilities. So it was cheaper and didn't leak.

Come spring when all the snow birds went north we both were laid off our jobs as we were the last ones hired.

We inquired about motel 6 school and were accepted we took our training at Scottsdale. Had one day a week off. They furnished us a place to live while we were in school for 6 weeks. On our day off we would go to Casa Grande to check on Kevin he still was not working and still wanting to go to Montana.

After our training was over we were sent to Santa Fe New Mexico. We were to have two weeks more training on the job there. Then the Manager was to go on Vacation and we would take over for him. When we arrived he told us they were leaving in two days and would be gone for two months. We had nice cleaning women they were Spanish and Indian. They would bring pot luck for their lunch once a week and always asked us to eat with them. I went to the store one day and in the meat market there were some kind of animal heads wrapped in saran wrap. They had their eyes and teeth but no skin. I asked the butcher what they were and he said sheep heads. I asked him what they were used for and he told me the Spanish and Indians in the area baked them for Sunday or holiday dinner and any that was left was what they used for shredded meat for their burittos and such. I never ate any more pot lucks with the girls again.

When we were packed up and ready to move to Arizona we went around to tell the boys and their families good by. Shianne was not very old but she asked me why we were running away. I guess that is how she seen it.

Before we left Montana we loaned Butch and Annette the money to make a down payment on about 3 acres out of Fortine about a mile across from Dry Lake. It had a small meadow and the rest was covered with brush and some nice pine trees. He put in a septic system. And had a well dug. They moved their trailer out there. With an awful lot of work it was turned into a very pretty place. Root Cellar and two gardens. Tool shed Tree house and a real nice pump house. They lived there about 10 plus years.

Dennis and Susan had bought another 5 acres that joined their property. Dennis is still building on their house.

Now back to our Motel 6 job. I was staying up till sometimes 2 AM looking for mistakes in the rentals and trying to make the money and rooms and TV rentals tally up. I had to balance the books and have the call in and the money deposited by 2:30 every night. I kept getting madder and madder at Jim as he was sleeping and not helping me.

He did have the maintenance of the grounds and the pool to take care of.

The day after Jims 60th birthday we received a call from Dennis May 17,1983 that he had a son Jacob Star born during the night and Susan and baby were fine.

When it was time for us to leave Sante Fe soon. I turned in our resignations. I was getting very up tight and confused. I could not do all the book work by myself for a 142 room motel, and oversee the laundry and cleaning. So I quit both of our jobs.

Kevin had left Casa Grande and gone back to Montana. He wasn't working and living with whoever would have him. A bad time here for a while. We loved him so much but knew at this point he had to make his own way, right or wrong.

We called Clyde and Doris we were coming back. We still had the trailer rented we had before we left as Kevin had been living in it. Clyde said Francisco Grande had been trying to get a hold of Jim. He called them and could go to work as soon as he could get there.

When we arrived back in town I went back and applied at TGY and was hired right on. I went into Domestics. Not my favorite spot in a department store but a job.

I was getting disgusted with it and found out they needed a morning waitress at the golf course. Applied and went right to work. It was a good job and the tips were great. After I had worked there for about 8 months we were all given pink slips. Getty Oil had sold the resort to a Mr. Lynn from Seattle and he closed the place up, Out of about 150 people they hired back 12 Jim was one of them. He was superintendent over the golf course for about a year or more.

We took a vacation and came to Montana to see my father who was in a nursing home in Eureka. Our sons and grandchildren. We had never seen Jacob as yet. What a sweet little one he was.
And so active.

I once more had my Montana fix. Back in Casa Grande I went to work at Sherries Cafe. We had to wear uniforms with puff sleeves and a gathered skirt with ruffles over the shoulders. A good place to work but I felt like a fat Holly Hobbit doll. I went into TGY one day for some reason and the supervisor over soft lines ask me if I was ready to come back to work. She said she had been transferred to another store and had no one to train to take her place. I turned in my notice at Sherries and told him when they went to white shirts and black pants I would come back to work for him.

My job this time at TGY, I had to do all the ordering for shoes, fabrics, mens, womens, childrens, clothing. Domestics and jewelry. I was over 22 employees to the point of making their schedules and being sure they were at work and the work was getting done. When it came time to straighten up the store after closing they could disappear faster than anything I ever seen.

I finally decided it was time for me to go to Whitefish and see if I could get Kevin straightened out. Jim would not move back. Paul Drager had taken the bull by the horns and was trying to get Kevin into the Army. He had been in the reserves for a couple of years. He didn't have a High School diploma, So Paul made an appointment at FVCC for him to take his GED. The first time he flunked the English part and passed everything else. They said he couldn't take it again for 6 months. By the time Paul and the Army Recruiter made a few phone calls he took it the next day and passed it that time. He had been living with some young people on lakeside but now was again living anywhere he could lay his head. We have Paul to thank for all his time effort and even hit a deer with his new car to get Kevin into the Army. This turned out to be Kevins salvation. They taught him to work and gave him some self esteem. Even though he didn't like the time he spent in there.

We gave up the trailer and Jim moved in with Doris and Clyde. We paid them $50.00 a week for him to stay there. Chrystal and her two little girls drove the pick up down to get me. She wanted a vacation and I needed a ride to Montana so I told her I would pay all the expenses for the trip. We rented a U Haul trailer to pull behind the pick up. That pick up either used a lot of gas or had a small gas tank. We gassed up in Casa Grande before we left and had to stop at Nothing Ariz. as we were nearly on empty. After leaving there we were driving along and Chrystal said that back window of the pickup cover sure looks funny in the rear view mirror. I turned around and looked at it and told her it was all shattered. We stopped at Wickiup and picked all the glass out, Went into a store and found some cardboard and taped that in the hole.

We gassed up again in Las Vegas and went on to St George. We found out where we could get a window put in the next morning. We stayed at a Motel 6. Kelly and I stayed in the room and Chrystal took Shandi and went down to call Mike. They hadn't been gone long and out the door Kelly went. By the time I got out the door she was no where in sight I looked all over for her. Finally went down to the phones to see if she found her Mother. Chrystal had not seen her. So the search was on. We finally seen her on the upstairs balcony, way down from where our room was, so everyone was finally in the room for a good well deserved night sleep.

The next morning after breakfast we found the window place. He told us this happens a lot in Arizona, when the sun comes up early in the morning and the heat hits the dew on the windows. They replace a lot of Motor Home Windshields that this happens to. Window repaired and gassed up again we head up that long trek through Utah. We had rain, wind, snow, you name it in March you can hit everything in Utah. Stopped this night in Pocatello Idaho I think.

On home today we hope. When we got up on the top of Monida Pass we needed gas again so went into the first town we came to that sold gas and paid something like $1.79 a gallon for it. I learned you never start over that pass without a full gas tank. We proceed on towards home. Stopped in Missoula and ate and got gas. On to Polson and gassed up one last time. Chrystal took me to Myrtle and Waynes in Whitefish and unhooked the U-Haul. I went to Mr. P's Cafe the next day and rented their little apartment over the jewelry store. Contacted the boys and they all came on the week end. Dennis brought his pick up and pulled the U-Haul over and parked it on Main street on Sunday which I had gotten permission for and they proceeded to unload and carry every thing upstairs to the Apt. Susan and Annette put everything away for me in the Kitchen.

I went two doors over to say hello to everyone I had worked with at Ben Franklins. Jack Sessler still had the store at that time and he asked me if I would come back to work? I told him I was only there for about three months. He said that was fine he needed some one right now. So I went to work. Kevin moved into the apartment with me. He went to Helena for his physical for the army. He had to lose 10 lbs. We got that off and Paul took Kevin and I down for him to take the bus. He was sent to Fort Leonard Wood Missouri, there he was put in the Tank division after being there for a while he was sent to Beline Texas. He hated that country down there, but was there till he was discharged.

I bought a Chev. pickup while in Whitefish and proceeded to eliminate everything I could not get in the pickup to take back to Arizona with me. I had a squeak in the hinges in the pickup doors and stopped to say good-by to Chrystal on my way up to tell Butch and Dennises family's good-by I mentioned the squeak to Chrystal and she got out her can of WD 40 and oiled them for me. No more squeaks. When I got to Butches he said Mom I think your truck is throwing out oil. Look at the doors. Sure enough oil all over both of them and on the side of the truck bed. He opened the hood and nothing there. Then it dawned on me we had been to generous with WD-4O. Washed it off and it was fine. I left Whitefish for Arizona by myself. Jim was going to meet me in Las Vegas. He would fly over there and we spent 3 days there before he drove us on to Casa Grande. I drove to Pocatello Idaho the first day. The next day I started on to Las Vegas. It is a good thing I knew the way and when I was in the middle of Salt Lake it dawned on me I could not see to read the road signs. Something was happening. When I arrived in Las Vegas I could not read the street signs. I had to find the airport. I kept heading in that direction and finally found it. Jim got from the plane and I handed him the truck keys. He had no idea what kind of vehicle I had bought. So it was a surprise to him.

When we got back to Casa Grande, the first week end he was off work we went to Phoenix and bought a 28 ft. 5th wheel trailer. It was old but real nice.

I asked him what was wrong with our TV it was all blurry he told me it was not. The moon looked like a big cluster of flowers. Something was sure weird.

I went to work at Francisco Grande as night auditor I worked from 11 p.m. till 7 am. I was there all by myself after the Cafe and pro shop brought their receipts at 12 am and the bars at 2 am. the night watch man checked in on me every two hours. Way out in the country and real spooky. There was the golf course tennis courts one cafe two bars the motel and the hotel. My eyes kept getting worse so I finally went to the Dr. He told me I had real bad Cataracts I was only 55 years old. He sent me to Scottsdale to a Dr. Carp. They found out I was totally blind in the left eye and had 20 400 left in the right eye. I was scheduled for surgery right away they did the left one first and I missed 3 days work with that one a month later they did the right one and I was out 4 days from work with that one. No trouble since. I see real good now.

Esther knowing we were living in a gated Senior citizen park could not resist sending me this little article she read, it is so cute I have kept it since and wish to share it here.

Child's view of a Mobile Home Park

After the Christmas break, the teacher asked her small pupils how they spent their holiday. Here's one little boy's reply:

We spent Christmas with Grandma and Grandpa. They used to live up north in a big house, but Grandpa retarded and they moved to Florida.

They live in a park with lots of other retarded people. They all live in tin huts. They ride tricycles that are to big for me.

They all go to a building they call the wrecked hall, but it is fixed now. They all do exercise, but not very well. They play a game with big checkers and push them around on the floor with sticks.

There is a swimming pool, but I guess nobody teaches them—they just stand there in the water with their hats on.

My Grandma used to bake cookies for me, but nobody cooks there. They all go to restaurants that are fast and have discounts.

When you come into the park , there is a doll house with a man sitting in it. He watches all day so they can't get out without him seeing them.

I guess everybody forgets who they are because they all wear badges with their names on them Grandma says Grandpa worked hard all his life to earn his retardment. I wish they'd move back home, but I guess the man in the doll house won't let them out.

—Author Unknown.

I hung this up in the club house and it got many a chuckle and a lot of copies were made of it.

I saw an ad in the Newspaper that they were taking applications for Restaurant manager training in the Casa Grande area. I made a phone call and set up an appointment. I was to meet a man from Phoenix at I thought he said Kentucky Fried Chicken at 4 p.m. . I didn't write it down. I went there and they didn't know what I was talking about but sure jumped in and started to do some cleaning up while I drank my coffee and waited for a half hour. I left a message and my phone number and started home. In driving down the street I seen Churches Fried Chicken and a light lit in my brain, that was where I was suppose to be. I wheeled into their parking lot and sure enough this was the place. The man was still there. I saw all these young people and asked him if he thought I was to old? He said not if you don't. He hired 5 people for training for one Management job. The rest were in their 20's. I was 55.

I gave a weeks notice at Francisco Grande as I had to report to a Churches Chicken in Tempe on a Monday morning a week from then. Three young women and one young man and myself showed up. The man lasted part of the first day and quit. He said he wore contacts and could not work around the pepper juice he might get it in
his eyes.

By the end of the week I was the only one left. They all thought to be a manager you just told other people what to do. They didn't want to do the scrubbing and cutting chickens and everything else that went with it. I had 6 weeks of on the job training in Tempe where I learned to do all of it from scrubbing the vent system to repairing motors. You can't ask someone to do something you have not done yourself. In this instance you just come up through the ranks fast.

After my 6 weeks there they sent me to California for 3 weeks schooling in the class room. I was handed a round trip ticket to Los Angeles. There I was told to get on a city bus to a certain street and get off at the corner of such and such and there was a Motel there that the class was staying at. I found it, there were 52 of us the average age was 24. We had orientation that night. They told us we were in the Watts district so there were to be no one leave the motel by themselves. Always two or more of us went to eat. That is the only place I went. There were two to a room. After about 3 days I had my room to myself for about a week. My roommate was from Tucson and when they found out where she was spending her nights she was kicked out of school.

The next bunch that came in I got a new roommate she was a nice quiet girl from some where in New Mexico. We had to learn Scheduling, how to work the computers, set the cash registers, make out reports and always have everything documented. We had to pass a California test to be a health inspector to be a manager. You could be an assistant Manager without it. Out of our whole class only 6 passed that test. It was a very informative school, I had a lot of this training before but each business has their own way of doing things. I received a Watch which I still wear for coming in first in the class.

Back in Casa Grande I was offered a Job as Manager in the Phoenix area or Assistant Manager in Casa Grande. For the little difference in wages and the long drive I took the Assistant and was there for some time. I don't eat chicken so would go next door to McDonalds and get my lunch.

I needed new Glasses so went to Lee Optical in the Mall across from Churches and had my eyes tested, and ordered new glasses. When they came in I was over getting them adjusted, I was the only one in there and the manager and one of the other girls were discussing how older people were giving them trouble trying to adjust their heavy glass lenses so they would stay on their nose in the heat in Arizona. I told them they just needed an older person in there that could talk to them. They would get along better with them and maybe could explain to them why plastic lenses were better in a hot climate and much improved as far as scratching and such now than they were when they first came out. Konie Kukowskie was the manager and she said when can you come to work? I told her I had a job, she asked how much I was getting paid? When I told her she said if you want to work here we will send you into Phoenix for two weeks training and we will pay you $1.00 more an hour than you are making now plus commission. I filled out an application and went to Churches and gave my two week notice and in two weeks started for Lee Optical. It was a very good job. I repaired glasses, filled prescriptions, taught people how to put in their contacts. Pick out frames to complement their looks.

While I was working there we received some red glass frames. I was going to buy them and the girls told me I was to old for red frames.

Esther had bought a 14x70 mobile home and was trying to find a nice court to put it in. It was sitting at the factory in Oregon. She was living in an apartment. In the spring of 1985 she was called and told that they had a spot for her in Meadow Manor in Kalispell. The Mobile home was moved and she moved in. She has been there every since.

In 1986 Myrtle and Wayne bought a 14x70 Mobile home that was all set up in the same court. They moved from the house they had been renting in Whitefish. So now there were the Sisters Two within a block of each other. We are still in Arizona.

Butch and Annette and their little Nichole are still in Fortine he is working at Plum Creek. Kevin is in the Army in Texas. Dennis is doing Contract work and he and Susan and their three children Yosha, Shianne and Jacob are still building on their house up Therrault Creek out of Eureka. I am getting tired of the hot weather, Summer Monsoons and all that stuff in Arizona. I want to come home to the Mountains of Montana and where our Grandchildren and sons are.

We also have a new Grandson in Maryland. Bill and Virginia adopted Wayne Jim who was two years old. He came to them from Korea. Two prouder parents you would never see. Wayne is Deaf like his parents are. They are building a new four bedroom house in Clarksburg Maryland it sits on top of a hill. They built it all on one floor because Sis has a bad back and didn't want stairs to climb. The only stairs are to the basement.

On May 10th of 1987 Dennis called us that their baby boy Mathew James had arrived. Susan was in labor for a long time and could not deliver him. Dennis took her to the Whitefish Hospital and he was delivered by cesarean. A beautiful big boy.

Myrtle and Wayne were in Arizona this winter also and in Feb. they rec. a call from Terry and Jane that they had adopted a baby girl. Lizzy joined the family.

We had put in for our vacation for the end of August to come to my 40th class reunion. Esther called me June 24th 1987 that Dad had a stroke and had died. I told her I would try to change my vacation time so I could come. She said there was nothing I could do now so just leave it as it was. I did not come to Dad's Funeral. Myrtle and Wayne were on Vacation in Illinois and Missouri and they did not get back either.

We came up in August and were at Dennis and Susans house on August 27th 1987 The phone rang and it was Doris in Arizona to tell us Clyde had died that morning. I told her we would come right home and she said no, She had him cremated and that her brother and Sister in law from Phoenix was there with her and she was all right. Before when he was in the Hospital he had asked us if we would take care of her after he was gone as he feared she had Alzheimer's We told him we would.

They had a memorial for him before we arrived home.

After our class reunion and visiting Dad's grave to say my good-bys we went back to Arizona and Back to work. Doris called me one day and was crying she said she didn't have enough money in her check book to pay her rent. We had got her social security all straightened out for her when we got home and Clydes Veterans pension stopped but I knew she hadn't spent a lot and should have enough to pay her bills. I told her when I got off work I would be right over. I asked her if she had worked up her last three bank statements. She told me she had. Now this woman was a Bookkeeper for years I just didn't realize how bad she had gotten. I asked to see her check book and the bank statements. She had checked off the returned checks on the statements but didn't know, or remember that they were having their Social security checks direct deposited. When I told her she had three months checks she had never entered as deposits in her check book. And how much she had she was real happy. She told me she had paid all the Dr. and hospital bills that came in for Clyde. When I asked to see them I discovered she had not sent any of them into their supplementary insurance. She had paid the balance herself. So I sent them all in so she would get reimbursement on them. We decided at this time she could not live alone. We moved out of our apartment and moved in with her. We paid for the trailer parking. Come May when Jim turned 65 we were planning on moving to Fortine. Butch was putting in a place for us to park our trailer we had sitting in Kalispell. We had bought it from Shirley Barret and had it in storage there in their trailer park.

Doris decided to sell her Mobile home and move to Montana. We put it up for sale and it finally sold. May 17th 1987 we loaded everything into a U-Haul truck. Put my car behind it. Jim drove the truck I drove our Pickup and Annette had flown down to drive Dorises car. We knew she could not drive it that far. Or we would lose her on the way. Annette really did enjoy the Sun and the swimming pool while she was there. It took us three days to get to Fortine. When we arrived in Kalispell, Doris , Jim and I stayed at Myrtle and Waynes. Annette went on home she took the pick up to Fortine.

In the meantime Butch had been putting in two trailer spots between his trailer and the road. He put in another septic system and water and we had power put in. We took Doris shopping and she found a 14x70 trailer and we had it delivered to Fortine. We found a trailer mover and had ours delivered also. Jim helped Butch get the ditches filled up and they hooked everything up for both trailers. Dennis built porches on both trailers for us and we were real comfortable. Took Doris into the bank and got her money from her other trailer sales in the bank. She and I went to town to take our Montana driving tests and she only got two questions right. We decided then that her driving days were over.

That fall we went huckleberry picking with Dennis and family. Doris came and asked me if she could set in the car with that young couples baby. She said they asked her to the baby was asleep and they wanted to pick berries. I told her she could and that was her nephew Dennises baby. She said oh I thought they were strangers.

Annette had two big gardens and I showed her how to can. We canned vegetables, made jam, canned fruit, made pickles. Had a busy summer.

I cooked at Chrystal lakes and baked the bread and pies until they closed the Cafe. Jim worked there as a Marshal on the golf course part of the time. One day he came upon all this back up of golfers waiting. He asked them what the hold up was? They told him there was a woman swimming. They guess she must have gotten warm. He had to go get her back on the golf course, to get things moving.

We had bought an Airstream trailer this summer and had joined the Libby Dam Good Sam group. Our very first camp out was at Fawn Creek camp grounds at Libby. We enjoyed it. Or I did Jim stayed in the camper most of the time. I enjoyed the card playing I had not played cards for many years.

Our next camp out was to Idaho to Silverwood.

Once we got there we had fun, even rode on a boat ride and got all wet. Going up the hill out of Troy the pickup heated up and started to steam and smoke. We pulled over and so did everyone else behind us. It was the thermostat, it had sealed shut. Jim took it out and when we got to Bonners Ferry we went to a car parts store and bought a new one. He put it in that night and everything was fine. On our way back we were following Bill Badgley and he had a flat tire. So everyone stopped again.

Before we moved to Montana Dorises Neighbors in Arizona had asked us what we were going to do with her? They informed me she was not their responsibility. I told them we knew that and we were taking her with us.

On December 6th 1988 Jim and I left for Hawaii. Butch and Annette said they would keep an eye on her for us. The day before we were to leave we went into Eureka to get the money for our trip out of the bank. Doris had an excess of money in her checking account as she wasn' t paying any thing but her lights and phone. On the way into town I told her to make out a check for two thousand dollars and I would put it into her savings. She did and gave it to me. She and Jim sat in the car while I went into the Bank. When I came out she said "Just how much money do you need to go to Hawaii" I told her I had not taken her money and gave her her deposit slip. Then she was O.K.

We came to Kalispell and Myrtle and Wayne took us to the Airport. We were to catch the 6 AM plane. It was grounded in Spokane in fog and was not coming in. So we had to wait till noon. I called the travel Agent and she had to set everything back for us. We flew out of Kalispell at 1:20 PM. We flew to Salt Lake then Los Angeles and on to Hawaii. We were flying along and I was watching a lightning storm bounce on the clouds below us. They had us all put our seat belts on because of turbulence a short while before this. All at once it felt like the bottom fell out of the plane. Purses flew pillows flew and the airline attendants flew. Water came out of the coolers. The Pilot came on and said we had lost 500 feet in altitude. Everything was under control. We were 20 minutes out of Honolulu I asked Jim if I screamed? He said you and about 400 other people.

We arrived in Honolulu at 11 P.M. so lost nearly a day there with our canceled flight out of Kalispell. They took us to our Hotel we were one block from the beach. There was no door on the lobby and a lot of open spaces under the roofs on the first floor. The birds flew in and out. I guess that was pretty to some people but if you can't stand fluttering birds like me!! Well!!

The next morning we went to a Hotel they had told us to go to for orientation. We had a continental breakfast and scheduled our tours we wanted to go on. We crowded as much into 6 days as we could. We were supposed to have a car for a day but never picked it up. We decided we could see more from tour busses than we could running around in a car and not knowing where we were going. We took a circle Island flight one day. We were picked up at our Motel at 7:30 AM and taken to the airport. Seen Amelda Marcoes private airplane It was out by the small plane we were to get on. We flew over Lanai. This is known as the Dole Pineapple Island. Also at one time was where the Women Prisoners were put. Mainly those that committed adultry There was fresh water there and they could raise their food. Then we were flown over Kahoolawe. This was a bombing range during WW II. There are still a lot of landing barges and sunken ships along the shores. This was the Island that was the men's prison many years ago. It was a death sentence to be sent there. There is no water so you can't raise anything there, and it is to far to swim to any other Island. Then they flew us over an island that doesn't have a name it is the top of an old volcano sticking up from the ocean it is shaped like a half moon. The pilot told us people go there to scuba dive. He also told us he fly's these flights in the winter and fly's smoke jumpers out of Missoula Mt. in the summer.

We then landed on Hawaii at Kona. While the plane was being serviced we were taken into Kona to see the town and the black sand. People leave messages for each other along the Highway with white rocks writing on the black sand with them.

We took off from here and flew over Mauna Loa Volcano. I felt the plane was standing still and wanted to push it on. Jim was setting in the Co-Pilots seat and he said we were cruising at 160 MPH but it didn't feel like it to me. We then were flown down over the Hawaii National Volcano Park and to where lava was flowing into the ocean. Sure was putting off a lot of steam. Then took off over the rest of the big Island. Seen snow on the Ski slope and seen lots of water falls

Coffee plantations. Then on to Maui. We landed at Kahulul and were taken by bus to a golf course for our lunch. We were not there to long. Then we flew over Molikai. I would like to go there some day and see where the Leper Colony was. Maybe another time. Our next landing was on Kauai. We landed at Hanamaulu. We were taken by bus to the river and all went on boats to the Fern Groto. It was beautiful. All Married couples were remarried in the Groto. We had a snack there before we boarded our plane to take our last leg of our journey back to Honolulu. As we went over all these Islands the pilot knew Jim was interested in the Golf Courses so he buzzed down over and told us about each of them. Some of the other people on the plane may not have been interested in them. On leaving Kauai he flew us around the back side of the Island and showed us the grand canon of the Islands. Really beautiful. He said during WWII a lot of the natives went into the Mts. And some of them established homes there and stayed. He also pointed out the Island of Niihau. He said they had no phones or electricity or any modern conveniences there. You have to be a full blooded Hawaiian to go on the Island and he could not fly any closer than he was there. We flew on around the Island then headed back to Honolulu. The sun was behind us and the pilot got the plane between the sun and a cloud and there was a perfect shadow of the plane on the cloud. We arrived back at our Hotel at 8 p.m. a day well spent.

The next day we took a circle Island tour of Oahu by bus. They showed us where the Japanese came over the Mts. with their airplanes. There is a highway goes completely around the Island. We seen pineapple farms. Stopped and tasted fresh pineapples out of the fields. Seen the house the man lived in that wrote the Little Grass Shack song. Seen schools, churches and were told any senior citizens that had lived there twenty years when they retire do not have to pay any rent and the apartments looked real nice. We stopped at a sea world for a while. Seen the Blow Hole. The beach where Blue Hawaii with Elvis Presley was filmed. Also the beach where the beach scene in From Here To Eternity with Burt Lancaster was filmed. It was a tiny beach. We came back to our hotel very tired this day, but had tickets to an impersonator show that night. We seen an Elvis Presley, Marilyn Monroe and The Pointer Sisters impersonators. It was a real good program and we enjoyed our Whole Day.

One evening we went to a Luau It was a lot of fun walking around in the sand. Lots of drinks I ordered blue Hawaii and Jim ordered a Maitie. We are not drinkers so didn't know what we had ordered. That way we both got to try both of them. They dug a roasted pig up from a pit and we got to taste poi well every one has their own opinion of that. There was a lot of fresh fruit. It was an experience. We later somewhere were shown how they pound the roots to make poi.

The next day we took a tour of Pearl Harbor. Jim had been in Pearl Harbor some time after the bombing but while there were still ships laying on their sides and etc. He said it really was different now. It is real emotional when you are standing on the walkway over that ship that is sunk and know how many men's bodies are still in the ship and you can see oil drops seeping up.

After we left there we went up on the hill to the military cemetery, we seen Ernie Piles grave. There are big Steel doors in the hillside above the Cemetery. I asked what they were? We were told that was bunkers that they kept ammunition in during the War and were now only used for storage. We went from here to the Dole Pineapple factory. Their Water tank is shaped like a Pineapple. They took us from the docks where the pineapples were unloaded clear through to where it was put in cans labeled and packed for shipping Sure smells good in there. Back to our hotel to rest.

This evening we had reservations for a Catamaran Dinner cruise. Then on to see the Don Ho show. I was afraid to go on the Catamaran. I thought I would get sea sick. (We had a cruise booked for January). Jim said if you don't get sick on this one you can stop worrying about getting sick on the cruise ship. Well it was a lot of up and down over the waves there in the harbor. We had Sushi on our plates Jim ate mine it was some kind of raw fish wrapped in sea weed. But the rest of the dinner was very good. I didn't get sick. After our dinner cruise was over we went to the night club to see Don Ho. It was a wonderful performance right down to Tiny Bubbles.

The next day we went to the Polynesian Center. The bus driver told us if you had a coconut palm on the boulevard you had to keep all the coconuts off it. It was a law in Honolulu since the 1930's. Some woman from Oklahoma had been hit on the head with one and had sued the city. He also told us there was a very good Sunday morning brunch on the top of the Hilton Hotel, he said it was rather expensive but well worth it. We decided right there and then we would go. It was our last day in Hawaii. We had a lovely day at the Polynesian Center. They show you culture from all the Islands in the Pacific. So interesting. We also found out what the Poi we had eaten was made from. They boil Taro Roots then pound them into a paste and let it ferment. This has been a staple of the people there forever. On our way back we were taken to the inside of where the volcano was that took the top off of Diamond Head. This Driver was very informative about everything.

Our last day in Honolulu we went to the Brunch the bus driver had told us about. You go up in a glass elevator on the outside of the building. The restaurant is the whole top floor with windows all around. You look out over the beach, the ocean and the town. There were 14 tables of food. Everything from scrambled eggs to Prime Rib. The waiter kept bringing us clean plates. I finally told him no more we were full. He said in Hawaii you don't eat till you are full you eat till you are tired. We told him we were that also. Now we get our bill. We had not asked how much it was. Well not that bad it was $34.00 total. We went down and walked the beach to the Kodak culture center. We seen the program there and took pictures. Seen a lot of Hula Dancers. We walked back through the business section of town to our Hotel to pack for tomorrow The beaches in Hawaii are so beautiful. All of them. We really liked the town of Kona on the big Island. There are so many people there. On all of the Islands. The Hospital in Honolulu is built on a hill and there are very few windows towards the beach. One of our tour guides told us the reason for that is the architect that built it had the blue prints turned backwards and all the windows face the hill. By the time they discovered this it was to late. All the elevators in this hospital are large enough to drive an ambulance into them. And that way they can be taken to any floor to unload.

We returned home from Hawaii and Myrtle and Wayne met us at the airport. We stayed with them in Kalispell over night then went home to Fortine. The Kids had gotten along OK with Doris while we were gone. The next day I went over to her house and was sitting at the kitchen table telling her about our trip and she said " I don't feel so good." She slumped over on my shoulder. I was there alone with her and her mouth went a little crooked and the saliva was running from the corner of her mouth. I got her in on the love seat in the front room and went and got Jim. We took her to Whitefish to Dr. Miller. He said she had a slight stroke. They set up an appointment for a cat scan the next week. It showed that the front lobe of her brain was black. We don't know if it was the stroke or if it had been coming on for some time.

We had gone to Dennis and Susans for Christmas We got stuck on their road going in and Doris and I walked on into the house and Dennis went back and pulled Jim out with the pickup. We had a wonderful time that day with all our children.

We went ahead and went on our first Cruise, it was with Carnival Cruise Line. We were on the Tropical. Wonderful. We left Kalispell and flew to Los Angeles and were picked up at the airport by the cruise line. They took us to the dock. We stood in line according to what your name started with. Jim had given our luggage to a porter and we were told it would be in our room. He failed to tell us it might take 4 or 5 hours to get there.

We got all checked in and found our room. I had been a little tight and booked us an inside room. There were curtains but when you pulled them aside there was a wall. With my claustrophobia it is a good thing we weren't in there very much. We had twin beds a small bathroom and adequate closets and drawers plus two life jackets. No luggage. We proceeded to look the ship over, as they were using the elevators to move tons of luggage we had to use the stairs.

We were up and down and located everything. Kept going to our room to put things away and nothing there. We found a place on the lido Deck to have lunch. Every thing is included on your ticket except liquor and gambling They feed you 10 times a day if you want it. We pulled away from the dock at 4 p.m. still no luggage. Jim said I probably tipped that guy to take our luggage and he didn't even put it on the ship.

We ate the early shift in the dining room and were at a table with six other people. Really nice dinner companions. We ate with the same group all through our cruise. We mentioned our luggage and only one couple had gotten theirs before dinner. We had a wonderful waiter and bus boy they were from the Philippines. After dinner we went to our room and our luggage was there. We unpacked and as it was nearly bed time I put my nightgown on my bed instead of in the drawer. We went to some kind of entertainment that evening. When we came back our beds were turned down with a mint on the pillow and my night gown was pleated and curled like a snake on my bed. We really got a big laugh out of that. The Cruise ships have stabilizers on them and are as smooth as your bed at home we slept like a baby.

We went down the California coast for two days. It was so pretty for January. We seen Porpoises and a lot of Whales. The third morning we pulled into Puerto Vallarta. You could either stay on the ship, go out onto the dock and walk around or take a bus tour of the area. We took the bus tour. There were little boys on the dock with iguana's up on their shoulders. They were trying to get every one to give them $2.00 to have their pictures taken with them. I didn't even want to get near them.

The beach is lined with beautiful white hotels. The driver told us everything there is built with man labor and by hand. He showed us some men putting tar on a house roof. It was in five gallon buckets and they were walking up a ladder with them on their shoulders and dumping them and some other man was spreading it around. He said the road we were on was not finished and they had been working on it 15 years but with no equipment it took forever. We went down the ocean shore and he pointed out the houses Elizabeth Taylor and Richard Burton own. They are across a canal from each other. Then we went on down to the place where the movie "The night of the iguana' s" was filmed. We went to a place and you could either have a coke or a Mexican beer. I know where all the little 8 oz. coke bottles are. In Mexico. Then back to the ship and a fine meal and wonderful entertainment.

The cruise director on this ship was really great. We pulled out that night for Mazatlan. Arrived there the next morning. We took another land tour. They took us to see the man dive from the cliffs into shallow water. He dove as the wave came in and then when the wave went out he stood up. We seen fishermen along the coast line. A Golf Course, then on to a plaza where there were all kinds of stores. In Mexico on these land tours they keep handing everyone margaritas. This time it was when we were all seated in a plaza to watch the young Aztec Indian men. They tied ropes around their ankle and came down head first from a real tall pole while one of them danced on the top. They all made it fine. Really great to watch. We bought some souvenirs here then back to the ship. We were late pulling out this evening as they had a Mexican Ballet come on the ship it lasted longer than they expected, it was beautiful. Also had a Mexican band.

This night the water was a little choppy going across to Carbo San Lucas but not bad. The harbor here is not deep enough for a big ship so we anchored out in the harbor and were taken into the docks on a small ship. Quit a feat to get from one to the other as they were both going up and down. We had a tour of the harbor in a glass bottom boat. We went around the tip of the BAHA peninsula Really pretty but, our boat driver didn't speak English so couldn't tell us much. We seen some seals, and some different fish. Then back to the ship. There were a lot of small fishing boats coming in and they told us the ones flying a flag with a marlin on it meant they had a catch.

We shipped out a little earlier this day as this was the night of the Captains cocktail party. Every one gets dressed up for this. It was real nice. Then more shows. Jim played some bingo along the way. We didn't go to any dances. We went to horse races. And ate a lot. One morning Jim got up and got ready for the day and told me to take my time and meet him on the lido deck and we would go eat breakfast. When I found him he was drinking coffee but there were plates on the table also. I found out he was eating breakfast on the lido deck and then later with me in the dining room.

The first evening out they had a life raft drill where everyone had to put on their life vests and find out what life boat they were to go to. Kind of scary but good to know.

This last day out there was a demonstration of ice carving up by the pool and all kind of games. A tour of the galley. Real interesting. This night they had a midnight Buffet with all the ice carvings and carved food and any kind of food you might want. Really a gala affair. The waiters came in dancing with trays of food on their heads, and all kinds of performances. We had dropped the camera in Hawaii and it went into many pieces, we put it back together and it took good pictures on this trip also.

We again seen a lot of whales along the coast. Arrived back at the dock in Los Angeles and were taken to the airport. Didn't have to long a wait till we were on our plane headed for home. A great experience and wanting to do it again.

WHY IS A SHIP CALLED SHE ?
BECAUSE there is always a great deal of bustle around her
BECAUSE she has a waist and stays
BECAUSE it takes a lot of paint to keep her looking good
BECAUSE it's the upkeep, not the initial expense, that breaks you
BECAUSE she is all decked out
BECAUSE it takes a good man to handle her
BECAUSE she shows her topsides, hides her bottomsides AND when coming into port, she always heads for the buoys..

When we got home Annette told me she had been taking food over to Doris but she didn't think she was eating it. We looked in her freezer and she had put it all in containers and frozen it. Washed the dishes and returned them. She was living on ice cream and cookies. Also could not remember anything. I started writing her checks for her to pay her utilities. She could not even do that anymore. I would take her meals as she would not come and eat with us. Then I would sit right there till she ate them. One morning I had fixed her poached eggs and toast. For some reason I felt Jim should go over with me. She was not sitting in the front room like she usually did. I called and no answer. We went back to the bed room and she was lying on the floor by the bed. She had clawed the wall trying to get up till her fingernails were all bloody. Jim picked her up and put her in bed while I called the Eureka Ambulance.

While we were waiting for them to get there she kept saying they came after me in a big black car but I told them I could not go till I told you I was going. She had a black eye and the whole side of her face was bruised. We found where she fell. She must have been on the toilet and passed out or fell getting up. Her glasses were lying on the bathroom floor by the tub. They were broken. She apparently crawled into the bedroom. It was not long till the ambulance arrived. Barbara Morgan was driving and Clarabell Dierman was with her. They got her loaded in the ambulance and I went with them. Jim came later in the car. Those gals were tops in my books taking care of people. When we arrived at the Whitefish Hospital they called Dr. Bill and he said he thought she had another stroke or maybe a series of small ones. She was in the Hospital for five days. She could leave, I was going to take her to our place and the Dr. said no you put her in a nursing home. You are trying to make a 36 hour day out of 24 hours and you will end up getting sick also. One should never make any one promise to take care of someone for them till they die . Because when the time comes you can no longer do so you feel so guilty. I made arrangements to have her taken to Mt. View Manor in Eureka. I knew they had given our Father such good care there. She kept trying to get out of bed so they had to posy her. She was in a wheel chair one day and decided she wanted out. She found some little manicure scissors in her purse and cut the straps. She tried to stand up and fell. They got her settled down again and she was in her bed and posied when she asked the women in the other bed who was sewing if she could borrow her scissors and she cut herself out again and fell out of bed. They told everyone not to give her any scissors. She went down the hall in her wheel chair asking every one if she could borrow some scissors.

Jim ended up in the Kalispell Hospital to have surgery. I was there with him and Wayne called me he had gotten a call from Dr. Bill in Whitefish that they had Doris back in the Hospital. She had pneumonia and the Dr. wanted me to come right away. I left Jim in the Hospital and went to Whitefish. The Dr. said they could keep her comfortable till she passed away but there was no hope of her living.

The next day February 17th 1989 Jim was released from the hospital and I took him home. He was to stay quiet and off his feet for a few days. We stopped on our way through Whitefish to see Doris. She was on oxygen and asleep. She looked real peaceful. We went on home. At 11 P. M. we received a call from the Hospital that Doris had passed away. I called her half sister in Seattle and all she said was-Where is her money? They did not realize that Doris and Clyde had lived on the money they got when they sold the stores in 1965 all this time. There was very little left. When I told Jim what they said he got mad and started pacing the floor and started to bleed again.

I called his Dr. in Kalispell and he told me to get him back to the hospital. But he said he can't ride in the car that far and they were having a terrible Ice storm in Kalispell, so I had better call the Ambulance. This I did and told him I would be down the next day.

I had already made arrangements to have Doris picked up at the hospital and have her cremated and the remains sent to Arizona to be interned where Clyde was. Her family did not ever ask me that I can recall what I did with her. I set down and wrote letters to the other relatives about her passing away.

Jim was in the hospital for another 5 days before he could come home.

I went and hired an attorney to probate Dorises Will. As she had crossed out one word. She changed and to or it made her will null and void. She had put Jims name on her car and trailer titles with her as she wanted him to have them. But because she didn't have with the right of survivor ship on them and they were not married. They had to go into the estate. Her sister and her oldest brothers three daughters contested the will and it was in court ever so long and finally went to the Montana supreme court and they put it into intestate and it went to her half sister and the nieces. None of whom had came to even see her or help with her. They called me and told me if we had not taken her to Montana she would not have died. No thank you or anything. But she was a very dear lady and I would do it again if I had to.

We sat it out in Fortine neither of us were working. We had bought the airstream trailer and it was sitting in the meadow. One day the middle of September the phone rang and I answered it. It was Jims old boss at Francisco Grande he wanted him to come back to work. Here they were going into winter and having all kinds of trouble with the water system. Jim told him he would come back if they paid him the same wages he retired at. They said they would call him back. When they called back they said they couldn't do that as they only wanted him to come take care of the water. He said then get some one else, an hung up. The next morning at 5 A.M. the phone rang and they asked him how soon he could get there? He told them he would leave the next day. We packed the trailer for him he hooked onto it and took off. He had a good trip and parked the trailer where we had been before.

The first part of October Paul Drager was driving to Arizona he had a place out of Phoenix. I proceeded to get the trailer in Fortine all ready for the winter. It was parked right by Butch and Annette. They would water my plants for me and watch things. I came down to Myrtle and Waynes and he picked me up there. It took us two and a half days and Jim met me at Pauls place in Phoenix and took me on to Casa Grande. I went back to Lee Optical and the gal they hired to take my place was still there and still is now eleven years later. I went to Wal Mart and was hired in Domestics. I worked there till we came back home the next May of 1988. When I left they told me if I came back the next winter to come see them if I wanted to work. I worked for them every winter till 1993. As a cashier every year except the first. And part time in customer service.

When I was at Lee Optical I kept wanting red frame glasses and the girls told me I was to old for them. When we went back and I was no longer working there I went and bought my red frame glasses and have worn them every since. They are kinda hard to find now.

When we came back to Fortine the next spring Kevin was out of the Army and living in Whitefish. Butch got him a job at Plumb Creek mill. He was working through the labor contractors. When he was nearly ready to get on full time he ups and goes back to Whitefish. He was doing odd jobs there and finally got on at a convenience store.

Myrtle and Wayne spent three winters in Arizona while we were there we really enjoyed having them. And went to see a lot of things with them.

We had a pet deer at Fortine and he loved cookies. This was before Doris Died she sure enjoyed him. When he got to big he was taken to the golf course so he would not get shot in hunting season.

When Yosha and Shianne were little and taking Ballet. I may have already told you about the pink Ballet slippers. They told me they had to have pink slippers, I could not find any so I ordered them. They were there by the time of their recital. We went to the program and there were two little girls with pink slippers the rest were dancing in their white sox. Yosha was to the point of being all arms and legs she danced with some long scarves Shianne kept pulling up her tu-tu till it was clear up under her arms but they were so cute. And they both still like ballet.

We spent our summers in Fortine. We watched Nichole play a lot of baseball she was good she started playing when she was five years old and she was very good. We still went to Arizona for the next few years. Jim worked at Francisco Grande and me at Wal-Mart. While I was working at Wal-Mart this winter I went out to go home one, night, pulled onto the Highway and went to look in the rear view mirror and I didn't have any. Some one had stolen all the mirrors from every Ford on the parking lot. Also while working there that winter they broke into the pickup topper and took all of Jims tools. Everything back there, a new battery and tools. They took everything except his golf clubs. The police said they didn't know where to get rid of them. They would get them next time. There was no next time as we didn't even carry a spare tire after that.

In the spring of 1991 Chrystal put her trailer up for sale. We bought it and sold ours at Fortine. We moved to Kalispell. Here were the SISTERS THREE all within a block of each other again.

We left Casa Grande to come home and went by way of Riverside California to see Jims Sister Lou Ella and family. Then went across Los Angeles to highway 101. It took us all day to get across Los Angeles on the free way. We then the next day proceeded up thru all the towns on the coast to San Jose where Lee and Karon were living. That is Myrtle and Waynes youngest son. Myrtle and Wayne were there. We had planned on only staying over night, but Lee came in and said did you know you don't have a window in the front of your camper? We all went out and had a look and the only thing there was the screen. We don't know when we lost it. No glass inside as the screen kept it from blowing inside. We stayed on one more day and the men went and bought a glass and fixed our front window. Lee and Karen has two lovely children Amber and Justen. We went on the next morning. Stopped in Vancouver and saw Aunt Blythe and Uncle Vein then on up and over through Packwood and Randall where we once lived. Over White Pass and on to Davenport Washington and spent the night parked in Jo Ann Taylors yard and on home. When we were driving along the Kootani River between Troy and Libby they were working on the road and one spot had a lot of muddy water. Jim had his window down and we met a motor home, it splashed mud in the pickup right in Jims face and all over the roof inside it was dripping I could not help but laugh at him. He had the window down instead of using the air conditioner.

When we arrived home and Jim went to unhook the camper he noticed a crack in the hitch up by the camper. We used it that way all summer on our good sam outings but before we left that fall he had it spot welded. When we left that year we decided to go by way of Colorado and do some visiting on our way. In Wyoming the Pickup started acting up it would lug way down going up hills. Then take off OK on the top. We went to Judys in Boulder and stayed over night at her place. Then on to Golden and parked in Maggie and Virgil's yard (Jims Brothers). They took the pick up to have it looked at. The Mechanic said it was a loose wire he fixed it and we paid $35.00. We took off the next morning for Buena Vista. Came to a pass and it did the same thing again. We took it to two garages in Buena Vista. They said it was vapor locking and there was nothing we could do about it. They said keep jugs of water in the truck and pour water over it and it might help it cool down. We again took off for Arizona after visiting Jims old Boss and other people we knew in Buena Vista.

We left Buena Vista early in the morning to head for Durango . About to the top of Wolf Creek Pass the pickup stopped, We were on a two lane part of the road and on a curve. I directed traffic around us for about 45 minutes. A trucker stopped and he and Jim poured water by the gallon on the motor some where nothing happened. We sent for a wrecker with a passer by but they either did not find one or ignored us. The truck finally started and we limped to the top. We parked in a turn out and ate our lunch in the trailer. The truck started right up and we sailed down the other side. There is another small pass into Durango. You guessed it , it started again. I told Jim to find a place to park the trailer and a ford Garage. I was not leaving there till it was either fixed or he bought a new truck. We went to the ford garage and they could not get us in but they said there was a real good mechanic down the road about a mile. We went down to him and he took it right in. He checked the fuel pump and then the fuel filter!!!! That was it . It was so close to being completely closed you could not even blow through it. He put in a new one to the tune of $7.00 . There was one truthful man!! We took it up over the pass to Silverton and Ouray it worked fine. The next morning we again took off for Arizona. We stopped at the Canyon De Chelly National Monument. We parked the trailer and stayed there over night so drove all over to look at everything. The next morning we took off and stopped at the Petrified Forest and on to Meteor Crater.

While we were going around with Myrtle and Wayne we had seen Oregon Pipe and Saquaro National Monuments. While at Organ Pipe we were siting at a picnic table having our lunch. Myrtle and I were on one side of the table and Jim and Wayne were on the other side. Wayne told Myrtle not to move but look behind her. She told him that would be kinda hard to do. There was a road runner eating crumbs right behind us.

We went up through Sadona. It is very pretty there. Also Tuozagoot , Montazuma Castle and Casa Grand Indian Ruins. Above these ruins at Jerome we found a restaurant that served the deep dish fruit pies we found down there that we all liked so very much. Took a back road from Gila Bend one day and roamed around on the dessert. Wayne was getting a dead limb from a Cholla cactus and it threw one of its shoots at him it stuck to his forehead and when Myrtle pulled it of it sounded like she was breaking a fresh head of lettuce. That is the jumping cactus. We ate our picnic lunch and finally found our way back to Casa Grande. Another time we were in their ton towing rig and were at Jerome. We decided we wanted to go down a narrow street to see the old hospital. The truck was to wide. He had to drive on the sidewalk but we finally made it back down. We had a real pleasant day in Tombstone one time also. Didn't miss much there.

When we got settled in Casa Grand the crack on the hitch had opened up again. We went looking for another trailer. We found a 23 foot Airstream it was real cute and had twin beds in the bedroom. A much smaller bathroom. We bought it. Took our old one in for a trade in and brought the newer one home. The first night we had it , we got one of Arizonas rain storms. That trailer leaked like you cant believe. It ran out of every seam. Down the walls behind the beds through the roof, around the windows. We called them and took it back in for two or three Saturdays in a row They finally got all the leaks fixed except one by the front window. We never did get that fixed. This was the winter of 1992. We decided we would have one more winter in Arizona and call that enough. I was very happy with that. Kevin had been living in our trailer this winter. We came home in April and he moved out and to Whitefish.

We came home and Jim had not been feeling to good.

He had chest pains and the Dr. could not find out what it was. They had ran stress tests, tread mill and the whole works here, so they sent him to Missoula for a catheterization on his heart. When the Dr. Came out of surgery he was all smiles and told me there was nothing wrong with his heart. He said to take him back to his Dr. here and have them find out what it was. They finally found out it was a hiatal hernia.

While Jim was sick on May 21st of 1992 we received word Jim's brother Eugene who was two years younger than he is, had been diagnosed with cancer. He lasted only a couple of weeks. Jim was sick and could not go to the funeral. As children I think he was closer to Gene than any.

We came home and I went to work for K Mart for a short while. Had my reasons but didn't like that job so I gave my notice and quit. Went by way of Pamida on my way home and got right on in Customer service and as cashier.

In September we went back to Arizona. Jim went back to Francisco Grande to work and me back to Wal Mart.

In January I became sick. I worked one day that way then went to the Dr. as I had little bumps breaking out on the left side of my face. I have never had anything hurt so bad in my life. The Dr. Told me I had shingles and I was dehydrated. Go home and go to bed and drink two quarts of liquid in the next hour, such as gatoraid apple juice or grape juice. If not I had to go to the hospital for Iv's. She told Jim to take two or three days off work and take care of me. He said he didn't know how. She told him if you want to eat feed her if you have to go to the bathroom take her to the bathroom if you want a drink give her one. Well we made out all right and in three days I was feeling better. I had to take five pills a day at $5.00 a pill, for ten days. I had 87 shingles on the left side of my face. Below the eye and above the lower lip. They were all around and in my ear. I never want to have them again.

When we went on our Cruise in 1990 Myrtle and Wayne went with us we really had a good time.

We left Phoenix January 4 1990. We flew to Missoula they met us there and we stayed in a motel. We flew out of Missoula at 7:30 AM for Denver, Houston and Miami. Had Coffee and cake on the plane between Missoula and Denver. We sat in the very back seats, not a good place. The stewardess said that was the cattle car seat. We arrived in Denver around 11 AM and left there before noon . Had better seats. We had Lasagna, salad, bread and butter and a cookie for lunch. We were on a larger plane this time. It was raining in Houston real dreary. We had three hours in Houston and tried to call Jims youngest brother but no one was home. On a smaller plane and across the Gulf Of Mexico to Miami. Guess what they fed us for supper ? Lasagna but we did have a different kind of cookie. We were met at the airport by a very nice young man in a carnival cruise line bus. He took us to a Marriott Hotel. We had lovely rooms. Went to bed early to be ready for our big day tomorrow

We ate a breakfast buffet on the terrace . Then on to the lobby where there were a lot of people going to the docks. We were picked up about noon in a bus.. went to the pier and through inspection and onto the Celebration ship. Found our room. It had a nice big window and four bunk beds. Myrtle and I took the bottom ones. We then went to lido deck and had our lunch. We wandered around the ship and went to the room and put our clothes away. We listened to a Calypso band, had a life boat drill. We were in the Horizon dinning room. We had a real good spot in the dining room at table 278. The first night out was International night. Wayne had Baked Chicken. Myrtle and Jim had sea food in a pastry shell. I had beef kabob on rice. Then we went to jackpot Bingo. At 10:30 we went to an introductory show. Found out Steve Cassel was the cruise director. He was the same one that was on the Tropical a year before when we went down the Mexican riviera. At Midnight we went to the Buffet to see how it was. Then to bed.

Sunday at sea. Jim and Wayne got up and went to the Lido deck for Orange juice coffee and rolls. Myrtle and I got ready for the day, we went and found them and then we all went to breakfast. Our waiter was from Honduras and our bus boy was from Jamaica. Our Cabin Stuart name was Gay Lapheous. I never found out where he was from. After breakfast we went to a travel talk show. We bought our tickets for San Juan, St Thomas, St Johns and St Martins. Went back to the room and took a nap. Got all dressed up and went to the Captains welcome aboard Cocktail Party. It was formal. They served cocktails and hot and cold hors d'oeuvre When this was over it was time for dinner. Back to the dining room. It was Italian night. I had Veal Parm, so did Myrtle Wayne had baked chicken and Jim had fish. The waiters and bus boys were dressed like Gondolier's. They came out with flaming cherries jubilees and all marched around and sang in Italian. The Mater De said they were from 17 different countries but no Italians. This evening we went to the Celebration stage show. It was very good, like a Las Vegas review. Then to bed. There was a ruff seas last night, but slept well.

Up this AM to a pretty day at sea. Had breakfast after Jim and Wayne had coffee on the lido deck. Myrtle and I found them and had Orange juice with them. Came back to the room and I slept till 11 AM Myrtle Wayne and Jim went to the horse races. Then to the casino I joined them there. We went to lunch Jim had eggs and shrimp Myrtle and I had Pork Chops, Wayne had egg

FoYoung.

Myrtle and I went to the Grandmothers party. We had champagne for refreshments. The men took a nap. We all played bingo and won nothing. We were getting close to San Juan Puerto Rico. We went up on the Lido Deck, the wind was really blowing. We could see the sky line. We watched for a while and wandered into the ice cream and cookie party. Had an early dinner so we could get into town to the Fiesta Flamenco Show. Tonight was French night. Myrtle Had Escargot (snails) and New York steak. Wayne and I had Veal with Mushrooms and apples. Jim had Red Snapper. Myrtle and Wayne had Crepes filled with strawberries. Jim and I had Neapolitan (pastry between a cream filling real good.

The Flamenco dancers were real good. San Juan is a city of high rise Buildings. A lot of which are apartments. It did not look to clean. The Theater had big tropical plants growing on the ceiling We had Pina Calata's to drink, really like a coconut milk shake. After the show we came back to the bus. (an open air one) and back to the ship. I went to bed the rest of them went to the Mexican Buffet. They brought me back a little taco and cake. My feet are real swollen. We can see another cruise ship all lit up way out there. From the window in our room. We are headed for St. Martin. We will be there in the morning. I can't get to sleep for a while and seen two other cruise ships from the Norwegian line. We have seen them now and then all the way from Miami. They were tied up at the dock behind us last night. We were all up early this morning to breakfast then to the Astoria room for briefing before we took off for our St Johns tour. We left the ship at 8:30 went on an open air bus to the other side of St. Martin. From there we all got on a ferry boat and were taken across a beautiful bay to St. Johns. They drive on the wrong side of the road there like they do in England. And they drive like there is no tomorrow. After the first shock we got accustomed to it.

On the way to the ferry we seen a lot of beached boats and houses with no roofs. Hurricane Hugo had gone through here a few weeks before this. These Islands are real tropical with trees not to many flowers. St. Johns island is the smallest one of the 3 virgin Islands owned by the U.S. From the Ferry we were put on more open air busses and taken to a beautiful beach. Here we were given refreshments of rum punch. Some people were snorkeling, some were swimming. We walked on the beach and got caught by a wave and got wet. It was really beautiful there. Then back to the bus and the Ferry. Arrived at the ship at 12:35. Ran on the ship to the bathroom and back out to the pier for our second tour.

Our second tour was again on one of the open air busses. Which are actually large flat bed pickups with benches across them and a canvas roof over you. We seen Megans Bay and Sir Francis Drakes seat. Jim and Wayne walked up 90 plus stairs to see Blackbeards Castle. Myrtle and I seen it from the bus. Went to the Coral World Aquarium, seen a lot of tropical fish. Back to the ship tired dirty and sandy.

Our dinner tonight was Oriental. Jim and Myrtle had stir fry. Wayne and I had mandarin Pork. We missed lunch yesterday but not really as we had Ice cream two different times. We all retired at 7 P.M. Really slept didn't even go to the stage show. We did all have a drink at the endless summer bar. You got to keep your glasses as a souvenir. Up and at em got ready for the day. Myrtle is amazed at how the room steward is in there putting up clean towels and etc. every time you leave the room. We went for breakfast, Myrtle had grits again-yuck. Out on the deck again. The water is so blue here. Just so beautiful.

We were on a regular big bus here on St. Martins. The roads are very narrow. St. Martins is all hills and lots of under growth. Our first stop was Phillipsburg which is the capital of the Holland side of the island. We saw a cemetery that had graves to the 16th century in it. Saw their Salt Lake.

Then on over to the French side, the capital of it is Marigot. We had about an hour there to wander around. Bought T shirts for the kids. Went to a market that the merchants had all their fresh produce strung out on the ground.

Back to the bus and they drove past The Mullet Bay Golf Course-real pretty. Past Fort DeMarigot up on the hill. Seen houses that are owned by Harry Belefonte, Jackie Onassis and many more stars. Had more rum punch and back to the ship. A great morning.

We had stopped at Cay bay to take pictures. There were remnants of a Cafe that Hugo had blown away.

Back on the ship we had a buffet lunch. Did a little gambling and took a nap. For dinner it was Caribbean night. Head waiters were dressed like pirates and the bus boys sailors. They danced with trays on their heads with flaming Flamba on them. That was our dessert.

We were rested from our naps so went to bingo and a talent show. Then to the 12:30 buffet of pizza and fruits.

We slept in a little this A.M. We all ate breakfast on Lido deck . During the morning we bought a video of the week. Watched the pig races and the ice carving demonstration. It was by the pool and lots of fun.

Then we took a tour of the galley. 100 people work in the dining rooms and over 100 in the kitchen. It is all stainless steal and tile and very clean. I had my picture taken with the head Chef.

We all refreshed and dressed for the evening. went to the Island in the sky for Pina Collates and Hot hors d'oeuvre's. On to the Dining room for dinner. Captains Gala Dinner. Steak and Lobster with baked Alaska for dessert. Myrtle and Wayne had strawberry soup. The Dining room was all decorated with balloons and streamers with hats and noise makers at each table. The staff sang Auld Lang syne to us. The show that night was called The best of Broadway. It was very good. Went and found our cameras to take pictures of the Gala Buffet before it was eaten. Back at 12:30 to eat it and to bed.

This would be our last full day on the ship. We went to breakfast then went to pickup the rest of our pictures that we wanted to buy, They take pictures all week long and you can buy them if you want. Then we went to the mens knobby knee contest. After this they had a debarkation talk. Then time for lunch. We then went and packed our clothes. Went to a party that was for newly weds and not so newlyweds. While up walking on deck we seen some flying fish. They come out of the water and really sail a long way before they re-enter. The men went to see the ships bridge. Jim always really enjoys this. We went to the male nightgown party. A lot of men dress up in women's night gowns and under clothes. It was fun. then on to the fun ship highlight party. we again had pina collates and hors d'oeuvre's There was a good Jazz band playing.

While waiting to go into dinner that night there was a couple standing behind us that had T shirts on that said Albuquerque balloon festival on them. I told them I had a daughter in law from there. They asked what her name was and I told them. He said that must be Susan. It turned out he has been her folks mail man for years I told them in the dining room It was going to soon be Myrtle and Waynes Anniversary and they were celebrating it a little early on the cruise. They brought them a cake to our table and a bunch of waiters and bus boys sang to them. Our waiter said we don't sing good but we sing loud. This was American night. We had Prime rib and baked potatoes. Very good. Next our luggage except carry on had to be put in the hall before we went to sleep. We had a big ship like ours ahead of us all day. We passed it this evening. Pulled into Miami about 7 A.M.

Up for our last breakfast in this beautiful dining room. Then to the Astoria lounge to wait to be cleared by customs. We disembarked about 9 A.M. The bus took us to the airport. Had a 5 hour wait. Ug. Then on to Houston. Jim called Dale and got him this time but we weren't there long enough for him to come to the airport. When we flew out of Houston they fed us on the plane!! you guessed it Lasagna again. We flew back to Missoula and drove to Kalispell. We spent 3 pleasant days with our kids and flew back to Arizona. Took the shuttle to Casa Grande and back to work. Every one should at least once in a life time go on a cruise. It is an experience you would never forget.

The next three months in Arizona were long and uneventful.

Except right after we arrived back from our cruise we received a call from Oklahoma that Jims Sister Margarett had passed away. We took off the next day and drove to Shawnee Oklahoma and stayed till after the funeral. She was 4 years older than Jim.

One year we were in Arizona, Esther came down to spend a few days. She and Paul had us up to his place in Phoenix for Thanksgiving dinner. It was real nice to be with family. Most of our Holidays down there were spent at the pot luck in the court. One elderly man started in September to remind me to make fudge and divinity for thanksgiving and Christmas. He would ask if he could take what was left over home. Of coarse I always gave it to him. One Christmas towards the end of our stays down there we had Sr. citizens plane tickets and we flew home for the holiday. That is the first time we met Irene, who later joined our family as Kevins wife.

The first part of May we left for home and were always trying to think of a different route for part of the way. We had heard so much about how wonderful the slabs were to stay at in California so decided to go home by that way. We left right after breakfast and were in Yuma about noon. Drove across the sand dunes to Imperial Valley. Then north to Brawley. We stopped at a rest area north of there and ate. Gased up in the next town. Then on to Nyland and found the slabs. What a mess!! We decided we could not sleep if we stayed there. So went on to a State Park at Bombey Beach on the Saltin Sea. Not to clean a place either with this polluted water. The sewer from Mexico empties into it they told us.

When we left here we went up through Dateland and Palm Springs. Then on to Riverside to spend a few days with Lou Ella and Bud. We left there and went to Las Vegas spent one night there and on towards home. When we arrived home Jim went back to work at Meadow Lake Golf Course. I didn't work for a while. We put our Air Stream up for sale and bought a small fifth wheel. Did some traveling with Good Sams. I learned to pull the fifth wheel.

In December, the 20th right before Christmas they found our brother Harold in his apartment dead. He had died from heart failure. He was buried in The Eureka cemetery by Grandma and Grandpa Baillargon. That is where Mother said he was to be buried when the time came. His funeral was right after Christmas.

We took off in March with the fifth wheel for Seattle . Stopped in North Bend and looked up Harold and Doris Wright. We had not seen them for over 30 years. Had a nice visit with them, they came to town and met us at a Cafe for coffee. Then on to Snohomish.

We visited with George and Meril McBride. Parked our 5th wheel in their yard. Went around and seen the other ones that were there we knew from our construction days. There were reports of a storm coming in so we headed south.

Stopped in Vancouver for one night to visit Aunt Blyth and Uncle Vein. Had a lovely visit at their home. We were talking about family and Aunt Blyth said there were always pictures hanging on their dining room wall of two old people. She thought they were Grandma and Grandpa Troy her mothers folks. She said they looked mean with a scowl on their faces. She does not know what ever happened to the pictures. He showed us a lot of slides of their trips. We took off the next morning.

When we arrived at Cottage Grove, Oregon and found a court and got parked, we looked up Don and Darleen Dennis they called Helen Norton who lives in Eugene and some other people Jim knew before we were married and we had dinner and a lovely visit. The next day we headed for the coast. We went down the coast to Fortuna California.

Here we found my cousin Jackie and her husband Ed. We parked in their driveway for the night. Uncle Alfred came over and had dinner with us. Clarence and Berta came over and visited in the evening.

We decided we had never been to Reno so we headed there. Beautiful country going over the Mountains. We spent one night in Reno and headed for Death valley. We spent the night in California and headed for Death Valley the next morning. We went up-up-up— Then Downdown and more down. When we got to the bottom we went into a little store and they said you don't pull trailers over that mountain. We did.

After parking for the night we unhooked the pickup and we went up to Scotties castle. That was interesting.

We seen a meteorite crater. And everything else we could crowd in before dark. Went out to eat and to bed. Left the next morning and headed south seen a lot of other pretty and unusual sights on the way to the south entrance to the park. We drove on over to California and parked at a state park for the night. The next morning the Pick up would not start. Lucky for us there was a Big Bus converted to a motor home had parked beside us. The man came out and told Jim he was a retired Ford mechanic. He showed him how to use a screw driver to start it. We were miles from a garage. We headed on in towards Riverside. Stopped for gas one place and had to use the screw driver again. We arrived at Bud and Lou Ellas late in the afternoon. Had intended to stay about three days. Jim and Bud decided they were going to fix the truck. They ended up with the dash out and everything, still would not start. I kept telling him there had to be a Ford Garage somewhere near.

After five days they took it to a garage and it needed a new part for the starter. Very minor and not to expensive. We headed out the next day for Yuma Arizona. We parked there and went out to see Rosenbachs had a good visit. Also seen Opal Peterson and Helen Norton. Went on to Casa Grande the next day. Spent one night there and did some visiting with people we knew.

Headed for Tombstone and Douglas Arizona. Stayed one night in Tombstone then on to Douglas. Took a tour there a real interesting area. We stayed north and east of there that night. Took a tour of Douglas and into a mine.

This morning we took off of for Belen New Mexico Jim wanted to look up a man who lived there that was his boss at one time. We found them and had a nice visit. We parked in their drive way. Took off the next morning and intended to get to Shawnee Oklahoma that evening. While driving across New Mexico on a road we had never been on before, we seen a sign that said

Pueblo Mission. We love Indian ruins, so turned in the road we found it. Spent some time there it was a mission that was about 250 years old. It was the ruins of it but still quite well preserved. We found out there that there were two more within a forty mile radius. We went to the next one and seen it. By then it was getting late so we parked the trailer and spent the night, at Mountainair N.M. The next morning we went down to the third one. They all had a large mission in the middle and the Indian dwellings all around them. Each one had a museum also. We left there in the afternoon and drove till evening and stayed somewhere west of Oklahoma City.

We woke up to a cold rainy day. Took off for Shawnee. Arrived there in the late afternoon and decided it was to cold to stay in the trailer, so rented a motel. Then went and looked up Harold Jims Brother and called his nephew Max. We were there three days. Went to move the pickup one day and the wheels were frozen to the ground. We had a lovely dinner at Max and Elgas home one evening. The weather had broken the third day so we took off for Colorado.

We made it as far as Guymon and rented a Motel there. We made it to Judys house in Boulder Colorado the next night. We spent two days there. Always a joy to be at Judys.

Took off for South Dakota the next morning. We went to Custer. Still cold so we stayed in a motel there. Got situated and went to see Crazy Horse Mt. real interesting. It will be beautiful if it is ever finished. Went through the museum there also. Then went to a wild life preserve the next morning and saw lots of buffalo's and prairie dogs. Then went back and hooked up the trailer. We went to Mt. Rushmore it is really something to see. We really enjoyed it. Took off from there and went to Sturgis. We stayed there over night. Everyone in the businesses there were telling us how they looked forward to the Harley David rally every year. When we left there we were bucking wind all the way to Kalispell. We stopped at Custers Battlefield hadn't been there for nearly 30 years.

Headed on home it took us two days to get here we went through Billings and Bozeman then up through Townsend and Helena. Went north of Helena and over Roberts pass and down through Lincoln and through the Swan and finally home. It was a nice trip.

I decided it was time for me to look for a job. We were at Costcos one day in April and I was talking to a Demo Lady I knew and she said why don't you apply here. I did and was hired. I went to work May 18th 1994. There were 6 of us in this bunch. One worked one day another about a year and there are 4 of us still there. We have nearly 4 years in now. It is a good job and we have a wonderful boss. I hate to have to some time quit but know my age will force it . I will be 70 this year. Jim is still working summers at Meadow Lake Golf Course.

We traded our 5th wheel in on a small Motor Home. We had it about two years , had fixed it all up but never used it much. We decided that was a lot of money tied up in something we weren't using. Put it up for sale and sold it the first day.

Jim came to work one day and told me he was going to trade off the pickup , he had found a 94 Subaru he wanted. Wanted his pickup back every since.

In early spring of 95 we had thermal pane windows and 3 new steel doors put in our house. In May I took two weeks off Jim hadn't started working for the summer yet and we drove to Seattle and then took a shuttle to Vancouver B.C. to catch a Holland American cruise ship. We were on the Rotterdam. This was a cruise we had looked forward to for years and this ship was he cruise ship from hell. We had requested a non smoking room !! The curtains and bed spread were dirty and caked with cigarette smoke. We had requested a table in the dining room with other guests as we were alone. We were seated at a table for two with a big pillar between us. Had requested early seating and were given late seating. Tried to get things changed but couldn't. So I ended up with a bang up asthma attach. All of our land tours we took. We had to wait for this large group to get on the bus first as they all wanted to sit together. We ended up siting in the back of the bus. One bus we were on the brakes caught on fire. Another tour we bought we were to go by bus to a lake and take a boat ride on the lake to a glacier. When we arrived the boat was frozen in the lake. They had to know that when they sold us the tickets. They cost us $25.00 each and we were all refunded $8.00. The only wild life we seen were two chipmunks. We did see a lot of eagles. But we can see them here at home. We saw a lot of pretty country and a few seals. Some glaciers. I would have enjoyed it more if I had not been sick. Jim was looking forward to Alaska King Crab and sea food on the ship. There was none. The entertainment was put on by the crew and more amateurish than a Jr. Play at high school. We stopped at Sitka, Juneau, Skagway, Valdez, and disembarked at Seward. We enjoyed the Russian Ballet we seen. The big fish they were cleaning on the docks. Lots of totem Poles. Then on to Anchorage. We stayed there two days. Seen where the Iditerod race takes off. Took a tour of Anchorage. We flew out of there at 2 AM The sun was just setting. A half hour after we were in the air the sun was coming up. We arrived back in Seattle early in the morning so went and picked up our car and headed home.

The morning we had left Seattle to go on our trip we had gotten up early so as to eat breakfast before we took off for Vancouver. Went to the Cafe in the motel and the waitress said we can fix you toast, breakfast rolls, cold cereal juice and coffee. Our Chef quit and left for Hawaii this morning. You cant tell me one of those middle age waitresses couldn't have stepped in to that kitchen and cooked eggs and meat. Anyway we had rolls and coffee. Our room had a terrible bed in it also and for $100.00 plus I got mad and filled out their card in the room when we left and turned it in at the desk to be sure they got it. When we arrived home we had a letter of apology from them and two free meals and a free night lodging with them. It had to be used within a year so needless to say they were never used. They did say the whole third floor would have new beds they didn't realize they were in such bad shape.

We left Seattle and headed north as we decided to drive across Canada. That night we stayed in Summas Washington in a very Quaint Hotel. It was decorated in antique furniture so pretty and pleasant. The next night we staid in Trail, British Columbia and then on home.

When we got home I stewed for a week over this very disappointing trip. I went to the travel agent to see if there was some way I could get the money back for the Plane trip we had paid for to start with. (The air lines went bankrupt). She asked me if I had paid for it by Credit Card? It was the only thing I had. I contacted the Credit Card, They contacted the bankruptcy court and we signed some papers and our money was returned to us.

Then I wrote Holland American and told them how I thought we got ripped off. This Cruise had cost us more than the other two we were on that were so enjoyable. Finally after months of corresponding, they sent us two vouchers of $300.00 off the next cruise we took with them. I sent them back and told them we would never take another cruise with them. They told me the Rotterdam had been decommissioned And was no longer in use.

When we arrived home I went to Eureka and bought 5 cemetery lots. Esther already had 3. She traded them in on 5 that joined mine on the east side. Myrtle bought two that join mine on the south side. So here we are again THE SISTERS THREE forever someday.

Early in 1996 we had steel seamless siding put on our trailer. They left the old siding on and put insulation over it before they put on the siding and rain gutters. It is a light blue and sure looks nice. Then we went ahead and had new carpeting put through out. We are quite comfortable now. And it looks real nice.

We had two cousins die not to far apart Frank O'Brien in Libby and Everett Roose in Oregon. They were both close to Esthers age one on each side of the family.

In June of 1996 our oldest Granddaughter was Married to Derik Kraus. They had a lovely wedding at Peaceful Lodge outside of Eureka. It was a big wedding. Yosha wore her grandmother Balderstens wedding dress, that she had worn when she and Gene were married at Annappolis It fit Yosha as if it were made for her. She was a gorgeous bride. Dennis and the little boys Jacob and Mathew all had tuxedos and looked so handsome. Shianne was maid of honor and she and the bridesmaids had lovely dresses. Susan was very much mother of the bride and looked so grand. There was not a dry eye I tell you. I had the honor of making her wedding cake and the mints. It was a gala day, but the weather did not cooperate. It was cold and windy and it rained. The wedding was out side. But it all turned out fine. The kids went to New Orleans on their Honeymoon.

In August Kevin Married Irene Lamb. She is a very special girl to our family. They were married in Whitefish by Dr. Kaufman at his church. Irene bought her dress and veil and I had the honor of helping her with everything. Her Father lives in Townsend. And her father and step mother were divorced so she had no one here to help and needless to say I enjoyed every minute of it. I baked their wedding cake and made the mints, decorated the tables and did the flowers. They had a beautiful wedding also. The boys looked quite handsome in their tuxes. Butch was best man and Laura a friend of theirs was brides maid. The reception was held at the patio of the Northern bar. We turned it into a pink and white fairyland. They went to Seattle on a short Honeymoon.

Wayne had a heart attack in 1993 they did a angioplasty here in Dec. and another in June. He was sent to Missoula for a by pass in Oct.. He has done real well since then. He exercises at the Summit nearly every day. Myrtle goes with him and swims. Myrtle is doing well except her knees have given out. This is why she swims. They still live here in the mobile home they bought 11 years ago. Sharon their oldest lives in Glascow. She graduated from Northern College at Havre with a degree in education. John came home from a stint in the Air Force and finished his college there also and he has a degree in education. John her husband has been a teacher in Glascow for 19 years. He was also the top Volly Ball coach for two years in the state for B schools in the state. Sharon works for the City of Glascow in their City Housing division. They have a nice comfortable home there. Tommy their son went to Airline school in Vancouver Washington. This is where he met Susana his wife. He works for Southwest Airlines and she works for a bank in Portland as a travel agent. Eva is in California she is being trained as a Camp Director for Church camps. They are all over the U.S. Tommy has been to Europe three times. Susan was with him twice. Eva has been over there two times. She and Sharon are leaving this spring for England and Scotland.

Terry and Jane have lived in Kalispell for most of their married life. Terry graduated from college at Bozeman with a degree in engineering. He worked in Omaha, Neb. for about one year. Then came to Kalispell and has worked for Morrison Maierle Inc. for over 24 years. He is branch manager of the Kalispell office. Jane has worked in the office of the Kalispell Diagnostic Service for 24 years. Anyone who may have gone to one of the Drs. there probably know her. Lizzie is a very active little girl and is in the 5th grade. They have a beautiful big house.

Lee Graduated from Carrol College in Helena last year. He is a C.P.A. Karon is a L.P.N. and works for the state. Amber works in Helena and is a fine young girl. Justin is a very active little boy. They have a lovely home. And are a great family.

Esther had bought a head stone for she and Clydes graves and had it put on two of her lots. I thought that was a good idea, one more thing the kids would not have to worry about. So I ordered one also and had it put on our lots. Esthers is Gray and plain with just the lettering on it. Ours is kinda rose color and has some flowers and entwined wedding rings and the printing. I told them I like foo-foo on things. Esther and Myrtle agreed I always did.

In February of 1997 Jim and I took off to go to California and take a two week trip. We left here early one morning in the 94 Subaru Legacy we had. Outside of Deer Lodge it sounded as if the bottom had fell out of the car. We lost power and then it took off again. We drove to outside of Butte and stopped for gas then parked the car and went in to eat lunch. When we came back out the car would not back up. I went in and called triple A . They told me they would come and tow us into Butte, but if it would go ahead and we could get out it would not hurt it any more to drive it on into town. They told us where there was a Motel close to a transmission shop. They were sure that was what was wrong with it. Well it would go forward and the car had left that was in front of us. Of course it was a Sunday. We went into town and parked where we could drive out. Registered at the Motel. The next morning we called the garage and they told us to bring it down.

It didn't take them long to tell us we needed a new transmission. They could not find a used one for two wheel drive and the four wheel drive would not fit After sitting in the motel for three days. They said they could order one from Japan, it would take from ten days to two weeks to get it and it would be $2000.00 plus shipping and putting it in. We debated should we take the bus home and get the other car and go get it when it was fixed? Or trade it in on a new car. We went for the last. So called Ford and Chevrolet garages they came and got us and took us to look at cars. We ended up getting a 96 ford taurus that had 18,000 miles on it. It had been a Ford executives car and was loaded we got it for a good price. So took off for California that day. When we left home we had reservations in Vegas for two days. I had to cancel those. We stopped in Mesquite the first night and called Vegas from there and made our Reservations for only one night this time as we had lost three days.

We spent a enjoyable night there and the next day took off for California. Sharons daughter Eva was working at a church camp at Wright Wood. We wanted to stop and say hello. We finally found her, she was way up in the mountains all by herself. It was a nice camp. After a short visit with her we went on to Riverside to see Bud, Lou Ella and Debbie. I had told them we would spend a week with them but with our time cut short we spent 5 days. We always enjoy being with them. They have a lovely home there and you can pick oranges from their trees year around.

We left here and went south through Julian and on

down the highway that comes out of San Diego. We had never been that way before. It is a pretty drive but the crookedest road you ever saw. We went on across to Yuma and stayed over night there. Took off the next day. We went to Wellton Az. looking for Phyllis and Richard Potuzak. We had not seen their new Motor Home so didn't know what it looked like. But could find no one that knew where the trailer court was we were looking for. We went on to Casa Grande. Spent a couple of days there then on to Nevada and took the road that goes north of lake Mead on to Mesquite. It is a pretty drive. We stayed at Mesquite over night. The next morning while we were waiting for the buffet to open Jim sat down at a quarter machine, He had three quarters. He finally stopped playing and cashed in $80.00. We ate breakfast and headed home. We stopped in Dear Lodge and went through the old Prison. What a terrible place. We went through the Ford car museum. Then headed on home. This is the last trip we have taken together.

The year before this we went to Oregon with Myrtle and Wayne to attend their grandson Tom's wedding he married a lovely girl from out by Salem Oregon her name is Susana. They were married in a park by a water fall and had a lovely reception there in the park Sharon baked the wedding cake.

Myrtle and Wayne also celebrated their 50th wedding anniversary. Their Children had a great party for them at the senior citizens in Eureka. Lots of people came.

I am so glad Bill, Virginia and Wayne were able to come to Yoshas wedding. Sis took a lot of pictures and Videos. She was very professional at it. We had a nice visit with them. They had planned on coming home for Christmas of 1996. Sis had not been home for Christmas for 26 years. They had been trying for about 18 months to adopt Yuri, he was 15 years old he lived in Minsk Belarus. They finally got their call to go after him some time in March. Bill and Virginia flew to Germany then on to Minsk. They spent some time there at the orphanage then took a train on to Poland. This is where they had to get Yuries Pass Port and Visa completed. All in all they were gone about 3 weeks. Bill said Sis lived on tea and bread over there she would not eat the boiled tongue and other things they were served. We received one E mail letter from her saying GOD BLESS AMERICA and that they had their boy and were home.

We heard no more. I had no idea she was sick. She had been going to the Dr. for 3 weeks with chest pains. They could find nothing wrong with her. Bill later showed me a fax she had sent to her Dr. and told him she could not stand the pain any longer and had to have an appointment to come in to the office. They gave her one in 10 days. On the 8th or 9th of June she wanted Bill to make her some raspberry ice cream. He did then he took the boys to the Bowling alley for their bowling. She got sick while he was gone, there was a friend there with her. They went to the Hospital. On the way Virginia slumped over and the woman thought she had gone to sleep. They were both deaf so she heard no sound from Sis. On arrival at the Hospital they said her heart had stopped. Because she was only 46 years old they started it again. They did not know it had been about 15 minutes since it happened. So when they got it going again she was Brain dead.

When Bill got home he had a message as to where she was. He went to the Hospital. Their Minister who is a hearing man but Ministers to the Deaf and interpreter for them was called to the Hospital. He called us and told me what had happened and he thought we should come. I called all the boys and they came and Dennis said he wanted to go. I called the air port and got a ticket to fly out the 10th. I had to go clear down by way of Texas but that was the only way I could get there. Friends of Virginia picked me up at the airport. Wayne and Yuri were with them. We went right to the Hospital. Sis was in a Coma and in the next two days she opened her eyes one time but I knew she seen nothing. She had a high fever and the day after I arrived they unhooked the IV's and only gave her oxygen. They assured us they would keep her comfortable.

During the night of the 12th they moved her into a private room from the ICU. When we got to the hospital that morning. I cleaned her face some around the oxygen tube into her nose. Then I asked the nurses if they would give her a bath. They cleaned her all up and put a clean gown on her. They put cream on her hands and arms. We were putting cool wash cloths on her forehead she was so hot. I was holding her hand and stroking her arm when she breathed her last. My precious daughter died at 11:35 on June 13th 1997. This is something no parent should have to go through. We should go before our children. She died from Coronary artery disease. The Minister insisted that someone go and get the boys who had stayed home that morning. He said they were both 16 years old and old enough to know that their Mother had died and not just left them. They both took it real hard. Yuri said I had a mother for 3 months.

Dennis got in late that afternoon. He did not get to see her alive but was sure a comfort to me to have him there.

During all these days the Deaf people of the area had been bringing food to the house.

Bills Mother ,Father, two brothers and two sisters and Dennis and I were there. We all had to get back home. The Funeral was held two days after she died. It was a lovely Celebration of her life. It was held in their Church. The whole ceremony was in Sign Language and also spoken. She was so very well thought of on both her job and with everyone who knew her. Everyone Bill works with at the Internal Revenue was there also all her coworkers from the Department of Transportation. A lot of the ones who graduated with her from Galladet University. It was a huge Celebration. One of their friends made a collection of photos from her whole life and there was a viewing also. Beautiful songs and one I had never heard. A very rousing song was played last it is called Dancing with the lord. After the ceremony her body was taken to the mortuary for Cremation. They had a coffee punch and cookie and visiting session in the basement of the church. It was real nice. Dennis got a flight out the next day. We were on different air lines and I could not get a flight out till the next day. When I got home the wonderful women I work with gave me a beautiful card with $100.00 in it to help with my trip. Going back to work was hard. It has taken a long time to start to heal and I may never completely do so. Jim wishes now he would have gone with me. I wished he were there also.

In July Bill and the boys came to spend a few days with us. It was good to have them but hard to not have that other smiling face with them. Sis was such a joker and a pleasure to have around. They spent some time up in Eureka with Dennis and Susan. They all went up the Flathead and went on a float trip. I took them up a little way into the park and to the maze. They seemed to enjoy it.

In August Esther became a Great Grandmother. Dick became a Grandfather. Charley was born to Stephani and Chris, Esther wanted to go back to Conneticut to see him but did not want to travel alone. I took a week off from work and went with her. We flew into Kennedy Airport in New York. Dick was there to meet us. We drove to Fairfield where he and Beth have a lovely home. We met Charlie he is a beautiful big baby boy. Blond, Blue eyed doll. They took us to see so many things. We went out to dinner at the Country Club one evening. Dick, Beth , Mathew, Christina, Chris, Stephani, Charlie, Esther, and Me. It was lovely. Mathew and Christina are finishing up law school this year and will be married in August. They are a real nice family.

Beth took Esther and I to a Greek restaurant for lunch one day and to a Hungarian one for Dinner one night. We seen long Island bay, and so many beautiful old old houses. I had never been in that area before and wish Jim could have seen all these things with me. Dick took Esther and I in his new Mercedes up into the northern part of the state to see the fall colors. They were beautiful. When we left for home we went to the airport by Limousine Dick was leaving an hour after we did to fly to Europe on Business. We arrived home tired but had a lovely trip and did see Charlie. And I rode in a Mercedes and a Limo. I had never been in either one before.

We had been home about a month when Esther received a call from Clyde on day that he was having Chest pains he thought he needed something for gas. She went and got him what he wanted and took it to him. He did not want to go to the Dr. She came home and later he called again . She went and picked him up and took him to the Hospital. He had a heart attack. They did a angioplasty and his heart was O.K. But something happen in doing this and he had an artery bleeding into the leg. He got gangrene and they took the leg off above the knee. He was in the hospital for 15 days then passed away.

Dick and his family came out and Clydes cremains were interned in the Eureka cemetery . It was a cold crisp morning but the cemetery was beautiful every tree fence and everything was covered with hoar frost from the heavy fog that night before.

This has not been a good year for us. Paul Drager has been in the hospital and nursing home for about three months. Last week his son David sold his Mobile home and moved him to Billings so he will be closer for him to take care of.

Prior to Clydex getting sick Esther had made arrangements to move her Mobil home to another spot where she could see the Mountains. It was moved while she was at the Hospital one day. Everything moved fine. So now she is in between Myrtle and I.

THE SISTERS THREE
Are still within a block of each other.
"In every life there is a story."

Taken around 1930. Mother Eva Shenefelt holding me, Helen, between one and a half to two years old. Myrtle about four years old, and Esther about nine years old.

Francis and Eva, Mom and Dad's wedding picture

Sara and John Shenfelt.

Sinai and Stephani Ballargon

Esther Myrtle and I as we took off on
our Memory walk.

Helen DeLong, Myrtle Richmond, Esther Paul,
and Harold Shenefelt

Our last family photo taken 1981. Left to right back row: Tom (Butch), 35 years old, Dennis, 31 years old, Kevin 18 years old. Front row: Virginia, 32 years old, Jim, 59 years, Helen 53 years old.